# Combat
# Search & Rescue

# Combat
# Search & Rescue

Andy Evans

ARMS AND
ARMOUR

Arms & Armour
An Imprint of the Cassell Group
Wellington House, 125 Strand, London WC2R 0BB

First published 1999

*British Library Cataloguing in Publication Data*
A catalogue record for this book is available from the
British Library

ISBN 1-85409-339-8

Distributed in the USA by
Sterling Publishing Co. Inc., 387 Park Avenue South,
New York, NY 10016-8810

Edited and designed by DAG Publications Ltd

Printed and bound in Great Britain by
MPG Books Ltd, Bodmin, Cornwall

# Contents

# Preface

The idea of using a 'dedicated team' to undertake hazardous combat rescue missions originally began—as, it seems, did most of the forward-thinking aviation ideas of the twentieth century—with the German Luftwaffe during the Second World War. Because of the demands placed on the Luftwaffe as a result of its over-water operations, crossing from mainland Europe to Great Britain, it saw the advantages of using Messerschmitt Bf 110 fighters to fly armed escort for slower seaplane rescue craft which could sweep in to recover downed aviators. Thus began the role of combat search and rescue as we know it today—an armed fighter operating alongside slower recovery vehicles.

Before the advent of today's dedicated CSAR platforms, existing aircraft were modified to carry out the rescue role, and, again, until the introduction of the helicopter, 'air-droppable' kits were released from such aircraft to downed aircrew either over land or in the water. Of course, aircraft are now far more powerful, and the combat situations they face more sophisticated and intense. However, the premise has remained the same, and has been expanded down the years to meet with the demands of the time.

Combat SAR continues to be one of the most hazardous and yet most rewarding missions undertaken by the aviators assigned to the rescue services. Combat SAR aviators are amongst the most respected community in the military sphere. Bar stools are relinquished without a second thought, and firm handshakes are always the order of the day. To attempt to recount every act of heroism would require many volumes. However, presented here is a historical and topical tribute to the Air Rescue Forces, and to the many aviators who owe their very being to the unselfish actions of a few élite men, and women, many of whom have made the ultimate sacrifice . . . 'That Others Might Live'.

**Andy Evans**

# Acknowledgements

Grateful thanks are due to the following, for their unselfish support for such an ambitious project: the United States Department of Defense; Byron 'Hook' Hukee; Maj Ed 'Blade' Walker; Gary Roush, Maj Frank 'Zoid' Simmons USMC; Capt Ian 'Blondie' Walsh USMC; Capt Jim 'Jinx' Jenkins USMC; SSG Evacuation Platoon Sgt Mike Curtis, of the 872nd Medical Company USAF; M/Sgt Mario Roiz AFSOC; Capt Roger Williams AFSOC; T/Sgt Mark Cunningham AFSOC; Lt Alan Vinson AFRES; Derek Armitage, from the Army Air Corps Museum; and Jerry Shore, at the Fleet Air Arm Museum. Thanks go also to Gary Madgwick; Tony Thornborough; Jon Lake; Graham Causer; Gary Parsons, of the f4 Aviation Photobank; Dale Donovan, RAF Strike Command PR; GKN Westland PRO; Textron-Bell Helicopters; Sikorsky Helicopters; Boeing Helicopters; Bertrand Deelest; Rick Llinares and Tom Hunter; and the Jolly Green Association.

**Andy Evans**

# 1

# World War II to the 1960s

## Air Sea Rescue Under Combat Conditions

Combat SAR is reported to have begun around the time of the Battle of Britain, when elderly Heinkel He 59B-2 seaplanes painted with large red crosses, escorted by orbiting Bf 110s, began landing on the water to pick up downed aircrew—from both sides of the war. The He 59 was a large, twin-float biplane, already obsolete, powered by two 485kW BMWVI 6.0ZU engines. Nevertheless, its four-man crews lumbered in at speeds of around 220kph and retrieved many grateful fliers. Despite its old-fashioned appearance, the He 59 remained in first-line service until 1943 and achieved much success in the search and rescue role.

The Royal Air Force, the Royal Navy and their allies were not slow to pick up on this methodology, and also made use of the escorted seaplane tactic to recover pilots who had been forced, by one means or another, to 'ditch in the drink'. Britain began by setting up a number of Air Sea Rescue (ASR) squadrons, with aircraft like the ungainly SupermarineWalrus (affectionately known as the 'Shagbat'), the Avro Anson and theWestland Lysander pressed into the search and rescue role. The increasing tempo of operations over Germany, and the continuing day and night raids undertaken by Bomber Command and the US Eighth Air Force, meant that many more aircrews were liable not to make the sea crossing before their engines gave out or they were forced to ditch. Amongst the ASR units formed around that time were Nos 269, 275, 276, 277, 278, 281 and 282 Squadrons, whilst in the Middle East Nos 283, 284, 293 and 294 Squadrons were established, No 277 alone being credited with no fewer than 598 aircrew personnel saved from the total of over 1,000 rescued.

As the war progressed theWalrus began to be fitted with air-to-sea radar, primarily for anti-submarine operations, but by 1944 the air–sea rescue squadrons also had radar on board their aircraft, and were thus able to identify dinghies at longer distances and in poorer weather than had previously been possible. The 'Shagbat' was also utilised aboard aircraft carriers, undertaking the 'plane guard' duties nowadays associated with the helicopter, and it has been recorded that a number of successful British Pacific Fleet ASR rescues were conducted by the Walrus right under the noses of the Japanese.

The Walrus was eventually superseded in the latter stages of the war by the similarly configured but more powerful tractor-engine Supermarine Sea Otter, which itself later gave way to the embryonic helicopter. For longer-range rescue efforts the Allies relied on, amongst other aircraft, the legendary Consolidated Catalina and the huge Short Sunderland flying boat, and these aircraft also recovered numerous fliers from the briny. The Royal Canadian Air Force formed several anti-submarine squadrons on the East Coast of Britain as part of Coastal Command. Converted Lockheed Hudson bombers served very briefly in the search and rescue role in the late 1940s. One interesting feature of the Hudson's service was the fact that it was configured to carry a rigid lifeboat under the belly which could be dropped by parachute to accident victims. It was, however, the Catalina which became the most successful flying patrol boat of the Second World War, operated in all theatres by both the RAF and US forces.

### 'Cat's Tales': The Rescue of NAP Bill Pugh

On 15 October 1942 Capt Richard J. Teich and his crew were operating their Catalina flying boat on their assigned patrol route of 348–356 degrees from Espiritu Santo. 'Dick' Teich takes up the story:

'Out near the end of our sector, looking to the west on the horizon, I noticed what appeared to be a column of smoke, as though from a ship (position 08°31'S 165°42'E). I turned and flew over to investigate. As we arrived the smoke died out, but, circling the spot, we saw what appeared to be the wreckage of a PBY in the water. As we circled we noted a lone survivor holding on to some debris and waving one arm to us. The wind was not too strong but the swells were high, so I decided to try a landing. Circling around, I made an approach on to a wind line which passed through the wreckage. When we touched down we hit a swell which bounced us into the air. Applying full power, the next bounce was less hard and we finally stayed on the water. After landing we noticed many of the hull rivets had popped out, and water was squirting up like little fountains through the fuselage.

'The navigator ingeniously started ramming pencils into the rivet holes to cut down on the flow of water. In the meantime we started to search for the survivor. After spotting him we had to circle around to get him into the wind line. The first time around we missed him because he wasn't close enough, so we circled again. This time we slowed our approach and managed to grab and pull him aboard. It turned out to be NAP Bill Pugh, who indicated that his aircraft had been shot down by a carrier plane. In slowing our approach the starboard engine died, and one of the mechanics went up on the wing and hand-cranked the engine, which we finally started. When the mechanic was back inside we started our take-off run. At this point we had about 6 inches of water in the bilge. Somehow we managed to pick up speed and we started to bounce from swell to swell. To lighten the load, I ordered the jettison of the depth charges. Finally we picked up enough speed to just touch the swell crests and finally were completely airborne. Because of Pugh's condition I sent a message to base that we were returning. A signal came back which ordered us to continue to search for the Japanese force that had downed Pugh. After another two hours of searching, without contact, we returned to base because of fuel limitation. It was touch and go for a while and I wondered what I had done, but we had an angel on our shoulder so it worked out.'

### Gordon's Black Cat

Another memorable 'Cat' rescue took place on 15 February 1944 when Lt Nathan Gordon, flying his Navy Patrol Squadron 34 PBY Catalina on air–sea rescue duty south of New Ireland, received an urgent call that several 345th Bomb Group B-25s were down following a major attack on Kavieng and that crews were in the water just offshore. Under intense heavy gunfire from Japanese shore batteries, Gordon made four separate perilous water landings to rescue a total of fifteen downed fliers who would otherwise have certainly died. He returned to the naval base at Cape Gloucester to make an emergency landing with a mere ten gallons of fuel left in the aircraft's tanks. Gordon was later awarded the Medal of Honor, thereby becoming the first Navy flier to win such merit in the South-West Pacific.

The German notion of a dedicated combat rescue team was to gain greater credence in post-war conflicts, and with the birth of the 'rotary age' the idea, albeit still in its infancy, was then nurtured through the Malayan and Korean conflicts, up until the Vietnam War, when the principles that had already been laid down were to become the foundations for all future combat SAR work, through the Gulf War and up to the present day.

## 'Rotary Wings—Changes Things'

Without a shadow of a doubt, the one thing that made combat rescue a more viable form of military operation was the advent of the helicopter. Developed during the latter part of the Second World War, it was to have a massive impact on the world of aviation. At the end of the Second World War, in spite of massive production cancellations, the helicopter industry grew at a phenomenal rate, and the promise of what the 'chopper' could accomplish—especially in the assault and rescue roles, where it could move quantities of men and their kit, and easily access difficult or denied areas, as well as bring medical attention quickly to wounded servicemen—was a revolution for the campaign planners.

The box-like Sikorsky R-4 was the world's first production helicopter and the US Air Force's first service helicopter. The original military model, the XR-4, was developed from the famous experimentalVS-300 helicopter, invented by Igor Sikorsky and publicly demonstrated in 1940. The XR-4 made its initial flight on 13 January 1942 and as a result of its successful flight tests the AAF ordered threeYR-4As and 27YR-4Bs for service testing and flight training. Of these 30, one went to Burma and one to Alaska, while several others were assigned to the US Navy, US Coast Guard and Royal Navy, who adopted the name 'Dragonfly'. The helicopters showed such promise that the AAF ordered 100 R-4Bs.

Sikorsky's first post-war offering, the S-51, was an upgrade of an earlier model, the R-5A. This new machine, which first flew on 6 February 1946, seated four and embodied a large number of mechanical improvements. It dramatically proved its usefulness while serving aboard the aircraft carrier USS *Franklin D. Roosevelt* during a Caribbean training cruise. The risks involved with an aircraft 'ditching' when launching or recovering from a carrier were high, and, acting as plane-guard, the S-51 stood by in flight near the ship, where it frequently had opportunities to rescue pilots who crashed during landings and take-offs—on one occasion returning a Corsair pilot in less than two minutes after he had ditched following an abortive take-off! Specially trained SAR divers were carried on board the helicopters, and these personnel could be dropped quickly at the crash scene to aid the pilot and prepare him for recovery. The US Navy, very impressed with the S-51's capabilities, ordered a number of the machines, which they designated HO3S-1. The HO3S-1 went on to serve with the US Coast Guard in the search and rescue and utility transport role.

### Original Rescue!

The R-4 was first used in combat in May 1944. In a letter to a friend, Col Philip G. Cochran, Commanding Officer (CO) of the 1st Air Commando Group, wrote, 'Today the "egg-beater" went into action and the damn thing acted like it had good sense.' In early 1945 a YR-4 helicopter, limited in its load-carrying and altitude capabilities, was assigned to the 10th Air Jungle Rescue detachment in Burma. Lt Raymond F. Murdock learned to fly it and on his first rescue mission airlifted a severely injured PT-19 pilot, Capt Charles L. Green. Although Green had crashed only a few minutes' flying time from an airfield, it took two weeks to rescue him after combat engineers and others cut down trees, blasted stumps and levelled off a crude hillside landing pad in the thick jungle so that the underpowered and worn-out helicopter could operate. Lt Murdock compared the hazardous pick-up to 'landing in a windy well'. Murdock was accompanied on the mission by Sgt Donald Joyce, who flew as escort for the rescue. The US Air Force's S-51s went on to see extensive service in the

---

### Sikorsky/Westland Hoverfly

With the R4 being the world's first production helicopter, the British Royal Navy had a brief association with the type, naming it the Hoverfly, before replacing it with the more powerful Dragonfly, the Sycamore and subsequently the Whirlwind for shipboard and SAR operations.

The S-51 was an early post-war development of the H-5/R-5. Although intended for the civilian market, most S-51s went into military duties, operating with all the US military services as well as with the air forces of Australia, Great Britain and Canada. The H-5 was also the first military helicopter in the Royal Canadian Air Force, and they were used mainly for training and experimental work, although some performed search and rescue tasks. In total the United States built 214 examples, and 165 were manufactured in Britain. For rescue operations the H-5 could be fitted with external closed stretcher carriers.

*Specifications:* Powerplant one Pratt & Whitney R-985 AN-5 Wasp Junior 450hp radial engine; rotor diameter 49ft (14.9m); length 57ft 8in (17.6m); height 12ft 11in (3.9m); weight (empty) 3,810lb (1,728kg); weight (gross) 5,500lb (2,495kg); maximum speed 103mph (166kph); cruising speed 85mph (137kph); rate of climb 1,000ft (305m)/min; service ceiling 13,500ft (4,115m); range: 260 miles (418km).

---

## Westland Dragonfly

During the Korean War the Royal Navy had the presence of mind to lease a small number of the US Sikorsky S-51s for search and rescue and plane-guard duties. The value of the helicopter was immediately obvious, and the aircraft soon went into UK production as the Dragonfly HR.1, with an Alvis Leonides engine. Further models, the HR.3 and the HR.5, were also produced, the final example being delivered in 1953. The Dragonfly saw service aboard all Royal Navy aircraft carriers during the mid to late 1950s, until replaced by the Whirlwind. It also saw service as a land-based rescue platform, replacing the Sea Otter.

Korean War, recovering downed pilots and carrying out battlefield casualty evacuation.

Lt Carter Harmon is recorded as making the first AAF helicopter rescue during the Burma Campaign, operating behind Japanese lines on 25–26 April 1944. 1st Air Commando Sgt Pilot Ed 'Murphy' Hladovcak had crash-landed his L-1 light aircraft with three wounded British soldiers on board. Taxing his YR-4 helicopter to its performance limits, Harmon made four flights to the site, the final hasty lift-off taking place just as shouting soldiers burst from the jungle. He learned later that the soldiers were not Japanese, but an Allied land rescue party! The H-5 served as a rescue helicopter from 1948 to 1955, and one H-5 in the National Aviation Museum of Canada is dedicated in honour of Capt David J. Miller for the valour displayed during the rescue of six soldiers from behind enemy lines in Korea.

### The Birth of the US Air Rescue Service:
### Recovery During the Korean War

To give credence to the necessity of recovering its airmen from tight situations, in March 1946 the United States established the Air Rescue Service (ARS) under the Air Transport Command umbrella, to provide rescue coverage for the continental United States. However, by 1949 ARS aircraft covered all of the world's transport routes, and

## Bristol 171 Sycamore

The Bristol Sycamore was a four/five-seat light helicopter which first flew in 1947 and entered service as a search and rescue vehicle in 1952. Its radial engine characterised the limited power and inefficiency that its large size gave it, and placed it firmly in the annals of the initial development phase of the helicopter. Subsequent helicopters have used exclusively turbine engines, which have enabled designers to use the space and weight saved for carrying more cargo or passengers.

could be found in every combat zone that involved US or UN personnel. To perform all its recovery tasks, the ARS utilised existing aircraft, which were then modified to perform their new rescue role. The
Grumman HU-16 Albatross was the ARS's rescue workhorse from
the late 1940s right through to the early 1970s, and rocket units,
mounted on the fuselage, were employed to improve take-off performance.

Also finding service with the ARS was the Boeing SB-17, a rescue-
modified version of the famous B-17 Flying Fortress. Around 130 B-
17Gs were converted for the rescue role beginning in 1944 and ending with US Coast Guard service as late as 1959. By 1953 the ARS
had also adopted the SC-54D, a modified C-54 which could carry
four MA-1 droppable rescue kits. Each kit contained a 40-person
inflatable life raft that could be dropped more safely than the rigid
boats.

During the Korean War the increased use of helicopters on rescue
missions became the dominant factor in saving lives, and by the war's
end ARS crews had been credited with the rescue of 9,898 United
Nations personnel, 996 of which were combat saves. The Sikorsky H-
5A-equipped helicopter rescue units could be mainly found on Cho-
Do island, located just off the North Korean coast some 50 miles
north of the 38th Parallel. Other rescue aircraft and a ground control

---

## Westland Whirlwind

In 1952 the RN received 25 Sikorsky S-55 helicopters (designated HAR.21 and HAS.22)
under the Mutual Defence Aid Plan. These proved highly successful and resulted in an
order for licence-built versions a year later, the first of which, a Whirlwind HAR.1, flew
on 15 August 1953. The Pratt and Whitney Wasp (600shp)-powered HAR.1 and HAR.3
were built in small numbers between 1953 and 1955 and were soon followed by Alvis-
powered HAR.5s. All the HAR models saw extensive service in ships' flights, particularly as the plane-guard on board carriers.

The large surplus of Whirlwind HAS.7s saw their use in a commando transport role
from 1960 onwards, some being converted to HAR.9s with Rolls-Royce Gnome tur-
bines and entering service with SAR flights in 1967. The HAR.1, HAR.3 and HAR.5 had
been retired from service by the mid-1960s, but the HAS.7 continued as a training
helicopter until 1975. The HAR.9 left SAR service in 1977. A total of 37 various HAR
models and 120 Whirlwinds HAS.7s were built, in addition to ten HAR.21s and fifteen
HAS.22s. The HAR.10 search and rescue helicopter was also developed for use by the
RAF, and first flew in this guise in the spring of 1961.

*Specifications:* Powerplant one 1,050shp Rolls-Royce Gnome engine; rotor diameter
53ft (16.15m); height 15 ft 7½in (4.76m); length 62ft 4in (19.00m); weight 8,000lb
(3,638kg); maximum speed 104mph (167kph); hovering ceiling 15,800ft (4,816m).

## Sikorsky H-19

The UH-19B was the US Air Force's version of the Sikorsky S-55, an aircraft used by all US military services in the 1950s and 1960s. It was the first of the Sikorsky helicopters with enough cabin space and lifting ability to allow satisfactory operation in troop transport or rescue roles. The engine was mounted in the nose, leaving the main cabin free for passengers or cargo. The prototype was first flown in November 1949, and in 1951 the USAF ordered production model H-19s (redesignated UH-19s in 1962). After receiving 50 H-19As, the USAF acquired 270 H-19Bs with increased engine power. Many were assigned to Air Rescue squadrons as SH-19s (later redesignated HH-19s). For rescue service, a 400lb capacity hoist was mounted above the door, and the aircraft also could be equipped with an external sling capable of carrying 2,000lb. During the Korean War H-19s were used extensively for rescue and medical evacuation work. Other missions included observation and liaison. The H-19 also flew the first helicopter combat airlift missions during the Korean War while serving with the US Marine Corps.

*Specifications:* Powerplant one 700hp Wright R-1300-3; rotor diameter 53ft (16.15m); fuselage length 42ft 4in (12.90m); height 15ft 4in4.67m); weight (maximum) 8,400lb (3,809kg); maximum speed 112mph (180kph); cruising speed 92mph (148kph); range 330 miles (531km); service ceiling 15,000ft (4,572m); no armament.

intercept radar facility also occupied the island, despite the nearness to the enemy mainland. During the latter part of the war the 3rd ARS Squadron used the SB-29, a version of the B-29 Superfortress fitted with droppable boats, and these aircraft orbited along the bombers' route in case of casualties.

## Lt (JG) John Koelsh

Like many aviators of his time, John Koelsh lost his life in a brave humanitarian rescue on 3 July 1951 in North Korea whilst serving with a Navy helicopter unit. Information was received during the late evening that a Marine Corps aviator had been shot down and was trapped by the enemy in mountainous terrain deep inside hostile territory. Koelsh voluntarily flew his helicopter to the reported position of the crashed airman and descended below the low cloud cover in his unarmed aircraft, without fighter cover, to effect a rescue. Despite enemy fire hitting his aircraft, Koelsh succeeded in locating the pilot, who was suffering from serious burns. However, whilst the victim was being hoisted aboard the helicopter it was again struck by a volley of fire, causing it to crash. Koelsh quickly extricated his crewmen and the aviator from the wreckage and led them out of the area, evading enemy troops, in the hope that a fresh rescue could be attempted. The crew evaded capture for nine days until they were finally found.

Sadly, Koelsh died in captivity, but he was awarded the Medal of Honor for his courageous efforts and unfailing spirit.

Perhaps the helicopter most immediately drawn to the memory from the Korean conflict is the Bell 447 H-13 Sioux, a machine made even more famous by its appearance in the opening credits of the long-running television series *M.A.S.H.* Pressed into service as a medevac (medical evacuation) platform, the Sioux carried two stretcher panniers on its skids and transported wounded soldiers from the combat staging area to field hospitals.

After the Korean War the USAF Air Rescue Service resumed world-wide operations for rescue coverage and ARS squadrons flew hundreds of humanitarian relief and rescue missions. In 1966 the ARS was redesignated the ARRS—Aerospace Rescue and Recovery Service—to reflect its additional role of support for US space flights.

As mentioned, the Grumman HU-16B Albatross was the backbone of the ARS for over two decades. Grumman delivered a total of 297 Albatrosses to the USAF, most being of the SA-16A variety, and these were assigned to the Military Air Transport Services (MATS) Air Rescue Service. In one of the most daring and spectacular rescues of the Korean War, Lt John Narjaria and his HU-16 crew risked their lives to recover Capt Kenneth M. Stewart, an F-51 pilot downed behind North Korean lines. Flying under power lines and taking fire from enemy gun towers, the HU-16 landed in a shallow river, with harsh jutting rocks and floating debris present, and without lights, to rescue Stewart.

Because of the Albatross's increasing weight and decreasing performance, the Air Force sponsored a major modification programme in the mid-1950s, and this new aircraft, designated SA-16B, first flew in January 1956. The SA-16B differed from the SA-16A in having an additional 70in wing section outboard of the engine and a 39in wing-tip extension coupled with leading-edge wing camber to replace the leading-edge slots. Because of the extra wing area, the ailerons, fin and stabilisers were increased in size. The SA-16B became the HU-16B in 1962. All but 21 of the SA-16Bs were converted from the SA-16A. The USAF retired their HU-16s in 1973, some 55 being transferred to the Coast Guard. The Albatross started life as a Navy aircraft, and the initial Navy contract was for two XJR2F-1 prototypes, the first aircraft taking to the air on 1 October 1947. During development, the Navy had decided that its initial order would be for anti-

## Westland Wessex

In the United Kingdom, the Westland Wessex was a licence-built development of the Sikorsky S-58 (US H-34), and the Wessex HAS.1 was the first Royal Navy front-line helicopter to be powered by a turbine engine. The first production HAS.1 flew on 20 June 1958 and entered service in July 1961 in the anti-submarine, rescue and utility roles. Some HAS.1s were converted to HAS.3 standard with improved avionics (including a large dorsal radome for a search radar), but these were soon replaced by the more capable Sea King. The last front-line HAS.3 squadron re-equipped in 1971. The aircraft was due to leave second-line service in 1982 but its withdrawal was delayed because of the Falklands campaign. The HU.5 replaced the HAS.1 being used in rescue and utility roles from 1964 onwards. An interesting point is that on her last cruise before decommissioning, the Royal Navy's last conventional aircraft carrier, HMS *Ark Royal*, carried a pair of Wessex plane-guard helicopters christened, in true Navy style, 'Make' and 'Mend'. The RAF also adopted the Wessex HAR.3 in the rescue role, and the bright yellow painted helicopters were a constant comfort to both militarymen and civilians in distress. The Wessex continued in RAF service until 1997, when it was replaced by the ultra-capable Sea King HAR.3A.

*Specifications:* Powerplant one Napier Gazelle 165 free-power turbine, 1,600shp (1,193kW) maximum power; rotor diameter 56ft (17.07m; length 65ft 10in (20.07m); height 15ft 11in (4.85m); rotor disc area 2,463.4 sq ft (228.85m²); maximum take-off weight 13,600lb (6,168.9kg); maximum cruising speed 138mph (222kph, 120kt); Louis Newmark autopilot, dipping sonar and search radar.

submarine warfare (ASW) aircraft designated PF-1A. The Air Force became interested in using the Albatross as a search and rescue platform and ordered procurement as the SA-16.

During the 1960s the Royal Australian Navy (RAN) operated the aircraft carriers *Sydney* and *Melbourne* and purchased a number of Westland-built Wessex HAS.31s, primarily to provide anti-submarine cover and to give over-the-horizon targeting for Ikara-equipped warships. Again, their secondary roles were those of plane-guard and SAR. The RAN also employed the Bell UH-1D for shore-based SAR, and these machines worked with the carriers when they were in home waters, utilising the ever useful 'Billy Pugh' rescue net. The Wessex was finally replaced in 1967 by the Westland Sea King HAS.50.

In the 1960s the Dutch Navy operated the carrier *Karel Doorman*, which embarked the Westland Whirlwind and, from 1968, the Sikorsky SH-34J Sea Bat. The ship usually carried six Sea Bats from No 8 Squadron for plane-guard duties as well as the ASW role.

# 2

# Vietnam: Birth of the Dedicated Combat SAR

*It is my duty, as a member of the Aerospace Rescue and Recovery Service, to save life and to aid the injured. I will be prepared at all times to perform my assigned duties quickly and efficiently, placing these duties before personal desires and comforts. These things I do—that others may live.*—ARRS Code

During the mid-1960s and early 1970s the world of combat rescue was dominated by the war in South-East Asia. For reasons beyond the scope of this book, America found itself fighting a jungle war in Vietnam, serving to headline US policies to halt the spread of communism in that corner of the globe. As air strikes intensified, so did the list of aircraft and aircrew being shot down by Vietnamese fighters and SAM missile systems. Recovering those unfortunate fliers who came to grief in the inhospitable climes of South-East Asia began as a small affair, but, as losses mounted, so combat rescue began to gain importance.

As more and more aircraft and aircrew failed to return to base, so more specialised recovery teams were needed to pluck any survivors directly from the clutches of the enemy. The peacetime Aerospace Rescue and Recovery Service (ARRS), deployed to cater for the perceived recovery mission, was woefully unprepared and ill-equipped to meet the demands of war. However, as their capabilities increased and more specialist aircraft became available during the course of the conflict, so the ARRS crews began to gain the highest respect, and they went on to save 4,120 lives—2,780 of them in combat situations. The Air Force units were not the only rescue services in Vietnam, as the CIA's covert airline Air America was also in the country and was flying helicopter missions: because of its crews' superior knowledge of the terrain, they were often called upon to support rescue efforts.

The combat rescue premise was simple: a pair of helicopters would be called in to pick up survivors, covered by attack aircraft (under the control of an orbiting command post) and escorted by an airborne Forward Air Controller. Despite the impressive capabilities of the 'paraffin-burning' F-105 Thunderchief and F-4 Phantom, the USAF found that they were in desperate need of a slow, heavily armed aircraft with an extended loiter capability that could provide cover for the lumbering helicopters. Enter the A-1 Skyraider, an ex-Navy piston-engine 'bomb-truck', ideally suited to the mission. Despite their vintage style, the A-1s ('Spads') and their pilots went on to become among the most widely respected institutions of the war.

## The Helicopter War

Perhaps the most fondly remembered of the rotary-wing aircraft used for rescue missions in Vietnam were the specially procured and ever-faithful Sikorsky HH-3s and later the HH-53s—affectionately known as the 'Jolly Green Giant' and the 'Super Jolly Green Giant' respectively—which became familiar and much-appreciated sights in the skies above Laos and North Vietnam. In the early part of the war much of the rescue work was undertaken by the short-ranged, ungainly but effective Kaman H-43 Huskie, or 'Pedro', which was hastily pressed into service as a recovery machine although it had originally been brought into theatre to act as an airfield fire-fighting platform.

The ubiquitous Bell UH-1 'Huey' also played an important role in not only recovering airmen but also moving wounded soldiers, very often from heavily defended areas. During the early days of the conflict the armed services relied on the venerable Grumman HU-16 Albatross to provide SAR coverage, the aircraft serving until 1967, when it was replaced by the air-refuellable HH-3 helicopter. Within the rescue organisations, one of the most respected ranks was that of Pararescueman, a unique breed of fighting man whose bravery is sometimes overlooked in the shadow of the more glamorous aircrew exploits. The Pararescuemen's blood-red berets still serve to remind all of the sacrifices they have made in furtherance of recovery.

## Anatomy of a Rescue

Most of the rescue missions in Vietnam called for a seven-aircraft package and would begin with a briefing from 'Sandy 1', the leader of the rescue attempt. Also present would be the FAC (Forward Air Controller) or 'Nail', two 'Jolly' HH-3 helicopter crews and six 'Sandy'

20

Skyraider pilots. 'Sandy 1' would give the details of the timings, the ingress and egress routes, the loiter areas and the armament. Two of the Skyraiders would remain on the ground in reserve, the pilots sitting in their cockpits until needed. 'Sandy 3', 'Sandy 4' and 'Jolly 2' would take a high-altitude position as back-up, whilst 'Jolly 1', supported by 'Sandy 1' and 'Sandy 2', would enter the rescue area. 'Sandy 2' and 'Jolly 1' would loiter whilst 'Sandy 1' moved in to authenticate the crew and sanitise the area. This airborne back-up would be refuelled by an orbiting Hercules tanker and Command Post, 'Crown'.

Working with the FAC, possibly an O-1, O-2 or OV-10, 'Sandy 1' would contact the downed aircrew by radio or beeper and fly a line towards the signal, sweeping the area in the hope of drawing enemy fire. Once any enemy guns opened up 'Sandy 2' would be called in to clear the area, and, once secure, 'Sandy 1' would call in the 'Jolly' after marking the location with a 'Willy Pete' phosphorous rocket. When the 'Jolly' was a short distance away from the survivor the latter would be asked to 'pop' his orange survival flare so that the helicopter could move right into his position. If needed, 'Sandy Smoke Support' could be called in, wherein up to eight A-1s would fly in at low level to lay a smoke screen between the survivor and the helicopter. If enemy ground fire could not be surpressed locally, then Phantoms, Thunderchiefs or Super Sabres could be called upon to deliver some heavy metal.

From the seas, the US Navy and Marine Corps helicopter pilots had expected to be on assault, fire-suppression and plane-guard duties but soon found themselves having to transit 'in-country' to recover airmen who had had an unfortunate mishap in the skies of the North. In a similar vein to the Air Force, the Navy quickly adapted its assets to take in the rescue role, employing their shipborne UH-1 'Hueys', S-61 Sea Kings and CH-46 Sea Knights to recover their fellows.

## Cunning Communists

The Americans' bitter experience at the hands of the North Vietnamese in the jungles of South-East Asia served as a salutary lesson for the men of the rescue services, and galvanised their thoughts as to the wily nature of the Viet Cong soldier. While the rescuers were en route a downed airman would be in contact with them—and eager listeners would also be tuned in, hoping to pinpoint the survivor and set up an ambush. Experience had shown the recovery forces that sending a single helicopter was simply not practical: the cost in lives and hardware frequently far outweighed the cost of rescuing a single airman from the clutches of the foe. The helicopter crews developed a 'double-talk' language so that they could communicate effectively with the survivor in a form that eavesdropping enemy radio operators could not understand.

Many rescues, however, were far from the success that the bravery of the recovery crews warranted. The enemy often succeeded in hiding machine-gun positions close to a survivor, with troops near enough to use him as bait for the recovery helicopter, and the subsequent hail of groundfire might bring disastrous results for the 'Jolly'. All manner of tricks were employed to trap the unwary, for example the positioning of a Vietnamese communist soldier, dressed in a standard K2B American flight coverall, high on a ridge-top with a signal mirror and instructions to act like a downed pilot. This deception had only limited success, but it did lure at least one unsuspecting HH-53 into the trap, the helicopter falling victim to a lurking MiG or becoming prey to fighters returning from other sorties.

The addition of fighters and close air support aircraft to the rescue package was, however, by far the greatest deterrent. The use of low-flying, heavily armed aircraft, spotter planes and 'fast movers' to sanitise the area before the recovery crews moved in paid handsome dividends—and the diligent helicopter crews themselves were more than happy to spray the area with a few rounds from their 7.62mm miniguns! When approaching a survivor the crews tried to avoid presenting their vulnerable frontal arc to the enemy. The glass cockpit was the helicopter's weakest spot, although a well-aimed burst of fire on any part of the aircraft would almost certainly bring disastrous results.

## MiG Shot

On 28 January 1970 the crew of an F-105, 'Seabird 02', ejected near the Mu Gia pass over North Vietnam. Rescue forces soon arrived, and whilst Capt John Dyer in 'Sandy 01' was ascertaining the exact location and condition of the survivors an SA-2 SAM was fired at him, forcing him to throw his Skyraider around to evade the missile.

The 'Sandys' were escorting a recovery formation of four 'Jollys' arriving from west-north-west at about 10,000ft. 'Jolly 19' was the

## Kaman HH-43 Huskie

The HH-43 Huskie helicopter was manufactured by the Kaman Aircraft Corporation in Bloomfield, Connecticut, and was initially designed for base fire and crash rescue. With its auxiliary equipment, the helicopter could be used for the aerial pick-up of survivors, fire control and suppression, crash entry and survivor removal, and immediate first aid. However, the slow, unarmed and ungainly Huskie was adapted for the rescue role early in the war and won the nickname 'Pedro'. It had a combat radius of only 75 miles, but this was increased by adding extra fuel drums strapped into the cabin. The HH-43s were credited with saving more lives than any other rescue helicopter in the whole of the war.

The Huskie was a redesigned version of the Kaman H-43A helicopter with twice the interior space and payload capacity. It featured a Lycoming T53-L-1B gas turbine engine. The H-43B had an intermeshing rotor known as a 'synchrocopter'. The two main rotors were driven by the twin shafts of a single transmission and they were mounted side by side on individual rotor pylons. The Huskie was the winner of a 1956 Air Force competition for a helicopter that would excel in local crash rescue missions. The initial deliveries of this helicopter were made in 1958 and production continued for another decade.

The helicopters saw extensive duty in Vietnam, where they rescued thousands of fliers. Huskies set performance, endurance and safety records during their crash rescue and disaster assistance missions. They were already in use with the US Navy when delivery of the first H-43As to the USAF's Tactical Air Command began in November 1958, and by mid-1962 the USAF had changed the H-43 designation to HH-43 to reflect the aircraft's rescue role. The final USAF version was the HH-43F, with engine modifications for improved performance, and some Fs were used for rescuing downed airmen in North and South Vietnam. A Huskie on rescue alert could be airborne in approximately one minute, and usually carried two rescuemen/fire-fighters and, hanging beneath it, a fire suppression kit. It often reached crashed aircraft before ground vehicles arrived, spraying foam to open a path for trapped crash victims to permit their escape.

*Specifications:* Powerplant one Lycoming T53-L-1B gas turbine, 860shp at take-off; length 25ft 2in (8.01m); height 15ft 6in (4.72m); main rotor diameter 47ft (14.32m); gross weight 5,900lb (2,675kg) ; maximum cruising speed 120mph (193kph); maximum rate of climb 2,000ft/min (610m/min); HOGE 18,000ft (5,486m); maximum fuel VFR; accommodation 1 pilot plus 2 passengers; first flight 27 September 1956.

primary low helicopter and he decided to refuel early. A single HC-130, 'King 03', and 'Jolly 19' headed west at about 7,000ft to conduct the refuelling and then began holding west along the border of Laos, waiting to see how things were going to develop. They were receiving several 'MiG threat' calls, but none of the crews was familiar with the reference point, 'Crab', being used by the radar operators.

Shortly afterwards the whole formation began wildly calling 'MiGs!'; then there was a flash and suddenly 'Jolly 71' disappeared in smoke. 'King 03' immediately dropped his tanks and headed west into the weeds and the now disconnected refuelling 'Jolly 19' did the same. Apparently two marauding MiGs had seized upon an easy opportu-

## Rescue Equipment Aboard Helicopters

*MA-1A Rescue Basket* Used primarily over the water to recover inert victims. The basket could be trawled through the water to accomplish the recovery. The MA-1A was cumbersome and difficult to manoeuvre through the cabin door and it was not the rescue device of choice.

*Forest Penetrator* This was the most widely used rescue device since it could be used for a multiple pick-up. With three fold-down seats and three slings, it could be sent down through trees with much success. With an attached flotation collar, it was used for many water rescues.

*Rescue Sling* Also known as the 'horse collar', this was very unfamiliar in use to many of those to be rescued. A crew member was usually sent down to make sure it was used properly.

*Rescue Seat* Much like the Forest Penetrator, the Rescue Seat had three seats but these were in a permanent 'down' position. It was not to be used for recovery in areas of dense foliage.

*Stokes Litter* This was a very difficult rescue device since it took up so much room in the cabin and was cumbersome to handle. It was only used in a situation where the victim needed to be immobilised.

*Fire Suppression Kit* Two types of FSK were used, the soft-hose kit and the later hard-hose FSK. Both kits carried the same amount of foam and water, 83 gallons of mixture, yielding 690 gallons of expanding foam. The device had 50 seconds of continued use and could reach up to 50ft on full stream, which proved to be ample because of the 'rotor wash' behind the helicopter. The objective was not to extinguish the fire but to cut a path to the burning aircraft and hold the path until the other fireman could accomplish the rescue. The soft-hose FSK weighed some 1,000lb when full and was about 5ft long, 4ft wide and 3ft 6in high; the hard-hose FSK weighed about 1,250lb when full and measured approximately 9ft long, 4ft 6in wide and 4ft high.

nity and made one high-speed pass through the holding helicopter formation, firing as they went and escaping to the North. 'Jolly 72' was in loose trail with 'Jolly 71' when the missile and MiG passed them on the right and hit 'Jolly 71'. The aforementioned F-105 crew, although having ejected safely, never made it into the POW system.

## A Typical SAR Rescue Package

Day one, late afternoon, December 1969. The crew of 'Roman 02', a Navy two seat F-4 Phantom, were reported shot down in an area known as 'Delta 25', just north of Mu Gia Pass along Route 101 in North Vietnam. Fast-FAC F-100F 'Misty 51' was quickly employed to put air strikes in the SAR area to protect the downed fliers. As daylight began fading fast, the decision was made to bed down the survivors for the night and they were advised that a first-light effort would be made to recover them the following day. Those involved at this stage were the Fast-FAC two-seat Super Sabre, on the scene; and, to coordinate the area, 'Crown', a command and control HC-130, and 'Waterboy', a GCI site.

Day two of the rescue began with 'Misty 51' again arriving in the area, to re-establish radio contact with the two survivors. They were properly authenticated, and the SAR force was directed to proceed into the area. After the hand-off of on-scene command from 'Misty 51' to 'Sandy 01', the rescue force was fully committed. Both survivors were successfully picked up and the forces egressed the area. On the scene for the recovery were 'Misty 51', the Fast-FAC; Sandys '01' to '04' (A-1 Skyraiders); HH-43 'Jolly Green 19'; 'Crown', the orbiting command and control HC-130; 'Misty 12', a replacement Fast-FAC which arrived in the area towards the end of the rescue; and 'Bison Flight', a strike package of F-105 Thunderchiefs.

## Authentication

All aircrews in South-East Asia completed an authentication card as part of their processing prior to their first flight in-theatre. The individual crew member would list five personal questions along with the answers. The responses to these questions could only be answered by the person who completed the card. For example, one question might be, 'What is the name of your dog?', the answer being 'Butch'. These authentication cards were kept on file at wing intelligence for use if a crew member was shot down. The theory was that if the man on the ground could not correctly answer the question, then he could not be a genuine survivor, but rather an impostor who was attempting to lure the rescue forces into a trap.

Capt Robert Castle, an A-7E pilot from VA-25 aboard the USS *Ranger*, was shot down in Laos approximately 17nm from NKP on 28 December 1970. A rescue team was despatched, comprising a single HH-43 'Pedro' flown by Capt Bobby Lay of Det 9, 38 ARRS, four 'Sandy' A-1 Skyraiders and an OV-1 'Nail' FAC. The 'Pedro' was not the normal SAR aircraft that would be sent to such a scene, but it just happened to be the only helicopter available that day. 'Nail 46', the OV-1 with which Castle had been operating, called in the hit on the A-7 aircraft and stayed in the area on tactical frequency whilst the rescue party assembled. Two 'Sandys' were vectored from Da Nang to the area, and once on the ground Castle established contact via his PRC-90 and was briefed to stay put until help arrived.

Bobby Lay later commented on the rescue: 'It was a very slick, quick and dirty rescue. Castle was on the ground for only nineteen minutes before we picked him up, but it probably seemed like an eternity to the guy. He was very calm, well, at least, his voice was not above normal.' The only conversation from Castle was, 'Pedro, do you want me to pop smoke?', to which Lay replied, 'Negative'. The pick-up went smoothly, and Lay recovered a small piece of twig from Castle's harness, which he kept throughout the war as a momento.

Sgt Michael E. Fish, a Pararescueman aboard an HH-43 from Det 11, 38th ARRS, won the Air Force Cross as a result of a rescue mission following the crash of an Army Huey about 25 miles south-west of Tuy Hoa. During the course of 18 February five survivors were reported to be trapped inside the wreckage, and, on arriving at the site, Fish and a fire-fighter were winched to the ground. Despite sporadic enemy fire, three of the survivors were freed and hoisted aboard the HH-43, whilst another survivor and a dead soldier were gathered by a Huey. One injured man remained trapped, and Fish stayed with him overnight following the departure of the rescue task force due to a shortage of fuel. The next morning the task force returned, again to enemy fire, freed the trapped survivor and evacuated the area.

Maj Robert Wilson of the Takhli-based 357th TFS/355 TFW, was on a combat mission in an F-105D when he was hit by ground fire over south-western Vietnam. The signal from his rather inadequate AN/URC-II survival radio reached an HC-54 Skymaster command ship, which vectored a flight of A-1s and a short-legged, Laos-based HH-43B to the rescue. Guided by the A-1s and Wilson, the PJ from the 'Pedro' plucked the Major from the foliage.

### Sikorsky's 'Jolly Green Giants'

As the 'Rolling Thunder' air strikes continued, the Air Force wanted to find a better way to rescue any downed airmen than using the rather limited HH-43 'Huskie'. The USAF was highly impressed with the transport and utility capabilities of the ex-US Navy Sikorsky S-61 Sea King amphibious transport helicopter and decided to procure a fully optimised variant to meet its own requirements. Sikorsky therefore developed the S-61R with two powerful T58-GE-1 turboshafts, pressurised rotor blades, a simplified lower hull and lateral fuselage sponsons into which were mounted two of the retractable tricycle landing gear legs. The revised design carried the USAF designation CH-3. The 'pod and boom' fuselage also incorporated a hydraulically powered rear ramp door which was fitted with a heavy-duty winch.

Operations in Vietnam, however, required a much greater capability, and this led directly to the development of the CH-3E, the 'Jolly Green Giant'. This new derivation was characterised by more powerful T58-GE-5 engines and a larger rotor diameter and fuselage length. The uprated type was first delivered in February 1966 and could lift 25 troops or carry twelve litters; it also carried a rescue hoist. The CH-3E was outfitted with self-defence and fire-suppression capabilities consisting of an Emerson TAT-102 gun turret on the outer edge of each fuselage sponson carrying a 7.62 minigun.

The HH-3E 'Jolly' was better configured for the rescue role, being fitted with protective armour, self-sealing fuel tanks, a retractable IFR probe and specialised mission equipment. Fourteen HH-3Es were ordered, but only eight were delivered, their numbers being boosted by a conversion programme that brought the remaining CH-3Es up to the same standard. The name 'Jolly Green Giant' came about after the first CH-3Cs arrived in Vietnam camouflaged in an overall green paint scheme. The colour coincided with an American television commercial advertising the Green Giant brand of vegetables and using the slogan 'Good things come from the valley of the Jolly Green Giant'. The name was soon adopted by the crews.

The first USAF pilot to accumulate 6,000 flying hours on the HH-3 was Maj Kyron Hall, and another valued rescue pilot was Capt Gerald O. Young. On one rescue, Young and his 'Jolly Green', plus a second HH-3, Army gunships, C-130 flare-ships and a 'King' ship, plucked a Marines reconnaissance team from the jungle where two helicopter rescue missions had already ended in disaster. Young's aircraft was shot down and, despite being badly burned, he nursed wounded soldiers and ran a diversionary effort to lure the approaching enemy soldiers. He was himself recovered and was awarded the Medal of Honor.

### Jollys in the Jungle

Typical of the 'Jolly Green Giant's mission are these two actual reports supplied from the archives of the 37th ARRS during the early 1970s in South-East Asia:

*Date: 18 July 1972*
*Mission Number: A-40-033*
*Flight Designation: Jolly Green 64*

*Mission Objective: Owl 02A*
*Location: 280/28/69*
*Saves: One Combat Save*
*Report by: AC Captain Mike T. Gerald, 37th ARRS*

'We were clocked on at 0015 while the Alpha crews were out making an attempt on Owl 02A, the pilot from of a downed F-4 Phantom. Alpha-1 was Jolly Green 66 (JG 66) and AH was Jolly Green 71 (JG 71). At 0045, JG 66 reported to have taken battle damage while pulling off of area of the survivor because of turbulence. He reportedly had a fuel leak and was returning to Channel 77.

'Jollys 72 and 64 were scrambled and airborne at 0100Z and proceeded to the area of Channel 69 declaring feet wet. While en route JG 66 said he thought he had damage to his flight controls and was declaring an emergency, and requested an intercept in the event of a water landing. Upon testing of miniguns JG 64 said he had one possible operational gun, and my aircraft had two good and possibly three functional guns.

'At this time, approximately 0130Z, JG 72 directed JG 64 to join up with JG 66 and escort him to Channel 77 while we proceeded to Channel 69 to be high bird for JG 71. We joined JG 71 and began holding feet wet while Sandys and FACs worked the survivor's area in an attempt to evaluate the severity of the turbulence and feasibility of another pick-up attempt.

'JG 71 and 72 briefed for air refueling, and refueled at 0213Z. JG 71 discovered he had no gas mask for his flight engineer and was going to return to Channel 77 to pick one up. JG 72 was going to also RTB for new batteries for the miniguns but was advised by JG 64 that he was airborne from Channel 77 and had extra batteries for us on board and would rendezvous at Channel 69. We proceeded to Channel 69 and awaited the arrival of JG 64. He arrived, the batteries were loaded and we requested to stay on ground alert, but we were told to launch with JG 64 to RTB and 72 to join with 71 and hold feet wet. At 0505Z Sandy 07 determined pick-up was not possible at this time and for all SAR forces to RTB. On the ground, problems of turbulence and ingress and egress were evaluated and the conclusion was drawn that the SAR attempt would have to wait until the winds died down.

'At 0900Z, another attempt was planned and JG 71 and JG 64 launched. Initial orbit was feet wet off Channel 69 (0917Z) which was subsequently moved to 280/28/69 at 0926Z. At 0933Z JG 71 was briefed that an attempt seemed feasible at this time by Sandy 01, now on-scene commander. The run-in began with JG 64 orbiting directly overhead at 13,000 feet just above a broken overcast layer of clouds.

'At 0942Z JG 71 was in the area and the survivor was briefed to pop smoke. The survivor was contacted visually at 0944Z and the Jolly's jungle penetrator started down. Sandy 01 asked the survivor to move to the penetrator if possible. JG 71 was vectored closer to the survivor and the survivor climbed on the penetrator at 0954Z and joined up with JG 64 feet wet at 1000Z. SAR forces joined up and RTB'd to Channel 77. The survivor was in excellent shape. Total time flown by this crew was 6.7 hours in 2 sorties. Negative ground fire.'

*Date: 18 July 1972*
*Mission Number: A-40-033*
*Flight Designation: Jolly Green 71*
*Mission Objective: Recovery of Owl 02A/B*
*Location: 1621N 10713E*
*Saves: One Combat Save*
*Report by: Captain W. H. Frederick USAF, Aircraft Commander, Jolly Green 71*

'Since the Alpha crews had flown during the night on 17 July and early morning of 18 July, the Bravo crews briefed at 0530L and assumed the Alpha Alert at 0700L, 18 July, in preparation for an attempted recovery of Owl 02A and Owl 02B, who were F-4 Phantom crewman shot down at approximately YD370 110. Nail 18, a Forward Air Controller (FAC) in an OV-10 aircraft, went into the survivors' area at first light and raised both crewman on the radio. Owl 02A had spent the night in a tree, suspended by his parachute harness, but had made a safe descent to the ground at dawn. Owl 02B was separated from his pilot but was talking to him as well as the FAC overhead. He reported a severe back injury and an inability to move.

'Having located the survivors, checked the weather and assessed the enemy's presence in the area, the FAC advised the launch of the Jollys. Jolly Green 66, Alpha Low, Jolly Green 71, Alpha High, Sandy 01 and Sandy 07 took off at 0715L and were directed to hold feet wet near Tan My while some air strikes were put in to secure the area around the survivors. Entering their orbit at 0750L, the Jollys climbed to 4,000 feet MSL in the holding pattern while the Sandy aircraft went feet dry for a first-hand look at the SAR area. Nail 20, another OV-10 FAC, also entered the SAR area at approximately this time to take over as on-scene commander from Nail 18, who was getting low on fuel. Low clouds in a scattered to broken condition at 6,000 to 8,000 feet MSL and moderate to severe orographic turbulence were serious limiting factors affecting the supporting tactical air strikes and the ability of the FACs and Sandys to maintain good visual surveillance of the SAR area.

'At 0810L the OSC directed the Jollys feet dry to a final orbit point at 280/28/69. The Jollys proceeded at 13,000 feet MSL to the new holding point, and Nail 20 came out to lead Jolly Green 66 to the survivors' area. Alpha Low went directly into the SAR area while Alpha High entered final holding. The only avenue of approach to the survivors which was open to Alpha Low was below the cloud deck where the FACs, Sandys or F-4 could not venture. Alone in this low-altitude regime of cloud-enshrouded mountain peaks, severe turbulence and enemy forces, Jolly Green 66 managed to raise Owl 02B on the radio and then caught a brief glimpse of his parachute. While manoeuvring for another pass over the survivor, Jolly Green 66 was caught in a downdraught and was nearly slammed into the mountain. Aircraft recovery was only possible after a descent to the treetops. At this time the aircraft also took numerous hits from enemy ground fire, forcing an abort of the rescue attempt. En route to Channel 77, the Jolly Green discovered bullet holes in the left auxiliary fuel tank and gradual loss of second-stage pressure as hydraulic fluid was depleted through bullet holes in that system's plumbing.

'The aircraft commander of Jolly Green 66 recommended that another rescue attempt not be tried until the weather improved in the SAR area. Jolly Green 71, still holding at the initial point, then assumed the role of Alpha Low and was joined by Jolly Green 72, the new Alpha High. The two Alpha aircraft were directed to hold feet wet again near Tan My while FACs and Sandys remained in the SAR area to direct supporting air strikes and to watch for weather favouring another rescue attempt. At some time between 1100L and 1130L the FACs lost radio contact with Owl 02B. Owl 02A reported hearing gunshots from Bravo man's area. Radio contact could not be reestablished with Owl 02B.

'The Jollys held at Tan My until 1315L, when it was agreed by Sandy 07 that the weather precluded a pick-up at that time. All SAR forces RTB at 1355L. During the afternoon the cloud deck lifted and went to a scattered condition, but the surface wind did not abate. Late in the afternoon a decision was made for another attempt to pick up the survivor just before sunset, when the wind might possibly slacken. The Alphas and Sandys re-launched at 1640L. The Alpha High crew transferred to Jolly Green 64 for maintenance reasons. Holding briefly at 1715L off Tan My, the Jollys were then directed to the final holding point, 280/28/69 at 1725L, after Sandy 01 had talked to Owl 02A. The winds had in fact decreased somewhat, lessening the orographic turbulence. The decision: Go.

'A Nail FAC rendezvoused with Jolly Green 71 as it approached the final holding point and the Low bird continued on directly to the SAR area, making a long, descending run-in at 150KIAS behind the Nail. After crossing an enemy trail structure at 10,000 feet MSL, rate of descent was further increased to get below the clouds in time to see Sandy's marker smoke. A brief glimpse of white marker smoke through a hole in the clouds prompted a steep 360-degree left turn in near full auto-rotation to avoid overshooting the survivors' location. Emergence below the cloud level occurred during the turn and, as Jolly Green 71 rolled out on the initial inbound heading, Sandy launched another smoke rocket to impact directly ahead, leading to the survivor. Jolly Green 71 started slowing down, called for the survivor's smoke at 1744L, and the pilot immediately spotted the survivor half way up a 60 degree slope at one o'clock, low. Entering a very high hover, the lower UHF antenna was selected and the survivor could be heard loudly and clearly on the radio. The flight engineer started the forest penetrator down while directing the pilot over the survivor. Thinking that there might not be enough hoist cable to reach the survivor, the flight engineer directed the pilot to lower the hover altitude.

'The hover altitude was reduced by approximately 150 feet, and suddenly the helicopter shuddered violently and entered a settling with power state as it lost transitional lift from the wind that had been blowing into the main rotor from the crest of a ridge 300 yards in front of the aircraft. A near-instantaneous recovery was accomplished by simply holding full-up collective, lowering the nose to gain 15 or 20 knots airspeed, and then hover-taxying 100 yards to the rear, following the engineer's vectors. This sequence was repeated a second time before the limiting descent altitude was established at 5,200 feet MSL, approximately 200 feet above the survivor and level with the ridgeline. Due to the steep terrain slope away from the right side of the aircraft, the pilot had no outside visual hover reference closer than 500 feet below the helicopter or ½ to ¾ miles to the side, so the co-pilot then took the controls and provided a rock-steady hover, utilising the near up-slope terrain on his side for hover reference.

'At 1725Z the survivor started up the penetrator, and as soon as he was clear of the trees Jolly Green 71 purchased additional hover insurance by increasing the hover altitude to 250 feet AGL to get farther into the envelope of wind that was blowing across from the ridgeline. The survivor was on board the helicopter at 1745L, and as Jolly Green 71 started an immediate climb to 13,000 feet MSL, the Pararescuemen were cleared to fire the miniguns to cover the Jolly's exit from the area. The survivor was in excellent condition considering his ordeal. There was no further contact with Owl 02B, and all SAR forces RTB, landing at Ch. 77 at 1845L.'

## More Jolly Reports

Sgt Thomas Newman, a Pararescueman aboard an HH-53, recovered a downed F-105 flier near Savannakhet in Laos. Newman was lowered through the jungle canopy to reach the survivor under intense enemy fire which threatened both him and his aircraft, so Newman requested they evacuate the area. A second HH-53 came into play, lowered its hoist and reeled in the pair from the ground. However, Newman had become entangled in the cable, so had to lower them again. Finally the pair were recovered, Newman with cuts and bruises and the pilot with a broken leg and arm.

Not all rescues were successful, either for the Pararescuemen or for the downed airman. Once such incident involved Airman First Class Charles King, part of the crew of an HH-3 from Det 1, 40th ARRS, who were involved in the rescue of a pilot in Laos. On 24 December a parachute was spotted, triggering off a Christmas Day recovery. Once established at the site, King was lowered, located the pilot and secured him to the hoist. At this point automatic weaponry opened up on the aircraft and King. King transmitted 'I'm hit, I'm hit! Pull up, pull up!', whereupon the aircraft initiated a immediate exit, snapping off the hoist cable. King was declared MIA until December 1978, when he was declared KIA.

More fortunate was Airman First Class Joel Tally—again a Pararescueman—engaged on his first mission as a member of the 37th

ARRS aboard an H-3. An injured F-105 pilot was down near Dong Ha, and he was surrounded by enemy soldiers, who set up a 'flak-trap' for the rescue forces. The first attempt damaged an H-3, the second severely damaged another and a covering F-105 was also brought down by ground fire. Finally an H-3 penetrated the defences and Airman Tally descended, found the pilot and called for a fast exit. Whilst the pair were being hoisted the H-3 was raked by enemy fire, causing over 40 hits. The aircraft dragged the two men away on the hoist departure, however, and on this occasion both survived.

Capt Wayne Stovall of the 40th ARRS flew repeated trips deep into North Vietnam to rescue two downed airmen following an initial attempt by another HH-53 which had been abandoned on account of heavy ground fire. Eventually Stovall succeeded in recovering the crew.

HH-3 pilot Capt Gregory Etzel from the 37th ARRS attempted to rescue a downed F-105 pilot from a heavily defended area on 2 July 1970, but the onset of darkness and fierce resistance prevented the rescue. The next day Etzel returned with a task force, with 'Spads' silencing enemy ground fire before the Jolly swept in and recovered the airman.

Sgt Michael Smith was the Pararescueman aboard a 'Jolly' during the recovery of a downed F-100F crew, when enemy fire made the helicopter's hoist inoperative and the Flight Engineer was forced to cut the cable. However, the 'Jolly' made four attempts to recover the PJ plus crew, eventually recovering the trio despite intense ground fire. Capt Leroy Schanberg, a pilot from the 40th ARRS, was awarded the Air Force Cross as a result of operations to recover an OV-10 pilot shot down over Laos.

The 3rd ARR Group evacuated 132 people from the citadel in the besieged city of Quang Tri to Da Nang, Vietnam. Five HH-53s of the 37th ARR Squadron were used for this mission. Thankfully no one was injured, despite the nearby presence of enemy forces. S/Sgt Robert L. LaPointe, a Pararescueman in the first HH-53, silenced enemy snipers with his door-mounted minigun and, when the helicopter landed, he organised the evacuees and maintained ground control until the second HH-53 arrived.

Following the enemy spring offensive through the DMZ on 30 March, rescue activity increased dramatically. On 13 April the 40th ARR Squadron was tasked to find USMC Maj Clyde D. Smith, who

# Sikorsky CH/HH-53 'Super Jolly'

The HH-3E, the Super Jolly Green Giant, is a twin-engine, heavy-lift helicopter. It is used for search and recovery of personnel and aerospace hardware in support of global air and space operations. It is also used for combat and special operations. The aircraft has the ability to operate from land or water, and its combat rescue-related equipment includes titanium armour plating, jettisonable external fuel tanks, internal self-sealing bladder-type fuel tanks under the cabin floor, a retractable in-flight refuelling probe, two 7.62mm machine guns, a forest penetrator and a high-speed rescue hoist with 240ft (72.8m) of cable. The Jolly Green Giant also has been used for astronaut contingency recovery. Several of the aircraft have been equipped with the mid-air retrieval system for the recovery of aerospace hardware.

The long-range helicopter has a hydraulically operated rear ramp for straight in-loading and a jettisonable sliding door on the right side at the front of the cabin. It has a gas turbine auxiliary power supply for independent field operations and built-in equipment for the removal and replacement of all major components in remote areas. The five-blade rotors are pressurised for quick, easy inspection, and both the all-metal rotor and aluminium tail rotor are self-lubricating. The horizontal stabiliser is on the starboard side of the tail rotor pylon.

The Jolly Green Giant has an automatic flight control system, instrumentation for all-weather operation and Doppler navigation equipment. Twin turboshaft engines are mounted side by side on top of the cabin, immediately forward of the main transmission. The aircraft also has a retractable tricycle-type landing gear. Despite the helicopter's power, its thin metal skin can be easily pierced—even a ball-point pen slammed against the fuselage could produce a hole—so it can only be imagined what a well-aimed burst of machine gun fire could do!

The HH-3E is a modified version of the CH-3 transport helicopter developed for aircrew rescue missions deep into enemy-held territory during the Vietnam War.

### Specifications

*Powerplant:* Two General Electric T64-GE-7s rated at 3,925shp (2,927kW)

*Rotor system:* Main rotor diameter 7ft 3in (22.02m); tail rotor diameter 16ft 0in (4.88m); main rotor disc area 4,070 sq ft (378.1m$^2$); tail rotor disc area 201.06 sq ft (18.68m$^2$).

*Fuselage and tail:* Length overall, rotors turning, 88ft 3in (26.90m); fuselage length 67ft 2in (20.47m) excluding refuelling probe; height overall 24ft 11in (7.60m); height to top of rotor hub 17ft 1½in (5.22m); wheel base 27ft 0in (8.23m).

*Weights:* Empty 23, 569lb (10,690kg); mission take-off 38,238lb (17,344kg); maximum take-off 42,000lb (19,050kg). (630 US gal); external fuel up to two 450 US gal (1,703-litre) auxiliary jettisonable tanks.

*Speed:* Maximum level speed, 'clean' at sea level, 196mph (315kph); cruising speed 173mph (278kph).

*Range:* Maximum range 540 miles (868km) with maximum auxiliary fuel.

*Performance:* Maximum rate of climb at sea level 2,070ft/min (631m/min); service ceiling 20,400ft (6,220m); hovering ceiling 11,700ft (3,565m) in ground effect, 6,500ft (1,980m) out of ground effect.

*Primary function:* Combat search and recovery, and special operations.

*Guidance system:* Doppler navigation equipment

*Armament:* Two 7.62mm machine guns.

*Load options:* 25 combat-equipped troops, 15 litter patients or 5,000lb (2,250kg) cargo.

*Crew:* 4 (pilot, co-pilot, flight engineer and Pararescue specialist; a flight surgeon may be included).

*Date first deployed:* 1966.

was down between Tchepone, Laos, and the DMZ. Capt Bennie D. Orrell, piloting an HH-53, approached the search area, and Smith 'popped his smoke' to show his location. The smoke drifted uphill before it emerged from the trees. When Orrell hovered at that spot, Smith made a 'max effort' run uphill to the hoist. He grabbed it, but Orrell encountered enemy fire and was forced to retract the hoist, not knowing that Smith was hanging on until the hoist had cleared the trees!

Eight HH-53 Super Jollys and three HC-130 tankers from the 40th and 56th ARR Squadrons, respectively, participated in Operation 'Eagle Pull', the evacuation of US personnel from Phnom Penh, Cambodia. One HH-53 inserted a combat control team prior to the evacuation whilst two HH-53s removed the fifteen military personnel from the capital following the completion of the evacuation. The Joint Rescue Coordination Center (JRCC), operated by the 3rd ARR Group at Nakhon Phanom, exercised operational control of the rescue forces. There were no ARRS injuries or casualties, although two HH-53s incurred hits from small-calibre ground fire.

'Gunfighter 82' was the crew of an F-4E assigned to the 366th TFW at Da Nang, 'Gunfighter 82A' being Lt-Col Arthur Blissett and 'Gunfighter 82B' his 'Wizzo', Lt Michael Murray. On the night of 17 December 1971 'Gunfighter 82' was shot down by a SAM near Mu Gia Pass about 65 miles east of Nakhon Phanom RTAFB, Thailand. Mu Gia Pass was a notoriously 'bad place' situated along the Ho Chi Minh Trail, and only a week earlier the crew of 'Ashcan 02', an F-105 'Wild Weasel', had been downed and successfully rescued from the same area. Two Super Jolly Green Giants from the 40th ARRS at NKP were scrambled and succeeded in retrieving the 'Gunfighter' pair.

### Drone Drama

On 21 July 1971 a single HH-3 'Jolly Green' was tasked to recover an RP drone and ended up being shot down by groundfire in the area just as it was picking its No 1 PJ by hoist. The 'Jolly' rolled over a couple times and ended up against some trees. The covering fighter crews involved in the recovery saw the 'Jolly' upside down on the downslope of a small clearing; the drone, its parachute in the trees at upper end of the clearing, was situated in the middle, and the 'Jolly's tip tanks were also visible, jettisoned in the area of the drone. The three crew members (pilot, co-pilot and FE) had scrambled out to the lower end of the slope, whilst the two PJs were located in the middle of the clearing. An Army medevac Huey was the first rescue helicopter on the scene and picked up the FE, who was suffering from severe back pains (later diagnosed as a ruptured disc in his spine), by having him grab the Huey's skids so that they could hover-taxi with him further up the slope to where the other PJ, who had extensive facial injuries (having been hit by a rotor blade as the helicopter went down), was located. The injured were packed up and the Huey exited successfully. About ten minutes later an Air America H-34 arrived and picked up the pilot and co-pilot with its hoist and horse collar. However, the hoist broke with the co-pilot 10ft up and the hoist operator reeled in the cable by hand as they exited the area. Another H-34 came in and picked up the re-grounded co-pilot by horse collar. The first recovery flight scheduled for the next day was given the task of determining whether the helicopter was recoverable, but it was greeted by so much groundfire that the 'Sandy' A-1s were directed to destroy the Jolly *in situ*.

# 3

# Sandy and Spad

The A-1 Skyraider was well-suited for several combat roles in Vietnam, flying rescue, close air support and forward air control (FAC) missions. In the rescue role the Skyraider pilot was required to locate the downed airman and protect him with the A-1's firepower. He became the on-scene commander of the recovery effort, controlling fighter-bomber strikes on hostile positions and escorting the helicopters during the pick-up of the survivor. On a close air support mission, the Skyraider pilot's ability to attack ground targets with pin-point precision made the A-1 an outstanding weapon to support friendly troops in contact with the enemy. In the FAC role, the A-1 pilot was an aerial observer and controller. In constant radio contact with Army units in his sector, he warned of enemy ambushes and then controlled fast-moving fighter strikes on the hostile positions.

The airman downed deep in enemy territory and the embattled foot soldier caught in a Viet Cong crossfire frequently depended on the Skyraiders for their very lives. Often running the gauntlet of heavy AAA fire, it is also true that the 'Spad drivers' were flying for their lives. Even before the pilot had dropped the aircraft's nose for an attack, clips of 37mm groundfire were already piercing the sky, coming out of the murk like a stream of molten metal. Sometimes the AAA was so thick that 'you could land on it', and many 'Spads' were hard-pressed to roll in without getting hit first. However, the Skyraider was at its most vulnerable when pulling off a target and getting flak from the rear. During the course of the conflict radar-directed guns became part of the North Vietnamese arsenal, and for the low-flying 'Spad' radar meant deadly accuracy: if the pilot failed to spot the muzzle flash, in all probability he would be hit.

A-1s came to Vietnam in the summer of 1964 and also became the workhorses of the Vietnamese Air Force and the mainstay of US Air Force counter-insurgency (COIN) operations. Eight thousand pounds of ordnance could be hung from its wings, and long endurance—in excess of four hours—made it an ideal aircraft for rescue escort, close

---

## Douglas A-1 Skyraider

The Douglas-built A-1 was a single-engine, propeller-driven fighter-bomber first saw service with the Navy in the Second World War. The A-1H was the single-seat model, while the A-1E was the two-seat 'wide bodied' version. Though the Skyraider could reach a speed of 400mph in a dive, it was slow in comparison with jet fighters. Its slow speed made the A-I more vulnerable to groundfire, but also gave the pilot more time to find the enemy's concealed positions. Furthermore, the aircraft's manoeuvrability allowed the pilot to make many firing passes on the target in rapid succession: it could be quickly turned and repositioned for another attack without leaving the immediate area.

The Air Force adopted the A-1 when it was retired from the Navy for use in Vietnam as a close air support asset. Instead of the myriad electronic 'gizmos' that were becoming commonplace in the jet world, the Spad was totally conventional and relied on traditional flying skills to make it perform. A 'tail-dragger' of the finest order, the Skyraider was a romantic aircraft, and one much loved by its operators.

Four versions of the 'Spad' were used in Vietnam, the A-1G, A-1H, A-1B and two seat A-1E. Painted in the disruptive 'jungle scheme' of two greens and tan, the aircraft operated mainly from Nakhon Phanom ('Naked Fanny', as it was colloquially called). Like the modern-day Harrier, it was said that one could dangle any amount of death and destruction from beneath the Skyraider's wings. By 1966 riot control munitions had been added to rescue missions, and these controversial weapons included CBU-19 cluster bombs and tear gas-filled CBU-30A anti-personnel bombs. Other 'nasties' included the BLU-52, which contained a cocktail of tear gas and napalm.

---

air support and FAC missions. Able to fly in poor weather, withstand small-arms and automatic weapons fire and carry a great variety of ordnance, the Douglas Skyraider was a favourite with fighter pilots and FACs.

## Spad Stories

The following are combat diary entries made by Capt Byron 'Hook' Hukee, a 'Spad driver' with the 602nd Fighter Squadron (Special Operations Commando) during 1970–72, and based at NKP. He flew many ground-pounding sorties in his trusty 'Spad' before moving to the 'Sandy' rescue mission. Here are some of his notes:

'I had now completed nearly three months of my combat tour in the A-1 Skyraider. During this period I had flown 33 combat missions worth 100.8 combat flying hours. With 167.1 total hours in the A-1, I guess the "powers that be" decided I could be entrusted with the single-seat models of the Super Spad, the A-1H and A-1J. This was a significant milestone, since it also meant that I would begin my "Sandy" checkout. Search and Rescue (SAR) was the most demanding and dangerous mission flown by the Skyraider during this time frame. It was also potentially the most rewarding.

*Date 27 Jan*
*Mission 34*
*Aircraft A-1H 135-257*
*Sandy checkout ride*

'[Hobo 23] Barrel Roll strike with Col [Jack] Robinson . . . "Supermarket" load . . . Col R. always got H's for his strikes . . . As I recall, my bombs were not super.

'As I read my diary entry for the 27th of January, 1972, I am amazed that I made no reference to the fact that this was my first combat mission in the A-1H. This was noteworthy since the entire flying schedule was now available to me, once I got my Sandy checkout. Colonel Jack Robinson was the wing commander of the 56th Special Operations Wing (parent organisation of the 1st SOS) at this time. He naturally picked his missions on the flying schedule and the squadron schedulers did the rest. I'm sure my wealth of experience flying with LtCol Barbena, the squadron commander, made me the obvious choice! The "Supermarket" load was one which had a little of everything. There was both "hard" and "soft" ordnance that allowed us to be effective against most any type target we might have encountered. The two Mk-82s we carried on this load were the hard ordnance that would be effective against hard targets such as bunkers or gun emplacements. The majority of the load was characterised as soft ordnance which meant it could be used relatively close to friendly forces. This included 2.75in FFAR, CBU-22 and -25, and Mk-47 white phosphorus bombs. And, oh yes, there were both 20mm and 7.62mm gun rounds. TACAN station channel 96 was on Skyline Ridge and was the only TACAN channel we could receive at low elevations in the "barrel". The strike on this mission was unremarkable. Col Robinson was on his second A-1 tour; he previously had served as squadron commander for one of the A-1 squadrons. He was also noted for his tour as Thunderbird lead when the team flew the F-100 Super Sabre.'

*Date 29 Jan*
*Mission 35*
*Aircraft A-1G 132-528*

'[Hobo 23] Sandy wingman check ride as #2 chasing [Lt Glen] Priebe with [Maj] Jim Harding in my right seat . . .

'Priebe stayed low and pressed . . . North of Sam Thong.

'This was a "check" ride although no paperwork was filled out to that effect, at least none that I ever saw. Jim Harding was the squadron ops officer and apparently wanted to see how his lieutenants were doing in the air. Jim was on his second tour; his first was as a FAC in the O-1 Bird Dog. He was destined to become the 1st SOS commander later in his tour. Sam Thong was a village north of Long Tien and south of the PDJ [Plaine des Jarres]. It was also the site of LS 20. This village with its karst-surrounded airfield was sited along a clear flowing mountain stream which never failed to catch my eye as I flew overhead.'

*Date 31 Jan*
*Mission 36*
*Aircraft A-1J 142-021*
'[Sandy 02] First Sandy ride as 2 with [Capt Randy] Jayne . . . Tango Orbit (Barrel Roll) . . . Strike in marginal weather at 096/55/96 with Raven 52.

'It didn't take long to get on the Sandy schedule after my last ride with the ops officer. I must have done OK. This mission consisted of a lengthy Sandy orbit, followed by an air strike south of the PDJ. The weather was dicey and we most likely got in, did our thing, and headed for home. There was no BDA mentioned in my log. Basically, each day's flying schedule consisted of two pairs of A-1 single-seaters (H or J) on SAR alert. The morning pair would "hot" cock their aircraft at first light (sunrise) and remain on 15-minute alert status until midmorning, when they would launch for an additional airborne alert period to cover the morning fighter missions in northern Laos and North Vietnam. The Linebacker campaign had not yet begun, but air-to-air and reconnaissance sorties were still being flown. Once the air activity diminished, the SAR command and control headquarters, through their mouthpiece King, would release the Sandys for a strike prior to their RTB to NKP. The afternoon pair of Sandy pilots would cock their aircraft so as to assume SAR alert once the airborne Sandys were released to strike. They would repeat the ground alert/airborne alert scenario. During my one-year tour, this same process was repeated at FOLs in Southeast Asia. At any given time, we had two Sandys on alert at Da Nang and either Ubon or Bien Hoa. The Ubon FOL shifted to Bien Hoa in early 1972 in response to increased communist activity in the tri-border area of Cambodia, Laos, and South Vietnam and An Loc, SVN.'

*Date 4 Feb*
*Mission 37*
*Aircraft A-1G 132-528*
'My first journal entry for 4 Feb 1972 [Hobo 41 with Maj Don "Major Major" Milner] Heavy Hook scramble to destroy a downed Cobra west of Ashau Valley . . . Hit it with soft ordnance with little visible effect . . . Worked with Mike 85.'

*Date  4 Feb*
*Mission 38*
*Aircraft A-1G 132-528*
'[Hobo 41 with Maj Don "Major Major" Milner] Loaded up 6 Mk-82s apiece at Da Nang to destroy the UH-1H . . . Had some difficulty relocating the target in marginal weather, but did find it . . . Dropped in pairs on my first pass, then singles (five passes) . . . Hit real close on a couple of passes, rolling it over . . . Major Major also got close on one. Back on the Hobo schedule again after my first Sandy ride, but somehow it didn't seem so bad, now that I knew both options were open for me. It helped to keep one sharp. Apparently there was a real need to destroy this Army helicopter. There is conflicting information in my journal as in two places it is referenced as a Cobra, but I also refer to a UH-1H, which is a Huey. I would suspect it was the latter as it was a mission relating to team insertion. This was an interesting demonstration of the limited effect our soft ordnance load had on some targets. I suspect we were anticipating the chopper to erupt in a huge ball of fire as we dropped a total of 8 canisters of CBU-25, 4 canisters of CBU-22, 4 pods of LAU-3 HE rockets, 4 pods of LAU-68 WP rockets, and 4 Mk-47 white phosphorus bombs on it. To say nothing of the 20mm and 7.62 mm strafe. A little embarrassing now that I think about it. We dropped into Da Nang to get a "bigger hammer". The total of 12 Mk-82s we dropped next would do the trick, we were certain of that. After some delay caused by the marginal weather, we rendezvoused again with Mike 85, an O-2 FAC out of Da Nang, and attacked the target once more. Again, there were no noticeable secondary explosions, but since we rolled it over a few

times it certainly wouldn't ever fly again, but perhaps the important equipment on board did survive? We'll never know.'

## Spad Down: Major D. Myers and Major B. Fisher

On 10 March 1966 Maj Bernard F. Fisher and his wingman, Capt Francisco (Paco) Vazquez, took off from Pleiku Air Base in South Vietnam's central highlands. A hundred and fifty miles to the north, near the Laotian border, lay the Special Forces camp in the A Shau valley. Twenty American Special Forces troops and 375 South Vietnamese soldiers were under attack by over 2,000 North Vietnamese Army Regulars. The siege was in its second day, and the defenders, who had been forced into a single bunker in the northern corner of the outpost, depended on American air strikes to slow the enemy advance. The North Vietnamese ringed the valley floor with more than twenty anti-aircraft artillery pieces and hundreds of automatic weapons, making it a deadly flak trap for the slow-moving A-1Es. One pilot described it as 'like flying inside Yankee Stadium with the people in the bleachers firing at you with machine guns.'

Fisher and Vazquez joined four other A-1Es orbiting high above A Shau. The pilots were handicapped by a deck of low cloud hanging over the valley. Maj Fisher had flown here the day before in bad weather, and if there was a way to get down through the murk he would find it. His luck held as he located a small hole in the undercast and led the formation of six Skyraiders down towards the jungle floor. The A-1Es broke into the clear to find that the ragged cloud ceiling lay only 800ft above the trees, obscuring the tops of the surrounding hills. They would be forced to operate at low altitude, constantly in the sights of the enemy gunners.

Skyraider pilots had nicknamed the narrow valley 'The Tube' because it was less than a mile wide and six miles long and provided little manoeuvring room for the bombing and strafing runs against the Viet Cong. Restricted by the weather and high terrain, the A-1Es could attack from just one direction. The pilots would be compelled to fly straight down the valley, deliver their ordnance during a hard left turn, continue the turn into a tight 180-degree escape manoeuvre and race back out of the valley. They knew that the North Vietnamese would fill the approach to the valley with a deadly curtain of fire.

Bernie Fisher led a string of four Skyraiders on the first pass down The Tube while an Army radioman described the hostile positions along the valley's south wall. The enemy gunners found the range, shattering the canopy of Capt Hubert King's aircraft with an accurate burst. No longer able to see out of the bullet-riddled windscreen and having missed death by inches, King pulled out of the fight and headed for Pleiku. After attacking and escaping successfully, the two remaining wingmen immediately returned for a second strafing pass. Maj Dafford W. 'Jump' Myers suddenly felt his machine lurch. He recalls: 'I've been hit by 50mm calibers before, but this was something bigger, maybe the Chinese 37mm cannon.' Almost immediately the engine started sputtering and cutting out, and then it gave out for good. The cockpit filled with smoke. Myers got on the radio and gave his call-sign, 'Surf 41', and said, 'I've been hit and hit hard.' 'Hobo 51', Bernie Fisher's call-sign, came right back and said, 'Rog, you're on fire and burning clear back past your tail.' Myers was much too low to bail out so he told Fisher that he would have to put the aircraft down on a small airstrip below and take his chances.

Though the airstrip was controlled by the enemy and flanked by heavy guns, 'Jump' Myers had no choice as he began a gliding turn towards the touch-down point. His forward vision was blocked by smoke and flame, so Bernie Fisher 'talked' him into a proper alignment and rate of descent. As the crippled Skyraider crossed the landing threshold, Fisher realised that it was going too fast to stop on the short strip. He warned Myers to raise the landing gear and 'Jump' retracted the wheels just before the aircraft settled on its belly. Fisher remembers: 'He had tried to release his belly tank, but couldn't, so it blew as soon as he touched. A huge billow of flame went up and the fuel made a path right down to where he stopped. He had skidded several hundred feet before he spilled off to the right side of the runway. The flame just followed him right on down, caught up with him and the A-1E turned into a huge ball of fire. I thought he would get out right away—usually you can get right out and run, but he didn't. It seemed like an awful long while. I estimated about 40 seconds because I made almost a 270-degree turn around him.'

Fisher continued to circle the airstrip and notified the airborne command post that Myers was probably hurt and trapped inside the blazing aircraft. He would learn later that 'Jump' was busy removing his parachute, helmet, gun and survival kit so that he could make a fast exit through the flames. Fisher still has vivid memories of the scene on the battle-torn runway: 'I continued my turn around on the east side of the strip and about that time "Jump" came out the right side of the airplane. I think the wind must have blown the flames away from the right side. He jumped out and ran, and it looked like he was burning. There was smoke coming from him, but I guess it was because he was so saturated with smoke in that cockpit. He ran toward the end of the wing, jumped across and ran a short distance to the side of the strip.'

Myers hid in scrub brush along one side of the runway opposite the enemy positions on the other side of the strip. He waved as Fisher flew directly overhead. Fisher now knew he was alive, but had no way of knowing if 'Jump' was badly hurt. Fisher was soon joined by Captains Jon Lucas and Dennis Hague, and the trio of Skyraiders made repeated strafing attacks to protect the beleaguered Myers. Ten minutes later the command post advised that the rescue helicopter was still twenty minutes away and asked Fisher if he could rendezvous with the helicopter above the overcast and escort the rescue aircraft down through the hole in the clouds. Twenty minutes, Fisher concluded, would be too late. 'I don't think we could have done it. If we had left him there, the VC would have soon been on him because they were all around him. They controlled the area, but he was pretty well hidden in the brush so we figured they didn't have him.'

Fisher therefore decided to make a daring landing on to the strip. A startled Myers saw the wide-body Spad, ran out of his hiding place and dived head first into the open cockpit of the A-1E as Fisher pushed the throttles to the firewall and made an impressive take-off. Fisher later received the Medal of Honor

### Spads from Both Sides: Captain George Merrett

During his combat tour in South-East Asia George Merrett served with the 602nd Fighter Squadron (Commando) from April 1968 to 1969, flying the Douglas A-1 Skyraider on 'Sandy' rescue missions and 'Firefly' strike/forward air controller (FAC) missions out of Udorn and Nakhon Phanom Royal Thai AFBs. About half-way through his year's assignment, he was scheduled to lead a morning two-ship 'Firefly' strike mission over the central part of the Plaine des Jarres in Northern Laos. He had just released ordnance over the target in a steep dive-bombing pass and started his pull-up when the engine began to run rough. Levelling off, he attempted to add power but the engine backfired badly. He was sure that he had taken a hit in the

44

engine from ground fire. The cylinder head temperature went to full hot, and, knowing that he was at least 100 miles from home base at NKP with only partial power available, he was unable to maintain level flight: the aircraft was slowly dropping, and he could not make it home.

Approximately 20 miles west of his position was Lima Site 21, located on the south-west corner of the PDJ. The site had an east–west narrow dirt landing strip used by the CIA and Laotian military and was surrounded by enemy territory. Merrett headed west for a forced landing, having the advantage of the sun over his left shoulder and a clear windscreen. His wingman contacted the Lockheed C-130 airborne command and control ship called 'Crown', reported his airborne emergency and asked 'Crown' to start a rescue effort. He then joined up in formation on Merrett's wing and helped him set up a partial-power dead-stick landing pattern. As Merrett touched down on the end of the dirt strip the field did indeed look short and narrow, but he applied brakes and easily slowed down and looked for a place to park the wounded Skyraider. Finding a flat spot off to the side, he taxied over and shut down the engine. The wingman radioed that he was heading back home to NKP and Merrett saw him fly away.

Within a few moments, a jeep drove up to the side of Merrett's aircraft and parked. The man spoke English and indicated that he was with the CIA. Merrett was reluctant to leave the Skyraider, but on the other hand felt might he be safer away from the plane, and certainly the 'Jolly Green' rescue helicopter would be unable to pick him up for at least ten or fifteen minutes—if then. Laotian men and women were walking around some distance away, not in any type of military uniform that he could recognise. He would easily be identified as an American pilot by his flying suit.

Soon he heard that wonderful sound of helicopter blades spinning in the air—*wop-wop-wop*. A Sikorsky HH-3 using the call-sign 'Jolly Green' landed on the dirt strip. Merrett gathered his helmet, maps, strike photos, checklist, survival vest and gas mask and jumped aboard. Once airborne, the 'Jolly' headed south to the nearest base, Udorn Royal Thai AFB, Thailand. The helicopter pilots contacted 'Crown' and reported that the Skyraider pilot was safely aboard, uninjured.

As the aircraft crossed the Mekong River separating Laos from Thailand, the command post called the 'Jolly Green' crew on the UHF radio. The Wing Headquarters at NKP had scheduled a Fairchild C-

123 Provider cargo plane to fly a group of Skyraider mechanics and tools to Lima Site 21 in an attempt to repair the broken aircraft. If the Skyraider could not be repaired by sunset, the crew would be prepared to blow up the plane to prevent it from falling into the hands of the enemy. It would take several hours to round up the resources, so they did not know when the C-123 would actually arrive. However, the command post ordered the 'Jolly Green' to reverse course and fly back to Lima Site 21. Headquarters said that a pilot would be needed to fly the Skyraider back to Thailand if it could be repaired, and Merrett was the pilot.

When the 'Jolly Green' landed back at Lima Site 21 the crew informed Merrett that it was too dangerous to leave the helicopter on the ground and that they needed to be airborne in case another rescue were required. They took off heading south-east. Feeling a little dejected, Merrett got out his .38-calibre revolver and re-checked the six shells in the chamber. Sitting under the wing of the aircraft, he wondered if the CIA type might have been a Skyraider pilot who had also made an emergency landing there some time ago and never got back home! The C-123 finally arrived with five mechanics and all kinds of tools. The repair was actually quite simple: a couple of magneto leads had evidently come loose. Within a short time he had started the engine and it was sounding as sweet as ever.

## Captain Melvin Elliott

On 19 October 1965 a flight of four A-1Es from the 1st Air Commando Squadron, then stationed at Bien Hoa AB, was scheduled for a combat mission in South Vietnam. Just before take-off the flight leader was told that they were being diverted to Plei-Me Special Forces camp, approximately 30 miles south of Pleiku. The flight departed and flew to Plei-Me uneventfully. Upon arriving just before dawn there was a flight of F-100s in the area working with a C-123 with a FAC on board. When the F-100s had expended their ordnance the A-1Es were directed into the area. The flight leader was told that the compound was in trouble from an attack by what was later determined to be regular North Vietnam troops—the first confirmed in South Vietnam.

The A-1 flight was operating on an FM radio frequency and had the flare ship as well as the American commander of the compound on the same frequency. During the attack the compound commander directed the A-1s to drop the napalm that he knew they had on board right on the perimeter of the camp. At times the pilots of the flight noticed that the igniters from the napalm cans were going over the wall into the trenches inside the compound. After all ordnance had been expended the flight returned to Bien Hoa without incident. Upon landing three of the four aircraft had several small-calibre bullet holes in them.

Two days later, 21 October 1965 (a Sunday), the pilots on alert had just taken off on their third mission of the day—which was the point at which they would have to be replaced—when the duty officer rounded up four new pilots to report to the command post as soon as possible. The four duly arrived, were briefed and assigned aircraft, picked up their flight gear and proceeded to the aircraft to 'cock' them for alert. They had just loaded their gear in the planes when the command post called and ordered two to launch. About two hours later the telephone rang ordering the second two aircraft to proceed to Lei-Me and rendezvous with a flare ship and an Army Caribou at 12.30 a.m.

After about an hour in the area Capt Elliott advised the flare ship that the flight would be able to stay in the area longer if it expended the external ordnance the aircraft were carrying—napalm, CBUs and rockets. Upon completing this, the flight again set up an orbit awaiting the arrival of the Caribou to resupply the compound. At approximately 2.15 a.m. Elliott asked about the status of the Caribou and was told that it had been cancelled for that night. He informed the flare ship and compound that they would have to leave the area shortly but that they could strafe any likely targets with their 20mm cannon before leaving. The compound marked an area with a mortar round and Elliott rolled in on a strafing pass. As he pulled off the target he noticed that things were quite bright; and, looking at the left wing, he saw that it was ablaze. He called his wingman and notified him that he was on fire. The wingman requested that he turn on his lights so that he could see him. Before the controls of the aircraft failed he notified all concerned that he was bailing out.

As he was attempting to bail out of the aircraft he became stuck against the rear part of the left canopy. His helmet was blown off immediately his head came out of the cockpit. At this point the aircraft was out of control and was rolling because of the fire burning through the left wing. After freeing himself from the aircraft, Elliott reached for the D-ring, but it was not in the retainer pocket on the parachute harness. However, he found the cable and followed it to the ring and pulled it. The parachute opened and shortly afterwards flares lit and he could see that he was going to land in the trees. After landing approximately 50ft above the ground Elliott bounced up and down to ensure that the parachute was not going to come loose. He then swung over to the trunk of the tree and grasped a vine nearby. Having lost his hunting knife during the bail-out, he was forced to abandon the survival kit that was a part of the parachute.

After climbing down the vine to the ground, Elliott sat and thought about the situation for a short time. He assessed what equipment he had: a 38-calibre revolver with five rounds of ammunition; a pen-gun flare; a strobe light; a two-way radio (which at times was a luxury to A-1 pilots); his Mae West; and a brand new 'chit book' from the Bien Hoa Officers' Club. On the ground, after gathering his thoughts he got out his radio and contacted his wingman, Robert Haines, who was orbiting the area. Elliott told him that he had him in sight, advised him when he was directly overhead and then instructed him to fly from his position to the compound and that he intended to attempt to make it to the compound. About 30 minutes later Haines had to leave the area and proceed to Pleiku as he was running short of fuel.

Elliott was proceeding towards the compound perimeter when a severe fire-fight broke out. At this point he found a likely place to hide out and stayed there for the rest of the night. Shortly after dawn he spotted an O-1 aircraft orbiting the area, turned on his radio and called him several times before getting an answer: in the mêlée he had forgotten his call-sign and had used his name when calling the Bird Dog. By identifying different landmarks the Bird Dog (which turned out to be an Army aircraft) pinpointed his position and the pilot told him that a Huey was coming to get him out. Shortly afterwards radio contact was made and he was told to get into the best position he could in order to get picked up.

The Huey arrived on the scene and Elliott moved from his hiding place on to a small trail through the brush. When the Huey came around with lights out he turned on his strobe. The Huey made two orbits and on the third circle came in and turned on his floodlight. At that point a 50-calibre machine gun opened fire about 50yds from Elliott's position. The Huey turned his lights off and left the area.

Elliott then put the strobe in his pocket and got off the trail into the brush and laid as low as possible.

About ten minutes later two people—North Vietnamese soldiers— came down the trail with a flashlight. At this point Elliott was about 20ft off the trail and flat on the ground. The soldiers were chatting and shining their flashlight from one side of the trail to the other. On one of the sweeps of the light it came to within about 2ft of him and then the next sweep was beyond him. After the soldiers had satisfied themselves that he was not in the area, he found a new hiding place and settled down for the rest of the night.

As dawn—Elliott's second on the ground—approached, he heard the familiar sound of a C-47 in the area. He got out of his hiding place and saw that it was in fact an AC-47 orbiting with the business side towards him. The aircraft made a couple of orbits, opened up with his guns, firing a short burst, and departed. After two nights in the jungle Elliott again made contact with a Bird Dog in the area and, by identifying landmarks, the aircraft again pinpointed his position. The USAF FAC said that he was going to throw smoke grenades to get a better position on the pilot. At this time another Bird Dog arrived and advised Elliott that a helicopter was coming to pick him up and that he should get into a suitable area, but on reaching the middle of a clearing Elliott contacted the FAC and was advised that the helicopter had been diverted on a higher priority mission. Once again he pinpointed his position with the Bird Dog, who said he was going to go for some food and water as he did not know how long it would be before Elliott would be picked up.

After thirty minutes he again contacted the Bird Dog FAC and was told to come on air again in fifteen minutes. During this time the downed flyer heard several pilots talking on 'Guard', many of whom he recognised as fellow A-1 pilots. The FAC said that an H-43 rescue helicopter was about five minutes out and that the A-1s would be dropping napalm along a tree line about 100yds from his position. Elliott was advised to move into the middle of the clearing as soon as the A-1s had passed over. He then spotted the H-43 coming in about 20ft off the ground directly towards him. The pilot got into position and was forced to hover because of the brush that was beneath the aircraft, creating a huge wave in the grass that Elliott was forced to crawl through. Upon reaching the helicopter he was found to be dragging a number of vines caught up from the undergrowth.

## Vought A-7D Corsair 'Sandy Sluff'

The Corsair II achieved its excellent accuracy with the aid of an automatic electronic navigation and weapon delivery system, and Corsair jets began to replace the lumbering but effective A-1 Skyraiders from November 1972. The A-7D was produced as a single-seat, single-engine tactical close air support aircraft. Although designed primarily as a ground attack machine, it also had a limited air-to-air combat capability. It was derived from the basic A-7 originally developed by LTV for the US Navy. The first A-7D made its initial flight on 5 April 1968, and deliveries of production models began on 23 December 1968. When A-7D production ended in 1976, 459 had been delivered to the USAF. In 1973 the USAF began assigning A-7Ds to the Air National Guard (ANG), and by 1987 they were being flown by ANG units in ten states and Puerto Rico.

The A-7D demonstrated its outstanding capability to attack ground targets while flown by the 354th Tactical Fighter Wing at Korat RTAFB, Thailand, during the closing months of the war in South-East Asia. In its 'Sandy' role it was equally outstanding, and on one rescue mission Maj Colin A. 'Arnie' Clarke, 'Sandy -01' (the on-scene commander), took part in a 75-aircraft, nine-hour-long rescue mission for which he received the Air Force Cross. Following the shooting down of a two-seat F-105G, Clarke spent a gruelling twelve hours aboard his A-7, taking four fuel transfers and suffering poor weather, bad communications and heavy ground fire. Clarke was hit repeatedly by 57mm AAA shells during his 'Sandy' fire missions, and despite constantly being low on fuel he stayed on station until the 'Weasel' crews were recovered.

Because the 'Sluff' was a different animal from the 'Spad', tactics had to change. The A-7 could not fly slowly enough to pace the 'Jolly Greens', so flew 'lazy circles' around the helicopters whilst leading them into the rescue scene.

*Specifications:* Powerplant one Allison TF41 turbofan engine of 14,250lb (6.462kg) thrust; span 38ft 8in (11.79m); length 46ft 1in (14.05m); height 16ft 1in (4.90m); weight 39,325lb (17,834kg) loaded; maximum speed 663mph (1,067kph); cruising speed 545mph (877kph); range 3,044 miles (4,900km); service ceiling 33,500ft (10,210m); armament one M61A1 20mm rapid-fire cannon plus 15,000lb (4 5672kg) mixed ordnance; crew one.

The PJ on the H-43 was hanging out of the door and Elliott stepped up on to the wheel. As soon as he reached up the PJ told the pilot he had him and away he went. The wheel rotated back and Elliott found himself hanging by his arm to the PJs. Elliott looked up at the PJ and told him in no uncertain terms that he was not going back down there alone, and the PJ immediately hauled him aboard. Elliott had spent some 36 hours on the ground.

### Twice Rescued . . .

Lt-Col Albert Volmer flew 100 F-105 combat missions during the Vietnam War and gained the dubious distinction of having been shot down and subsequently rescued twice! On 13 January 1965, while attacking a road bridge in Laos, his aircraft was struck by AAA and he was forced to eject. After a night of evasion he made contact with a civilian Air America C-123, which then directed another Air America asset, an H-34 helicopter, on to his position for a pick-up. The H-34, which was on a supply mission when the call came, landed in an open field, disembarked all the onboard personnel except the winch operator and proceeded out to make the rescue.

On 17 August 1967, again flying an F-105, Volmer was hit by AAA over North Vietnam. He nursed his stricken aircraft out over the China Sea before punching out, sustaining severe eye and leg injuries in the process. His wingman and two A-1 'Spads' provided cover during his parachute descent, and within fifteen minutes a brace of 'Jolly Green Giants' from the 37th ARRS arrived on the scene to make the rescue. Volmer spent the next two years in and out of hospital recovering from his injuries, but after 26 months he was returned to flying status.

The crews from the 37th ARRS who rescued Volmer visited him in hospital at Da Nang. As a momento the crew signed one of their 'business cards', which they presented to him on 18 August 1967, and for years after he carried it for good luck. The card read:

CONFUSED? FOLLOW THESE STEPS

1. Stay with chute/aircraft
2. Conserve flares and radio
3. Advise others of your position and condition
4. Stay calm . . . others have been rescued under worse conditions than yours
5. The bearer of this card, upon being suitably rescued, agrees to provide free cheer at the nearest bar to those making said rescue possible

37th ARRS APO 96337

TEMPORARILY SUSPENDED?

NEED A PICK-ME-UP?

Contact: [signed] Crown
[signed] Sandy
[signed] Jolly Green
[signed] Pedro

# 4

# Son Tay

Shortly before midnight on 20 November 1970, at Udorn RTAFB in Northern Thailand, 56 US Army Special Forces Troopers ('Green Berets') boarded two USAF HH-53s and one HH-3 for a mission deep into enemy territory to rescue 75 or more Americans held by the North Vietnamese authorities. These Americans, mostly aviators of all services, were being held under conditions that can be best described as horrible in all respects—tortured, suffering from poor diet and a lack of medical care, and devoid of hope for a return to freedom in a timely manner.

One hundred and sixteen aircraft from seven air bases and three aircraft carriers made up the force, which was under the command of Brig-Gen LeRoy J. Manor. The weather was clear, all aircraft had been thoroughly checked and were in A1 condition, the 'Red Rocket' (mission approval call-sign) message had been received from Washington, the troopers and air crew members were suited up, all exposed skin areas painted, and the command post communications had been checked and readied. The commander declared the mission ready and ordered the launch. It was to be a historic event.

By 1970 the United States had secured the names of over 500 Americans held in North Vietnamese prisons; many more were missing and presumed captured. Reports of the cruelty suffered by these men at the hands of their barbarous captors, along with reports of resultant deaths, were received from various sources. Anxiety, concern and anger among the next of kin, friends of the captives, commanders and government officials were very much in evidence throughout the country. What was being done to alleviate the growing concern? Negotiations were being conducted in Paris on a sporadic basis, depending on the mood of the North Vietnamese representatives. An attempt was made to reach an agreement whereby an exchange of prisoners of war could be made. After over two years of such negotiations, the results were nil. The mood of the country demanded that something be done to help these suffering POWs.

## The Task Force

During 1970 Maj James Trask was the commander of the USAF Special Operations Force with its headquarters at Eglin AFB, Florida. His responsibilities included the training of all Special Operations personnel and units of the Air Force and the coordination of these forces with the US Army and US Navy. Joint training exercises were conducted primarily with the Army's Special Forces under the command of Maj-Gen 'Flywheel' Flannigan and later Maj-Gen Hank Emmerson. On 6 August, by telephone, Maj Trask was summoned to the Pentagon and instructed to report to the Chairman of the Joint Chiefs of Staff at 0800hrs on 8 August. He was told that his Air Staff contact was Brig-Gen James Allen. He was requested to plan a stop at Pope AFB, North Carolina (adjacent to Fort Bragg), on the way to Washington and pick up an Army colonel who also had instructions to report at 0800hrs to the Chairman of the Joint Chiefs of Staff. His name was Arthur D. 'Bull' Simons. Simons was then the G-4 for the US Army XVIII Corps. Over dinner on Sunday evening at the Andrews AFB Officers' Club the two men speculated about the reason that they were being summoned to Washington, suspecting that, owing to the similar circumstances, they were being called for the same purpose.

Early in the morning of the 8th the team reported to Brig-Gen Allen and 'Bull' Simons reported to Allen's counterpart on the Army staff, Brig-Gen Clarke Baldwin. A brief preview of the reason they were called, plus a short meeting with the Chairman's principal staff member for Special Operations, Army Brig-Gen Don Blackburn, prepared them for a meeting with Admiral Thomas Moorer, the Chairman of the Joint Chiefs of Staff. The latter asked them if they were prepared and willing to take on an assignment to explore the possibility of rescuing some US POWs held by North Vietnam, with the ultimate responsibility of conducting a recovery operation should it be deemed feasible.

Their responses were immediately in the affirmative. Col 'Bull' Simons was appointed task force deputy commander. He was advised that the Secretary of Defense, Melvin Laird, had authorised the formation and training of a task force and that whatever resources were needed were to be made available to them. Admiral Moorer instructed them to advise the JCS as early as possible regarding the feasibility of such an operation, and, should it be deemed possible, when it would be ready to go. The group represented each of the four services, so it was truly a 'joint' effort. The assembled group consisted of 26 members.

Attention was next turned to the task force operational element, and an early decision was made to assemble an all-volunteer force. The ground element would be composed of men from the Army Special Forces and the air element would be from the Air Force. The insertion and extraction of the force, along with the rescued POWs, would be by helicopter. Eglin Air Force Base, Florida, was selected as the training site. Security was a prime consideration and the Eglin area was well suited because of its vast size—and the fact that it is a base where military personnel wearing different uniforms do not create speculation that something unusual is being planned. Moreover, the required air resources were located primarily at Eglin and at nearby Hurlburt Field. The group wanted 100 men possessing certain identified skills and preferably having had recent combat experience in South-East Asia. Although some believed that the number might be excessive, some degree of redundancy and a reservoir of 'spares' were deemed appropriate. About 500 men responded.

From that group 100 dedicated volunteers were selected, all in top physical condition. All the required skills were covered. The ground component commander selected was Lt-Col 'Bud' Sydnor from Fort Benning, Georgia. Sydnor had an impeccable reputation as a combat leader. Also selected to be a member of the task force from Fort Benning was another superb combat leader, Capt Dick Meadows: he would later lead the team that made the risky landing inside the prison compound. The air element (primary force) would include five HH-53s, one HH-3, two MC-130 'Combat Talons' and five A-1Es. The selection of crew members for these aircraft was based on experience and proven performance: all were well versed in recent combat operations. They were assembled, were given the same information as that given to the Army troops regarding the purpose of the project and were invited to become participants. All accepted.

By late August the joint task force was assembled in the Eglin area. Primary activity was at Duke Field, known as Eglin Auxiliary Number 3. A remote site—but one not far from Duke—was selected for the construction of a replica of the Son Tay camp. This is where the detailed training was accomplished, including precision helicopter operations. The CIA provided a scale model of the Son Tay compound.

The model proved to be a valuable device for detailed training of the raiders—especially the members of Meadows' assault element.

Aircrew training began with night formation flying involving dissimilar aircraft. As the crews became comfortable with the phase, low level was introduced as well as objective area tactics which included helicopter landings and extractions; air-drops by the C-130s of flares, fire-fight simulators and napalm; and close air support by the A-1s. During this training aircrews flew 1,054 hours without so much as scraping a wing tip or rotor blade, most of it at night with dissimilar aircraft in low level formation while blacked out—a true reflection of the superb skills of each and every aircrew member. Training culminated with two 5½hr full-profile missions flown for the benefit of JCS observers, who pronounced the force ready.

There were a number of important considerations for the mission. First, the raid would be conducted at night. Secondly, weather and moonlight were important, with cloudless skies ideal for air refuelling. Thirdly, surprise had to be achieved, and the element of shock had to be exploited. Fourthly, once launched, the operation had to be one of precision, with timing and navigational accuracy strictly according to plan.

The importance of light led to the selection of a 'window' during which the desired conditions would prevail. The period was 21–25 October, although the same conditions would be found during 21–25 November. The date of 21 October was selected. The plan was approved. Secretary of Defense Laird was briefed on 24 September and his approval without change to the concept was obtained. Higher-level approval would still be required, and on 8 October the plan was outlined at the White House. Dr Henry Kissinger reported that it would not be possible to get President Nixon's approval by the next evening because he was not available, but that he was confident it would be forthcoming in time to make the next 'window', 21 November. The delay was a disappointment, largely because of constant concern about an intelligence compromise. On the other hand, an extra 30 days were now available for additional rehearsals, more intelligence, refinements to the plan and possible improvements to equipment. The team made numerous changes during the extra 30-day period, the two most important of which were the addition of FLIR (forward-looking infra-red) to the MC-130s and obtaining a suitable night sight for the weapons.

55

Authorisation was received to visit COMUSMACV, Gen Creighton Abrams, and his Air Deputy, Gen Lucius Clay Jr, on 1 November 1970, and arrangements were made to confer with the US Navy commander of Task Force 77, which operated in the Tonkin Gulf, aboard the flagship USS *Oriskany*. It was requested that, concurrent with the raiding force approaching the Hanoi area from a westerly direction, *Oriskany* launch a force from the carriers and make a feint toward the North Vietnamese coast. The purpose was to deceive the air defence system of North Vietnam. Such a raid, which would appear on their radar, would convince them that an attack from the east was imminent and cause them to be unaware of the main raid approaching at low level from the west. The admiral agreed.

### 'Red Rocket'

On 10 November the two MC-130s left Eglin, destination Takhli in Thailand. Transportation to move the task force and its equipment for the mission was by Military Airlift Command and consisted of four C-141s. They departed Eglin on 14 November and arrived at Takhli two days later. By 17 November the force had closed at Takhli. A CIA-operated secure compound was made available to the force, and it was here that final preparations were made. 'Firebird' F-105 'Wild Weasel' aircraft were added with the mission of engaging surface-to-air missiles (SAMs) should any batteries become active; F-4s were also added, to provide protection against possible MiG interference. The F-105s were from Korat, the F-4s from Ubon and the A-1Es were based at Nakhon Phanom. All these bases were in Thailand. KC-135 tankers were provided by a SAC unit at Utapao, a base south of Bangkok. The helicopters originated from various bases and were brought to Udorn and prepared for the mission.

The CIA compound at Takhli became a beehive of activity. Weapons and other equipment checks were carefully conducted and ammunition was issued. Of the original 100 SF members of the force, 56 were selected for the mission. This was unwelcome news for the 44 trained and ready but not selected, although it was known from the beginning that the size of the force would be limited to the number considered essential for the task.

The 'Red Rocket' message was soon received. This meant that President Nixon had given his final approval to launch the mission. However, the planned date of 21 November now appeared to be in jeopardy. A typhoon in the area of the Philippines and moving slowly towards the mainland was forecast to bring bad weather to North Vietnam by the night of the 21st; the weather over the Tonkin Gulf would certainly prevent the US Navy from launching the diversionary force, and the weather en route to and at the objective would be unsuitable. It was a grim situation. The task force weather officer and weather support personnel from the 1st Weather Wing exhaustively analysed the meteorological patterns, and they predicted the formation of a high-pressure area over Vietnam and the Tonkin Gulf which would provide suitable conditions for the mission prior to arrival of the typhoon. The good weather, however, would prevail on 20 November, not the 21st. The decision was taken to advance mission launch by 24 hours.

Final briefings were conducted on 20 November. All were told the exact location of the objective area and that the latest information indicated that between 70 and 80 POWs should be at the Son Tay Prison. While the participants were confident that the plan had not been compromised, this would not be certain until the force had made the landings. If the enemy had foreknowledge of the plan, the reception would not be a pleasant one. However, even though the task force was small, it was extremely potent for its size: while it could be overwhelmed by a much larger force lying in wait, the enemy would pay a heavy price. Escape and evasion procedures were thoroughly covered. The mission force was fully 'go'.

For the troops 20 November was a day for crew rest and they were issued with sleeping pills. At 2200 hours the men boarded a C-130 and left Takhli for Udorn, where helicopters were waiting. Upon landing at Udorn the men transferred to three of the helicopters—two HH-53s and one HH-3—carefully re-checking all the equipment that had been deemed necessary for the mission that lay ahead. At 2318hrs the first helicopter launched and at 2325hrs the last. They were led by two HC-130 refuellers en route to an air refuelling area over Northern Laos. One of the mission planners pulled the cover off a large sign that read 'F— COMMUNISM'. All cheered and the tension seemed to subside.

Just as practised, the formation lead HC-130P refueller aircraft, 'Lime 1', got off on time, as did the rest, the HH-3 'Banana' and five 'Apple' HH-53s. The aircraft fell routinely into the seven-ship formation, three helicopters stacking high on each side of the leading HC-

130 at about 1,500ft AGL. There was a partial moon and some clouds when suddenly the call came to 'break, break, break!', indicating that someone had lost sight of the formation lead and the aircraft were to execute the formation break-up procedure. Each helicopter turned to a predetermined heading and climbed to a predetermined altitude for one minute and then returned to the original heading. The effect was a very widely separated formation, each helicopter 500ft above the other and at varying distances from the lead HC-130. Apparently a strange aircraft had almost flown through the formation and one crew had called the 'lost contact' procedure to avoid a mid-air collision. As it turned out, the rigorous planning for such possible events, and the training for such, resulted in a rather routine formation break and with a subsequent re-join being completed successfully. In the meantime, the helicopters had all topped off their fuel tanks from the lead HC-130 and had quite deftly exchanged formation leads from the original 'gas station' to the newly arrived and blacked-out MC-130 with all the fancy electronic gear.

The mission of the lead HC-130, 'Lime 1', was to launch from Udorn, join up with the six helicopters and take them to the North Vietnamese border after refuelling them. This was done in total silence without any incidents. The HH-3 stayed close behind the left wing in order to maintain the speed required by the rest of the formation. After leaving the helicopters for their final assault, the HC-130 immediately returned to Udorn for refuelling. It was then tasked to refuel as soon as possible and return to northern Laotian airspace in order to provide air refuelling and search and rescue support as needed. Happily, the weather in the refuelling area was clear and all transfers were accomplished without difficulty. All six helicopters then joined formation with the MC-130 'Combat Talon' for the low-altitude flight towards North Vietnam. Laos is a mountainous region, and precise navigation by the MC-130 crew was required.

In the meantime the five A-1 'Spads' had left Nakhon Phanom and joined formation with the second MC-130 'Combat Talon'. This formation was in close proximity to the MC-130/helicopter flight, and all were en route at low altitude for Son Tay. Close air support was the job of the A-1s because they were ideally suited to the task. They had a long endurance and carried a big load of ordnance, and their relatively low speed permitted small orbits which would keep them close by overhead should assistance be needed at short notice. Ten F-4s had taken off from Ubon to provide a MiG air patrol and five F-105 'Wild Weasels' had launched from Korat to provide protection from the SAM sites. The F-4s and F-105s would be flying at a high altitude, providing cover over the general area, and would not interfere in any way with the primary force. The Navy force launched on time with a total of 59 sorties.

As the primary force reached the Laos/North Vietnam border, the enemy radar's became aware of the Navy force coming from over the Tonkin Gulf. The diversionary raid was having the desired effect. The presence of the Navy on enemy radar caused near-panic within the North Vietnamese defence centres, and it became obvious that the North Vietnamese' total concern was directed eastwards: the Son Tay raiding force, coming from the west, was having a free ride. As rehearsed so many times, the lead MC-130 took them over the last mountain range and down to 500ft above the ground. At the IP they, along with 'Apple 4' and 'Apple 5', popped up to 1,500ft to fly directly for the camp. A single radio transmission with the last vector heading to the camp was made by the MC-130's navigator and they continued on, maintaining a disciplined radio silence.

Now the force were only four—'Apple 3' in the lead, with the HH-3, 'Apple 1' and 'Apple 2' following in trail, with 45-second separations between. Upon reaching the IP the MC-130 climbed to 1,500ft. The 130's mission at this point was to drop flares over the Son Tay Prison. Helicopters 4 and 5 were to provide a back-up and drop flares should the MC-130 heats not be effective. However, the flares worked as intended. The helicopters made a left turn and proceeded to a preselected landing area which was on an island in a large lake. There they would wait, to be called to move to Son Tay to pick up some POWs. The MC-130 made a right turn and dropped fire-fight simulators and napalm to create a fire as an anchor point for the A-1s. The MC-130 then left the area for an orbit point over northern Laos.

Immediately after the flares illuminated the prison compound, HH-53 'Apple 3', under the command of Capt Donohue, flew low over the prison, firing at the guard towers with his Gatling machine guns, the sheer number of tracer rounds immediately setting the bamboo and wood towers on fire. The plan called for neutralising these towers to eliminate that potential source of enemy opposition. Immediately following that pass the HH-3, whose crew was Herb Kalen, Herb Zender and LeRoy Wright and which was carrying a thirteen-man assault force, landed in a relatively small space inside the prison walls. So far all was going strictly according to plan and precisely on time. The landing was a hard one, but successful. Rotors contacted some of the tall trees which bordered one side of the landing area. It was anticipated that damage would occur and the plan provided for the HH-3 to be considered a loss; it was to be destroyed by means of an explosive charge with a timing device upon the departure of the troops from the compound. The hard landing caused a fire extinguisher to dislodge and crash against Sgt LeRoy Wright (HH-3 Engineer), who consequently sustained a fractured ankle. While undoubtedly this caused severe pain, the flow of adrenalin apparently was such that Wright ignored the pain and continued with his duties to perform as a member the assault force. (He was later awarded the Air Force Cross by President Nixon.) In control of the assault team was Dick Meadows, and his highly trained and rehearsed assault force, including the helicopter Air Force crew members, went into action immediately.

They announced with bullhorns that they were a rescue raiding party and were there to bring out the POWs. North Vietnamese military personnel exited the buildings in various states of undress and fired their weapons against the intruders. The raiders, however, having the benefit of initiative and a rehearsed plan of action and not suffering from the element of shock that was imposed on the defenders, quickly disposed of the camp contingent. Meadows' primary concern now was to enter the buildings to search for Americans held prisoner by the North Vietnamese. The timed explosive charge was placed in the HH-3 to ensure its destruction upon the departure of the raiders. With the use of another explosive device a hole was blown in the south-west corner of the prison wall through which the raiders and the POWs would exit. A command post would be established just outside the wall at the site of the hole. Simultaneously with the landing of the assault force, HH-53s 'Apple 1' and 'Apple 2' were to land opposite the south side and their troops immediately fan out and enter all the buildings in search of Americans and to prevent reinforcements from interfering in any way with the rescue effort. 'Apple 1', with 21 raiders aboard, mistakenly landed at a site enclosed by a fence that presented an appearance not unlike the Son Tay compound. It was approximately 200m south of the objective area. A fire-fight immediately ensued and the estimate of enemy killed ran as high as 200 (a number which may be somewhat exaggerated).

This raiding element was on the ground for no more than five minutes when the mistake was realised. Simons and his men re-boarded the helicopter and moved to the correct position. 'Apple 2', carrying the other force, had landed at the correct predetermined spot and, realising that 'Apple 1' was not with them, immediately put an alternative plan into effect. Within a few minutes, however, the primary plan was reinstated when the erring helicopter was back in place. Sitting in the holding area waiting to be recalled to pick up the POWs and ground forces, 'Apple' flight was also treated to a spectacular fireworks display. Between 14 and 16 SAMs were fired at the F-105 'Wild Weasel' aircraft, and one was at such a low angle that one of the departing helicopters had to take evasive action. One SAM was observed to explode and spray fuel over 'Firebird 3'. The aircraft descended in a ball of flames and appeared to be lost. However, the fire blew out and the crew continued with the mission. Another SAM exploded near 'Firebird 5', inflicting damage to his flight controls and fuel system. The crew later bailed out over the Plaine des Jarres and were picked up at first light by 'Apple 4' and 'Apple 5'.

While all the helicopters were engaged with the compound, the 'Peach' A-1s, which had arrived with the second MC-130, were going about their tasks. Almost immediately their pilots realised that one of the helicopters had gone to the wrong area, but they were helpless to do much other than support the troops as best they could. Because they were out of position, the A-1s were called upon to pay close attention to the road from the south, to make sure that the enemy did not take advantage of the situation. When the order came to shut down the footbridge between the Citadel and Son Tay, they lined up and headed east to take the bridge out with a couple of 100lb 'Willie Pete' bombs. However, Lead's run was too shallow and the WPs impacted short, but fortunately his 'run in line' was across a chemical factory and he 'greased it'. There was a beautiful display of different coloured flames, with the bright green ones going up way over the aircraft's altitude.

The A-1s continued to circle the camp about at 100–200ft AGL and when on the north side they dropped down to water level over the Red River. Again, because some of the ground troops were not in position to blow the bridge on the north side of the camp, they were also called to take that out as well, but they could not get enough altitude to drop any heavy weaponry and so they began to strafe it.

Then the coded message 'Negative Items' was reported to the command post. There were no Americans at the camp.

In disbelief, the officers hoped that the message had become garbled in transmission, but it was not to be. The raiding party was on the ground at Son Tay for 29 minutes, within one minute of the planned time of 30. They experienced no losses. Sgt Wright suffered a broken ankle and Sgt Murry a bullet wound on the inside of a thigh, a minor injury. The number of enemy killed was determined to be about 50. The helicopters were called in and the raiding party went aboard. After every man was accounted for, they launched for the long ride back to Udorn. The SA-2 missile sites quickly became active and were engaged by the F-105 'Wild Weasels'. A missile hit and severely damaged one 'Firebird' F-105. It began to lose fuel and an effort was made to return to the KC-135 tankers on an orbit over Laos. However a flame-out was experienced prior to contact with the tankers and the crew of two, Maj Kilgus and Capt Lowry, ejected, landing in a mountainous area, uninjured. The progress of this emergency was monitored at the command post and the location of the downed airmen was relayed to the crew of HH-53s 'Apple 3' and 'Apple 4' with instructions to search for and pick up the F-105 crew members. The pick-up was successfully accomplished after more helicopter air refuellings and flare drops; and all returned to Udorn safely, though only after one of the HH-53s, flown by Lt-Col Royal H. Brown, had been targeted by a heat-seeking 'Atoll' missile fired from a marauding MiG-21.

At Udorn the dejected force of raiders arrived in solemn mood. They were disappointed because their hopes of returning with POWs had been dashed. They had failed. This thoroughly dedicated group expressed the belief that they should return the next night and search again for the POWs. However, for many reasons this could not be done.

## The Aftermath

The North Vietnamese announced to the world that the US forces had bombed a POW camp. They also made various other allegations. While disappointed that they had not rescued any POWs, the Americans felt that the rescue attempt would result in an improvement in morale among the POWs, their next of kin and, in fact, the whole country. Participants in the raid, as well as the planners, were recognised by means of appropriate awards. Some were presented by President Nixon and others by Secretary of Defense Laird.

In the end the mission did bring benefits. The North Vietnamese, fearing a repeat performance but not knowing when and where, closed the outlying POW camps and concentrated all prisoners in the two main gaols in Hanoi city centre. These were the old French prisons of Halo and Culac. The number of POWs at these two prisons grew to the extent that POWs lived in groups, rather than in what for many had been solitary confinement. Morale immediately improved and, as a result, so did general health. Some POWs later stated that lives were saved. Prison conditions to some degree generally improved, for example regarding mail delivery and food. Morale among the next of kin, for the most part, also improved.

## Seeing Stars

During the course of the war, the need to retrieve personnel who were operating deep inside enemy territory led to the fitting of the Fulton STARS (Skyhook) recovery system to the Lockheed C-130 Hercules, the aircraft being given the interim designation C-130-I. The feasibility of using this airborne system—which provided for a line attached to a helium balloon secured to a person on the ground, who would then be hoisted aloft by the rescue aircraft snatching the line in mid-air—had been demonstrated in 1958, and the need to support rescue and unconventional warfare during Vietnam operations led to the STAR system being introduced to service.

The first trials were held at Pope AFB in North Carolina in 1965 using a C-130 fitted with a tubular device on its nose. The decision was then made to modify seventeen aircraft to C-130-I configuration with folding 'whiskers' on the nose and a broader radome to house additional avionics. The aircraft affected were 62-1843, 63-7785 and 64-0508, -0523, -0547, -0551, -0555, -0558, -0559 and -0561 to -0568. Assigned to the 'Combat Spear' detachment of the 314th Troop Carrier/Tactical Airlift Wing and then to the 15th Commando Squadron, 14th ACW, the C-130-Is perfected the use of this unique recovery system. Of the original aircraft, 64-0508 was hit by ground fire during an SAR mission near Phuc Yen, North Vietnam, on 28 December 1967 and crashed in Laos, a second was shot down in South Vietnam and a third was destroyed during a mortar attack at Nha Trang AFB. A fourth was lost in a mid-air collision in the United

States. The remaining thirteen aircraft—which were also officially designated C-130H(CT) and NC-130E—were eventually upgraded to MC-130 'Combat Talon I' standard.

# 5

# Dustoff

The name 'Dustoff' was derived from the radio call-sign given to the first aeromedical helicopter evacuation unit in Vietnam, the 57th Medical Detachment (Hel Amb), from Fort Meade, Maryland. This unit flew five Bell UH-1A 'Huey' helicopters, and was to service the 8,000 United States troops then on the ground in Vietnam. The unit was stationed at Nha Trang close to the US 8th Field Hospital, which had arrived in-country in 1962. The 57th initially communicated internally on any vacant frequency it could find, but in Saigon the Navy Support Activity, which controlled all the call-signs in South Vietnam, allowed the 57th to adopt 'Dustoff'.

This call-sign epitomised the 57th's medical evacuation missions, since the countryside was at the time dry and dusty, with helicopter pick-ups in the fields often blowing up dirt storms, blankets and shelter halves, often all over the men on the ground. The 57th had no radio call-sign of its own and one officer noticed the vacant call-sign 'Dustoff' in the Signal Operations Instructions. He assigned the call-sign to the unit and sought to make it official. During late 1963 the National Security Agency allocated the name 'Dustoff' to the 118th Airmobile Company, the 57th fought to retain the name and the 118th refused to use it.

It was at this point in history that the call-sign 'Dustoff', denoting aeromedical evacuation of the wounded from the battlefield, became a permanent feature of the conflict. On 11 January 1964 Maj Charles L. Kelly took up his post as the third commanding officer of the 57th. He was tough, stubborn, willing to take on the top brass and deeply committed to the 'Dustoff' concept. Kelly laid down the rules and adhered to them himself: there could be no refusal to fly a mission and the wounded always came first. July 1 saw Kelly hovering near the ground picking up casualties on a hot LZ, his ship having taken numerous hits. He was repeatedly advised by ground troops to abort the mission but he refused, remarking, 'When I have your wounded.' Quite suddenly the aircraft pitched up, nosed over to the right, and crashed. Kelly had been shot through the heart with a bullet which came through the open cargo door. He was posthumously awarded the US Distinguished Service Cross, the Vietnamese Military Order of the Medal of Vietnam and the Vietnamese Cross of Gallantry with Palm. He was the 149th American to lose his life in Vietnam and, such was the level of emotion surrounding his death, the name 'Dustoff' and the service for which he had given his life became cemented into the history of the war in Vietnam. Kelly's creed read simply, 'No compromise. No rationalisation. No hesitation. Fly the mission. Now!'

Throughout Vietnam virtually all evacuation helicopters thereby assumed the call-sign 'Dustoff' followed by a numerical designation (the exception being the air ambulances of the 1st Cavalry Division, which used the call-sign 'Medevac'). Though other call-signs regularly changed, both ground and aviation units refused to refer to these evacuation helicopters by any other designation. By adopting 'Dustoff' in those early stages of the Vietnam War, a legend was born; and to this day the call-sign 'Dustoff' is synonymous with the life-saving aeromedical evacuation mission.

During 1968, 35 'Dustoff' helicopters were hit by ground fire whilst carrying out evacuations; in 1969 the figure was 39. In 1968, during the Tet Offensive, an Infantry Rifle Platoon was engaged in a fierce fire-fight with a company-size enemy group. Unable to break off the engagement, and with members of the platoon severely wounded, an American helicopter gunship fire team arrived to provide fire support and attempt to break up the attack, and with them came two 'Dustoff' helicopters. The gunship team went about its business, strafing the enemy position with minigun and rocket fire, but still the enemy hung on, determined to fight. The situation on the ground was bad, with many severely wounded and the platoon taking further casualties.

Realising the desperate situation, especially for the seriously wounded, the pilot of one 'Dustoff' helicopter decided to attempt a winch-out of the two most serious cases while the gunships laid suppressing fire on the enemy position. Under fire and without thought for his own safety and the safety of his crew or aircraft, the 'Dustoff' pilot hovered his helicopter above the platoon's position while the two injured soldiers were winched up through the jungle canopy. The two casualties were then flown back to hospital. The gunships continued to blast the enemy position and eventually the enemy withdrew, allowing the remainder of the wounded to be evacuated. Some time later the pilot of the first 'Dustoff' returned in a different helicopter, still keen to help. On landing back at Ben Hoa, he had been informed by his ground crew that he had over sixty bullet holes in his machine and that it was no longer safe to fly. Undaunted, the pilot and his crew simply jumped in another helicopter and returned.

By late 1971 the American 'Dustoff' crews in the Mekong Delta had transferred the bulk of the daytime ARVN medevac support to the Vietnamese Air Force (VNAF). The VNAF medevac pilots, despite their vast flight experience, were not inclined to fly at night. The 57th Medical Detachment continued to fly night medevac missions in support of both American and Vietnamese forces in the Delta until late 1972, when the unit returned to the United States. Flying at night was a lonely experience: rarely were there any other helicopters in the air, and the few fixed-wing aircraft that were flying, such as the Army's OV-1 Mohawk surveillance aircraft or the Air Force's Spectre or 'Puff' gunships, were usually on a different frequency. The 'Dustoff' crews that had first-up duty typically flew ten to twelve sorties each night. Their only company was provided by 'Paddy Control', the Air Force controllers who provided radar coverage for most of the Delta.

The techniques used for locating the people on the ground and making a safe pick-up provided an interesting set of challenges. Staying alive and successfully accomplishing their missions depended upon the 'Dustoff' crews' developing excellent crew coordination skills. Everyone was depended upon to do his part. Mission coordinates were plotted on a 1:50,000 tactical map. 'Paddy Control' usually provided vectors to the general vicinity of the pick-up. From there, a safe landing could only be assured if two-way radio communication with someone on the ground was established. It helped if someone knew what they were doing. Many of the Vietnamese units had at least one American adviser who could handle communications with the 'Dustoff' crew. For other missions, a Vietnamese interpreter flew with the 'Dustoff' crew and handled communication with the elements on the ground. Several methods were used for identifying the landing area.

First contact was normally made by sound. Flying without external lighting and there being no other aerial traffic around, there was no reason to provide a visual target for an enemy gunner. To the men on the ground, the sound of an approaching Huey was unmistakable. Upon first radio contact, the 'Dustoff' crew would confirm their proximity to the landing site by asking the ground troops whether they had heard them, and, if so, from which direction were they coming. A typical response would be: 'We hear you, Dustoff. It sounds like you're north of us about two klicks.' In that case they would turn south and ask the ground contact to tell them if it sounded as if they were getting closer.

Once in visual range, the crew needed some type of light to identify the landing area. Among the possibilities were a hand-held strobe light, a flashlight, a flare, a small fire or four small fires built to form a 'T' on the ground. Most of the crews preferred the last, because it gave them not only a marker for the landing site but also something to line up on for their approach, the base of the 'T' being oriented along the recommended approach path. The least preferred method to mark a landing spot was the use of a flare, for two reasons: first, the flare would highlight the position of the ground troops, and secondly it adversely affected the night vision of the 'Dustoff' pilots. More often than not, a hand-held strobe light or a flashlight aimed at the helicopter was all they had to work with.

The radio operator on the ground would describe the landing area to them, including any obstacles and an estimate of the wind direction and velocity. They would also recommend a way out, based on obstacles, the location of the enemy, etc. Rarely did it make sense to go back out the way they came in, but it did happen. Using whatever they had to work with visually, and the landing area briefing from the contact on the ground, they would set up a rectangular landing pattern. This would help them stay oriented with the landing spot, making their approach to a point just short of the LZ marker.

The pilot not flying the helicopter called altitude and airspeed every few seconds as the aircraft descended. He also kept his hands near the controls. Some ACs even preferred that both sets of hands be on the controls during short finals. The landing light was delayed as long as possible for an obvious reason: without the light, enemy gunners had only sound and possibly a shadowy outline to aid in target acquisition, and once the landing light came on it was obvious where the Huey was located. Normally the crew took the approach all the way to the ground because of dust and debris but would hold the helicopter light on the skids—who knew what kind of surface they were landing on? It could be muddy, wet, lumpy or littered with stumps or stubs that could easily puncture a hole in the bottom of the aircraft or, more importantly, the fuel cells. Throughout the approach, the medic and crew chief hung out of the sides of the aircraft, watching for obstacles or enemy activity. Constant chatter on the intercom was a necessity to keep the pilots informed, since they could not possibly see all that was around and beneath them. At touch-down the landing light was switched off and the crew in the back supervised the loading of patients.

They were not to unplug from the intercom in case a rapid departure were needed. They usually had extra-long microphone cords that allowed them some freedom of movement outside the aircraft. Seldom did more than fifteen or twenty seconds pass before the crew in the back reported being ready to depart: 'Ready right.'—'Ready left.'—'Coming up.'—'Clear up left.'—'Clear up right.' The landing light was used on departure only if necessary to ensure that obstacles would be cleared; otherwise it was best for the pilots to regain their night vision as soon as possible. It was not unusual for a pilot who was flying to be coached by his AC—'Watch your torque, you're at 38, 40, okay nose her over.'—'We're still clear left.'—'Clear right.'—and off they would go, either to a small local hospital or perhaps to another pick-up. If there were Americans on board, they would head for the nearest US Army hospital. En route, the medic and crew chief would be busy treating the patients. This scenario would be repeated many times each night, night after night.

### Night Rescue of 'River Rat 3'

It was almost midnight at 'Dustoff' ops, when the phone rang.

'Dustoff, sir,' cried a young ground crewman.

This was the 57th Medical Detachment helicopter's call-sign, and one that meant another dangerous night in the Vietnamese jungle for the crew of one of the medical rescue units in Vietnam. Flying the 'Hospital Huey', identified by the red cross on its nose and doors, the crews recovered countless numbers of wounded soldiers and airmen during the course of the war. Presented here are a few recollections from Capt David Freeman, a 'Dustoff' pilot from the 57th Med Det.

Freeman ran to his aircraft, untying the rotor blades as he climbed aboard and strapped himself in.

'Clear' was the yell as he pulled the starter trigger The crew was with the pilot and co-pilot before the rotor was in the green, and they lifted off while Freeman called Ops on 'Fox Mike'.

'Dustoff Ops, this is 74. We're airborne. What have you got for us?'

'It's a river boat, 74. Let me know when you're ready to copy the coordinates.'

Freeman pulled his plastic-covered map out of the leg pocket of his flight suit and fumbled around in the left sleeve pocket for a grease pencil.

'Go ahead.'

'Coordinates are x-ray tango one zero four four zero zero. It's just south of Go Da Ha on the Vam Co Dong river.'

'Copy. What's the contact?'

Freeman pointed north-west to his co-pilot Dave Smith and turned his attention back to getting the details of the mission.

'Contact River Rat Three on thirty-eight twenty-five.'

'Roger.'

Freeman moved the ICS selector up one setting and contacted the Air Force radar controller on UHF.

'Paris Control, this is Dustoff Seven Four, off Long Binh, headed for x-ray tango one zero four four zero zero, squawking 1200.'

Paris advised: 'Radar contact three clicks north-west of Long Binh. Looks like three five zero for three five miles.'

'Roger.' He glanced at the RMI to make sure Smith was picking up the heading, then turned his attention back to getting artillery clearance. Freeman then switched back to the Dustoff Ops frequency to see what else he could find out about the mission. The RTO was just full of good news.

'The target has been in an ambush, seven four. When they called the mission in, they were still taking fire from one of the river banks. They've got two critically wounded.'

'Any chance for some guns?' Freeman enquired.

'Are you kidding?' came the response.

Paddy Control told the crew they were getting close and needed to turn a little more to the north. Smith turned ten degrees to the right and Freeman tuned to the tactical frequency they had been given.

'River Rat Three, this is Dustoff Seven Four.'

'Dustoff Seven Four, this is River Rat Three.'

'We're about five minutes out. What's your tactical situation?'

'Not good, Dustoff. We're adrift and taking fire from the river bank. The engine's got hit with an RPG. We're taking water, and I've got four wounded, two critical. Over.'

Not good was right—a disabled boat in the middle of a river taking fire, and the Huey carried no guns!

'Can you mark your position for us?'

'Affirmative, Dustoff, but we're still in the middle of the river. We're trying to get downstream where we can get ashore, but we've been a little busy.'

'That's okay, River Rat Three. We can use the rescue hoist to get your wounded if we can locate your position.'

In the back crewmen Pierce and Toomey began to rig the hoist.

'We've got you in sight, River Rat. Can you give us some lights for positioning?'

'We can give you our running lights,' came the reply, 'but you'll be a sitting duck if you come up over us now.'

'Roger that, River Rat. How bad are your wounded?'

'Pretty bad, Dustoff. I'm not sure a couple of these guys are going to make it.'

'We will do our best to see that they do,' said Freeman. 'Wait until you hear us approaching from over the river, then give us your running lights. We'll come overhead with the hoist. Put the two most severely wounded on the jungle penetrator first and strap them on tight.'

'Roger, Dustoff, and thank you.'

'Don't mention it.'

This was not going to be easy any way the crew tried it. Using the hoist and jungle penetrator required maintaining position directly over the pick-up site. That was difficult enough to do in the daytime over a stationary position, but at night it would be even more problematic owing to the lack of visual references.

Pierce and Toomey switched their microphones to 'hot mike' and were talking to Freeman constantly, who was flying the helicopter and looking outside, trying to keep his eyes accustomed to the dark and also endeavouring to locate visual references. In the back the crewmen were down on the floor, scanning the area below, and, having found the river, were guiding Freeman to it. River Rat obligingly turned on his running lights, which exposed him to more fire from the river bank. The 'Dustoff' was totally 'lights off' outside the aircraft, and Freeman flipped up the protective cover over the button that would allow him to cut the hoist cable in the event of its becoming entangled.

'Dustoff, this is River Rat Three. We hear you coming up the river near our position but don't see you.'

'Roger, Three, we've got you in sight. Hold your position as best you can.'

Freeman knew from his training that if he got too low the rotor wash would make it difficult to load the patients on the hoist and if too high the drift differential between the two craft would make it even more difficult. The crew continued their constant stream of instructions.

'A little forward, sir. Right there, now. To your right. Stop. Hold it. Now forward, right there, hold it steady. Hoist going down, sir. Ten feet, twenty feet, twenty-five feet, forward, forward, hold it.'

'Forward. To your left. Down just a little. Hoist on the deck. Forward. Stop. One patient on. To your right, to your right. Second patient on. Bringing it up.'

The crew kept up their chatter. Freeman was concentrating on the horizon, trying not to look at anything too close.

'Forty feet. Thirty feet. Twenty feet. Ten feet. Patients are on board, sir. Let's go!'

Freeman hauled the helicopter into a climb, feeling like the proverbial 'nervous wreck'. The actual mission had taken less than five minutes, but it had seemed more like an hour. The rear crewmen reported that both patients were still alive, and they continued to work on them. However, they needed urgent hospital attention, so the helicopter headed towards Long Binh.

'River Rat Three, this is Dustoff Seven Four. My medic tells me we need to get these guys to the hospital fast. Can the rest of your guys wait until we get back?' Freeman called.

'We can take care of the rest of these guys, Dustoff. You take care of those boys for us. They're good men.'

'We'll be back, River Rat. It'll take us about an hour.'

'Dustoff 74' headed for the 24th Evac, alerting the hospital by radio that they were inbound. Thirty minutes later they had unloaded the two men and landed to refuel. Then they headed back to the river. On arrival, they found that the patrol boat had managed to bank on the opposite side of the river from its ambushers. A clearing had already been marked for the Huey and Freeman quickly picked up the remaining wounded men. The uninjured boat crew elected to remain with their craft. 'Dustoff 74' took the wounded back to the 24th Evac.

## Sandy Down

Capt Dave Freeman and crew parked their UH-1 'Huey' medevac helicopter in the dust at the edge of the Lai Khe strip as a pair of Phantoms started napalming the area right across the road. A soldier ran over and told them that NVA tanks were less than a mile up the road and that they had better get airborne. Jumping in, the crew got organised—'one burning', 'two turning', 'three in the green'—and were ready to go. Lifting off and heading south, Freeman contacted the nearest FAC to find out where the action was so that they could stay clear.

'Covey Three, this is Dustoff Seven Four,' Freeman radioed.

'Go ahead, Dustoff Seven Four. This is Covey Three,' the FAC replied.

'We just lifted off Lai Khe and need a sitrep.'

'Roger, Dustoff Seven Four,' the FAC replied. 'Stay three or four klicks south and east of Lai Khe and you'll be clear. Don't get too far away, though. I may need you.'

'Roger,' Freeman replied. He continued heading south, still climbing, obtaining altitude.

'Dustoff, what's your fuel status?' Covey three called in.

'An hour and a half,' Freeman told him.

When they were above 3,000ft they turned back towards the east. Freeman saw two flights of Phantoms making bombing runs on a hillside to his left, while below a couple of A-1 'Sandys' were circling, waiting their turn. Holding up there for a few minutes, listening on the airborne C&C frequency, they waited for any call to aid. Watching the action, the crew were mesmerised by the awesome amount of firepower being displayed right across the road from the airfield that they had been using as a staging area for several weeks. Suddenly the FAC called up.

'Dustoff Seven Four, this is Covey Three. Over.'

'Go ahead Covey Three.'

'I've got a Sandy down.'

Freeman immediately lowered collective and turned north, scanning the area ahead.

'Where is he?'

'I'll mark it for you in just a minute. I don't see any movement down there yet.'

Freeman caught site of the O-2 FAC flying west over a small road.

'I've got you in sight, Covey Three,' Freeman announced.

'Give us a mark when you're ready.'

'Roger, Dustoff. I'll be marking with Willy Pete. Look fifty yards south of my mark.'

Watching the ground for signs of the white phosphorous rocket that the forward air controller would be firing from under the wing of his O-2, Freeman steeled himself for the pick-up. 'Willy Pete' was highly flammable and 50yds was about as close as he would dare put it to friendlies. However, it would show well against the green trees. Seeing the mark immediately, Freeman pointed the Huey for the white smoke, still descending.

'Watch it, Dustoff,' Covey cautioned. 'There are bad guys all over that hillside.'

'Okay, keep an eye out for us,' Freeman told him. 'What's the best way in?'

'You're doing fine,' the FAC responded.

Watching from this perch overhead, if somebody started firing at them he would mark the target for one of the Phantoms to take out.

'A hundred yards ahead,' Covey coached the Huey crew.

Down on the deck Freeman had a much better perspective and the wreckage came into view in front of them, but they were not too sure how to get to it. Hovering for a closer look, one of the Huey's medics called.

'Look over there, sir! At two o'clock—there he is!'

Freeman could not see him, but David Garcia, who was flying the right seat, did. 'I've got the controls,' Garcia said, and Freeman did not argue with him.

'You've got it.'

'Keep us covered, Covey,' Freeman radioed. 'We're sitting ducks down here.'

'Roger, Dustoff,' came the reply. 'There's a group of twenty or so bad guys headed your way from the north-west, but I don't think they'll get to you. I've got a little present on the way for them.'

'Okay,' Freeman replied. 'We've found your man. Looks like he's okay.'

The 'Sandy' pilot, a young Air Force captain, was on his feet with his .45 in his hand. The Huey was carefully hovered through the trees in order to avoid a rotor strike. When they came within five or six feet of the ground the 'Sandy' pilot jumped on board, grinning from ear to ear. The fuselage of the big old A-1 was still intact. It had done a good job of protecting the pilot during the crash. The 'Dustoff' came up out of the hole in the trees, and followed the FAC's suggestion to depart to the south-east, remaining low-level. He released the Phantoms and they obliterated the A-1, also dropping a load on the North Vietnamese troops who had been trying to reach the downed pilot before the rescuers did. The 'Sandy' pilot had been on the ground for less than ten minutes.

## Seawolf SAR

Early in the morning of 3 December 1971 'Paddy Control' contacted Dustoff Operations with an emergency scramble mission. A Navy Seawolf helicopter from HA(L)-3 had just given a mayday call near Tra Vinh, indicating that he had been hit by enemy fire and was going down. Freeman and his crew scrambled immediately, and 'Paddy' vectored them to the coordinates where he had last seen the Seawolf on radar. It took approximately fifteen minutes to get there. That fifteen minutes probably seemed like two hours to the Seawolf crew, so Freeman began asking the 'H' model Huey for all she could give without breaking airspeed and torque redlines. Not knowing whether anyone was alive and having no information about the tactical situation, Freeman started a search pattern, flying north to south with all eyes scanning the ground for a crashed helicopter or some signal from the Seawolf crew. Within a couple of minutes the crew chief spotted the wreckage and pointed it out. The helicopter was in an open area, easily visible and with plenty of room beside it for the Huey to land.

It looked as though the pilot had managed to get the machine on the ground with little external damage. From a tactical perspective, however, the location was bad: the crew were in an open area, difficult to defend and with little cover. Freeman made a low pass over the downed helicopter and saw four airmen. They were huddled next to their machine and holding off a squad of VC with their personal weapons. Their 'Mike' model Huey had a 50-calibre machine gun mounted in it, but it was facing the wrong way and could not be swung around and used for defence. As the 'Dustoff' pulled up from that low pass, Freeman got a call on UHF from another Seawolf helicopter which had also responded to the emergency call. The pilot told them he was less than five minutes away and would give them gun cover while they made the pick-up. Freeman told him that the gun cover would be appreciated but that five minutes might seem like a long time to the men on the ground. The Seawolf 'rogered' that and said it would make it in three.

Meanwhile the 'Dustoff' crew decided on what appeared to be the best plan of action. They came in facing the enemy location and, using the downed aircraft for cover, were able to land within 20–25yds of where the crew were making their stand. As they started running towards the helicopter all hell broke loose. At first the 'Dustoff' crew thought it was the VC firing a B-40 or something similar, then they saw the other Seawolf swoop low overhead, guns and rockets blazing. For a few seconds nobody on the ground was shooting at anybody else. The VC were all trying to dig as deep into the earth as they could. The crew from the downed helicopter scrambled on board the 'Dustoff' and they exited the way they came in, without taking any hits.

## Marine Corps Hueys

Like the 'Dustoffs' the 'Seawolves' also used the 'Huey'. Their Bell UH-1 armed helicopters were, in most respects, unmodified former Army machines, and these helicopters had already seen a lot of long and hard use, and those received directly from the Army units in Vietnam generally required a good deal of repair and rejuvenation before being sent out in Navy service. The UH-1B, which formed the backbone of the squadron's aircraft assets, was powered by a Lycoming T53-L-11 engine and incorporated a standard Bell UH-1 rotor head. Still another improvement was the UH-1M, the first examples of which were introduced into the unit on 15 June 1971. It was planned for HA(L)-3 to equip entirely with the 'Mike' model, but the heavy demand for its engine, which was also used on the UH-1H and AH-1G, kept the Navy on the low side of the priority list, and by December 1971 only eleven of the Seawolves' gunships were UH-1Ms

The USMC's UH-1E was basically an Army UH-1B to which minor modifications were applied to make it suitable for use by the Marines. Chief amongst these modifications were a different electrical system and radios, a rotor brake and an aluminium fuselage, and the 1E was the first turbine-powered helicopter to enter service. Flying medevac, escort, recon team inserts and extractions, assault operations, direct fire support of engaged Marine ground units, TACA duties and convoy escort as well as other missions, Huey 'slick' operations had Marine aircrews over-committed throughout their entire tours. If ever the Marine Corps got its money's worth out of any aircraft, it was the Huey.

## POW Rescue Attempt

On 22 December 1972 the 'Dustoff' crews were informed that Army Intelligence had determined that a number of American POWs were being held in a camp in the lower region of the U Minh forest. Some time before Christmas they were going to be moved to the coast and picked up by boats that would transport them to Hanoi. The 'Dustoffs' were to be included in an attempt to rescue them before the prisoners were moved. The mission was in the hands of the 188th Assault Helicopter Company, but the 57th Medical Detachment was to send two crews along to pick up the prisoners in case they needed medical attention.

Just south of Can Tho, Freeman and his crew joined up with several helicopters from the 188th. There was a C&C ship, accompanied by six Cobras, and five 'slicks' loaded with combat assault troops. The guns were to create a diversion while the 'slicks' dropped the troops in to secure the area and release the prisoners. Then the 'Dustoffs' would come in to pick up the freed prisoners while the guns flew cover. The 'slicks' would pick up the troops and they would all head for home. The plan's success depended upon immaculate timing and knowing exactly where the 'bad guys' and the prisoners were located.

Conversation in Freeman's helicopter was subdued, but much was said with eye contact and the business-like precision with which the men carried out their routine tasks. The helicopters from Can Tho were circling in a wide orbit south of the airfield, waiting for the 'Dustoffs' to arrive and for everyone to join up in formation. Freeman picked his spot and fell in behind the 'slicks' on the right side of the staggered trail formation.

The Cobras flew off to either side of the main group, and when all were all joined up the C&C ship broke radio silence with one short comment on FM: 'Flight's up lead.' The lead 'slick' then turned south with the whole formation in tow. The mission profile called for the helicopters to arrive at the site of the POW camp at daybreak. All the crews had plotted the mission coordinates on their tactical charts just before take-off, but it was the lead 'slick's job to get them to the right place. The POWs were located 45 klicks south of Quanh Long.

## Bell UH-1 Huey

The Bell Model 204 was for many the classic helicopter design. Winner of a 1955 design competition, it first flew on 22 October 1956 under the designation XH-40. Production followed as the HU-1A, and despite its official title, it was universally dubbed the 'Huey'. In 1962 designations were re-worked and it became the UH-1A, coincident with the type's first deployment to Vietnam. Its first uses were in the escort role, the helicopter being hastily adapted to carry 7.62 miniguns and rocket pods. The more powerful UH-1B introduced shortly afterwards brought greater armament with door-mounted guns. Able to carry seven troops, the UH-1B was partnered by the UH-1D with a larger cabin for up to twelve troops or six stretchers, and the design gained fame as the workhorse of the war. 'Everything that moved went by Huey': 'Dustoffs' retrieved wounded whilst 'Bullshit Bombers' dropped leaflets and 'Bugships' sprayed pesticides—no job was too big or too small.

*Specifications:* Powerplant (UH-1B) Avco Lycoming T53-L-11 turboshaft delivering 716kW and turning a two bladed rotor with a semi-rigid head. Armament—door-mounted M60 machine guns and/or skid-mounted forward-firing 7.62mm guns and/or rocket launcher tubes. Crew 2.

The helicopters refuelled in the pre-dawn darkness, departing the Quanh Long strip; the 'guns' took off first, then everybody else fell in behind. There would be absolute radio silence. The C&C ship supposedly had contact via the scrambled KY-28 FM radio, and the success of the mission depended upon total surprise, which would be hard to achieve with so many aircraft heading south at the same time.

The group were half-way between Quanh Long and the POW camp when the mission commander came on the air-to-air radio with a short, simple statement: 'The mission is off, boys. Let's go home.' Somewhat bemused, the lead 'slick' began a turn back to the north. The mood was sombre as the 'Dustoff' crews walked back into their operations room. Finally the cancellation was explained. 'They had the prisoners in bamboo cages,' they were told. 'They had them close to the river. If we had come in, they would have dumped the cages into the river before we could have stopped them. The prisoners would have all drowned.'

## Dustoff Statistics

Vietnam was the 'helicopter war'. To the wounded, no sight was more welcome than the Iroquois helicopter with the red cross emblem painted on the nose, top and sides. It meant immediate treatment and a swift journey to a hospital for medical attention—the saving of valuable minutes that were for some the difference between life and death. The average time from being wounded to hospitalisation was one hour.

The UH-1 Huey was fitted to carry six patients with at least one member of the crew of four being a fully trained first-aid man, able to give treatment from transfusions to reassurance. Medevac helicopters flew nearly 500,000 missions, and between 1965 and 1969 there were 372,947 casualties evacuated by helicopter—and this figure included US troops, Allied troops and civilians. At the peak of Allied involvement, 116 Bell UH-1 'Dustoffs' were in service, operating among the eighteen hospitals scattered throughout Vietnam. Eighty-three per cent of wounded were able to return to military duty; 2 per cent of wounded died in hospital, compared with the Second World War death rate of 4.5 per cent. There was a much higher percentage of deaths from small-arms fire compared with the Second World War and Korea, and this was attributed to the lightweight, high-velocity rounds in modern weapons such as the AK 47 and the captured M16s: these weapons, with a rapid-fire capability, caused multiple injuries, with small entry and large exit wounds. However, without the use of the helicopter for rapid evacuation, the death toll in Vietnam would have been far greater.

## Bat-21

In one of possibly the most bizarre rescues of the Vietnam War, Lt-Col Iceal Hambleton was plucked from enemy territory in North Vietnam after 11½ days on the ground, the subject of the largest rescue operation in USAF history. On Easter Sunday, 2 April 1973, Hambleton was flying as a navigator aboard an EB-66 electronic countermeasures aircraft of the 42nd Tactical Electronic Warfare Squadron, whose call-sign was 'Bat-21' The aircraft was struck by a North Vietnamese SAM, and Hambleton was the only crew member to eject safely from the aircraft, landing near a busy highway junction on a communist supply route. Intelligence sources indicated that the area contained over 30,000 enemy troops, and, indeed, whilst awaiting rescue Hambleton directed USAF strike aircraft which destroyed many of the enemy's vehicles on the road.

Intense ground fire prevented the first attempted rescue, so a plan was devised to direct the survivor by radio contact, using his URC-64 handset, with a FAC O-1 Bird Dog to a safer pick-up point. Hambleton was later quoted as being enthusiastic about the performance of the URC-64, despite its frequent immersion in water and other hardships. USAF reconnaissance aircraft photographed the area, and later analysts laid out a course for him to follow to a river two miles away. In order to guide him safely past enemy camps, gun emplacements and unfriendly villages, a code was necessary to spoof any 'listeners' as to Hambleton's position or route. As a keen golfer, Hambleton had a detailed memory of various golf courses he had played, and this was used as the code, citing various 'holes' at certain courses to establish the direction of travel and the distance for each segment of the journey to guide him downstream to the intended rescue point.

Travelling only at night, he reached the tenth day, exhausted and having had nothing to eat or drink since bail-out save for a few ears of corn and some rainwater. The last 'hole' called for him to float downstream, where he was finally met by a Navy SEAL, Lt Thomas R. Norris, and a Vietnamese Ranger, who had managed to steal a boat. Despite several enemy ambush attempts, he delivered Hambleton to a waiting USAF helicopter, which took off under intense enemy fire.

Lt-Col Hambleton's experiences were later put into print and formed the basis for a Gene Hackman-led movie. However, neither medium captured the complexity of the operation, the exotic technology or the number of people involved in the rescue. In all, 234 medals were issued for the 'Bat-21' recovery, and Norris received the Medal of Honor for his role in this and another related rescue.

## Bat-21: A Different View

US Air Force Col Darrell Whitcomb has talked of the B-52 bomber strike against the North Vietnamese during the massive 1972 Easter-tide Offensive, and the shooting down of the Douglas EB-66 electronic warfare aircraft. As in numerous other events, the story has many different perspectives. Col Whitcomb, a former FAC, tells the many-sided story of the attempts to rescue two downed American airmen in the spring of 1972.

As noted earlier, Air Force Lt-Col Iceal Hambleton (call-sign 'Bat-21 Bravo') was the navigator of the EB-66 that was shot down while leading the B-52 bomber strike. 1/Lt Mark Clark was the navigator of a North American Rockwell OV-10 FAC aircraft shot down in an early attempt to extract Hambleton. The efforts to locate and rescue both men—later sensationalised in the 1988 movie—actually involved separate Army, Air Force and Navy operations. What follows is Darrell Whitcomb's account of the Air Force operations.

At approximately 3.15 p.m. on 6 April, US Air Force Capt Fred Boli took off from the American air base at Da Nang in a Douglas A-1 Skyraider fighter-bomber ('Sandy'). With Boli, whose call-sign was 'Sandy 01', were three other A-1s, '02', '05' and '06', and two Sikorsky HH-53 rescue helicopters, Jolly Greens '67' and '60'. A few minutes later two more 'Jolly Greens', led by Capt Mark Schibler, took off as back-ups. The task force had two possible objectives. Col Hambleton, the EB-66 survivor, had now been on the ground for four days and needed to be resupplied. Therefore one A-1 (Boli's) was rigged to drop him a Madden resupply kit together with food, water, ammunition and extra radios. A rescue attempt could also be made if Boli, the 'Sandy' leader, felt that the situation warranted it. It would be Boli's call.

Lt-Col Bill Harris, commander of the 'Jolly Green' squadron, was concerned about the mission. Harris knew that there was still likely to be a significant enemy presence around the two downed Americans. He discussed the situation with his commander, Col Cecil Muirhead, in Saigon. Muirhead and his staff were also worried and were monitoring the continuing rescue effort very closely. Harris had intended to fly as aircraft commander on the lead 'Jolly Green' during the 6 April mission, but he had participated in one of the earlier pick-up attempts, when the helicopters had been badly shot up, and his squadron colleagues persuaded him that he had already done his share. When Harris reluctantly stood aside, Capt Peter Chapman stepped forward and insisted that he be allowed to fly as aircraft commander on the mission. Harris was deeply impressed with Chapman's volunteering, especially since Chapman was not next in the duty rotation and, in fact, had orders to return to the United States to fly with the presidential air unit at Andrews Air Force Base in Maryland. But Chapman's attitude was typical of all of the men in his squadron, who were ready to risk their lives to save others.

With Chapman in 'Jolly Green 67' were 1/Lt John H. Call III, co-pilot; T/Sgt Roy D. Prater, mechanic; Sgt William R. Pearson and T/Sgt Allen J. Avery, Pararescuemen; and Sgt James H. Alley, photographer. The gaggle of aircraft proceeded to a holding point southeast of Quang Tri, where Jolly Greens '67' and '60' and Sandys '05' and '06' circled while Sandys '01' and '02' entered the battle area to assess how dangerous it might be to attempt a pick-up. There they took over from the two FACs on station, Capt Harold Icke ('Bilk 11') and Capt Gary Ferentchak ('Nail 59'). Icke and Ferentchak had been working the area jointly and were finishing off the preparatory air strikes.

The two back-up 'Jolly Greens' were on hold at a position east of Hue, just off the South Vietnamese coast. Boli noticed a friendly tank position approximately 6km south of the survivors and decided to make the final holding point for the helicopters right over them. However, he was very concerned about the five enemy battalions that intelligence had told him were directly around the survivors. He spent the next 30 minutes trawling the planned ingress route for the helicopters, using his 7.62mm minigun to strafe anything that looked suspicious. Neither Boli, in 'Sandy 01', nor 'Sandy 02' observed any appreciable enemy reaction, but they did receive some enemy SAM signals on the radio while they were checking out the area. At 4.15 p.m. Boli directed the two FACs to terminate the air strikes so that he could overfly the survivors' immediate area. He requested that Icke and Ferentchak as well as 'Sandy 02' and both Hambleton and Clark, on the ground, all listen on the same radio frequency and watch while he flew low around the survivors' positions. Boli also tried to drop the Madden supply kit to Hambleton, but the arming wire on the device failed and the kit did not release from the aircraft (Boli did not know that, however, until he landed back at Da Nang). Boli also strafed a few suspected NVA locations with his 20mm cannon and had 'Sandy 02' drop cluster bombs on other locations, widening his area of search as he did so. Boli directed the FACs to hit several places with more air strikes. While all of that was going on, Boli ordered 'Jolly Green 60' to hold south-east of Quang Tri and ordered 'Jolly Green 67' and Sandys '05' and '06' to proceed to the final holding point. As the aircraft were repositioning, Capt Boli began his final briefing for all the participants in the rescue attempt.

They would first try to pick up Hambleton, he said, then—depending on how the situation developed—they would try to extract Clark. The two would be picked up either by 'Jolly Green 67' or one of the other helicopters. But the briefing was rudely interrupted by a SAM call, which forced all the aircraft to dive for the deck to avoid the missiles. Boli noted that the SAM launches were not accompanied by any anti-aircraft artillery (AAA). At 5.10 p.m. 'Sandy 03' joined the force with a full load of white phosphorus, which could be used to lay a smoke screen. Boli finished the plan briefing—'Sandy 02' would lead 'Jolly Green 67' in with a series of smoke rockets to pick up Hambleton and then Clark, in that order, if the area was quiet. 'Sandy 02' would then join with Sandys '05' and '06' in a 'daisy chain' around the 'Jolly Green' to provide suppressive fire. 'Sandy 03' would lay a series of well-placed smoke screens and then join the daisy chain. 'Sandy 01' would orbit above to direct the operation and call ground fire. At 5.15 p.m. Boli determined that all the requested targets had been struck to his satisfaction. He had the FACs and remaining strikes hold high and dry while he re-entered the survivors' immediate area to brief them and take one last look.

He reviewed the plan and situation in his mind. He knew that it could be a trap, but the preparation had been thorough and the trawling and probing had been intense, and the enemy response so far had been slack. It was time to go: Boli directed the task force to execute the pick-up. 'Sandy 02' immediately laid down his marks for the helicopters to follow to Hambleton. 'Sandy 03' put down his smoke screen. Sandys '02', '05' and '06' began the daisy chain to protect the vulnerable helicopter and began dropping cluster bombs and strafing with their 20mm cannon anything that looked in any way threatening. A slight shift in the wind caused some of the smoke screen partly to obscure Hambleton's position, but the confusion was quickly resolved and the force pressed on.

Overhead, in the swirling mass of aircraft, Capt Ferentchak took out his camera and began to take pictures. He wanted to record what he thought was going to be a historic rescue. As 'Jolly Green 67' crossed the river near Cam Lo, the helicopter began to take ground fire from all quarters. Seconds later, as it approached to within 100m of Hambleton, Boli called for the survivor to pop his red smoke so that the 'Jolly Green' crew could locate him. Almost simultaneously, someone on 'Jolly Green 67' called, 'I'm hit.' It was later determined that they also had added, 'They got a fuel line.' Hambleton heard all of this on his survival radio and, realising the gravity of the situation, did not pop his smoke and reveal his position.

The crew of 'Jolly Green 67' fought to control their damaged aircraft. Boli had briefed the helicopter crews that if they began taking ground fire, they were to exit the area immediately on a south-east heading. Realising their desperate situation, the crew began to turn their craft to escape the cauldron of withering fire. The North Vietnamese gunners seemed to increase the intensity of their fire. Boli ordered the other 'Sandys' to cover the wounded 'Jolly Green', and he began strafing in front of the lumbering helicopter as it tried to gain speed. But instead of turning south-east as briefed, the crew began heading due east, towards the enemy concentrations north of the river nearby. Apparently one of the crew members on the 'Jolly Green' was holding down his microphone transmit button, since numerous calls directing the helicopter to 'Turn south, Jolly, turn right!' were blocked. The crew finally turned south about 1km east of the planned route after Boli had warned them not to cross over a village full of enemy troops. As the 'Jolly Green' crew made their turn, Boli flew up behind them and strafed the enemy soldiers. 'Jolly Green 67' overshot its turn and took up a heading to the south-west. Boli ordered the helicopter to turn back to the left. Someone else came on the radio and told it to turn right. Boli tells the story from there: 'Jolly hesitated, and again I ordered, "No! Turn left Jolly, turn south." He initiated the turn, and I was about to order him to climb when, as I passed on a strafe pass, I observed a fire suddenly break out between the middle of the left engine and the main rotor. Immediately pieces flew off of the tail rotor and struck the main rotor, causing it to disintegrate. Jolly Green 67 continued to roll left and crashed on his left side about ten kilometers south of Nail 38 Bravo's [Lt Clark's] position. Fire immediately spread throughout the aircraft. No beepers were ever heard . . . The time was 1740.'

On the tactical frequency, Boli began calling, 'Jolly's down! Jolly's down!' 'Jolly Green 67' lay on its side, a heap of burning, smoking wreckage. It would continue to burn and smoke for several days, with intermittent explosions of the ordnance on board. The fire would become so hot that some of the metal would melt into the ground. There were no survivors and there would be no search and rescue attempt. Instead, the names of six more Americans—Chapman, Call, Prater, Pearson, Avery and Alley—were added to the mounting bill for Hambleton. Boli conducted a roll call of his task force. All others were present. Capt Schibler, leading the two back-up helicopters, monitored all of this and immediately began to move his two aircraft to the holding point, where he encountered the rest of the force. The two groups of aircraft quickly joined with an orbiting aircraft and tried to sort out the disaster. All the pilots agreed that there were apparently no survivors from 'Jolly Green 67' and that another attempt to rescue Hambleton and Clark did not appear justified at that time, since there was still a strong enemy presence in the area. As the task force leader, it was Boli's call. He agreed that the area was just too hot: they would abort the mission.

Boli then turned on-scene command over to Capt Icke, with another list of targets to be struck, told the survivors to remain hidden and accompanied his shaken force back to base. Back at Da Nang, the men of the rescue forces were stunned by the tragic loss of 'Jolly Green 67' and its crew. Col Harris was very upset. The loss of 'Jolly Green 67' confirmed his earlier fears that the search area was just too dangerous for helicopters. Once again, Harris called Col Muirhead in Saigon, and this time Harris told him that they had to find another way. Muirhead agreed with Boli's decision and Harris's recommendations to terminate the rescue attempts by helicopter. Muirhead then notified his superiors that 'all reasonable actions had been accomplished' and that the area was just too dangerous for a helicopter pick-up.

In their hiding places near Cam Lo the two survivors had been witnesses to the 'Jolly Green''s downing. Lt Clark later recalled that there had been so much firing going on that he could not distinguish who was firing at whom. But as the 'Jolly Green' passed over him heading south, he could tell that it was not gaining altitude. When he heard it crash, Clark was devastated. His immediate thought was, 'I really cocked this up. Six more guys dying because I f——d up.' And then the realisation set in that he was not going to be picked up that day. Clark felt desperately lonely. Colonel Hambleton —'Bat 21 Bravo'—cried for the six brave men who had lost their lives lost trying to save his own. Although he was tired, hungry and demoralised, the 53-year-old navigator resolved then and there: 'Hell, I'm going to get out of this, regardless.'

Hambleton and Clark did get out—but not by helicopter. No more of the vulnerable machines would be sent in. Instead, a small ground team was despatched, commanded by US Marine Lt-Col Andy Anderson and led by Navy SEAL Lt Tom Norris. Within a week the team would infiltrate behind enemy lines to rescue the two downed fliers. It was a risky and dangerous mission, but it got done. The two lucky fliers returned home as heroes. Nothing could be done, however, for the brave crew of 'Jolly Green 67'. They were lost forever, part of the larger cost of the war. It would be 22 years before their remains would be found and returned to the United States.

## More from the BAT: 'Blue Ghost 39'

On 2 April 1972, near the demilitarised zone (DMZ) of Vietnam, a US Air Force FAC pilot, using the call-sign 'Bilk 34', broadcast an urgent radio plea over the emergency-only 'Guard' frequency that was routinely monitored by all pilots flying in the South-East Asian theatre. The request was for assistance in rescuing any survivors of an EB-66 radar surveillance aircraft that had just been shot down. The plane had been struck by a surface-to-air missile fired by the North Vietnamese Army near Cam Lo. A general alert warning of the possibility of further SAM attacks in that vicinity was also issued on 'Guard', noting the time in minutes after the hour at the end of his message. A single parachute had been observed to open, followed by a desperate call for help, so at least one survivor was confirmed.

Flying his model UH-1H Huey helicopter near Quang Tri to observe the three-day-old invasion by the NVA, Army Lt Byron Kulland, a 'slick' pilot with F Troop, 8th (Air) Cavalry, 196th Light Infantry Brigade, answered the call as 'Blue Ghost 39', his call-sign while in the air. Together with co-pilot WO John Frink, he had only arrived in the country a few weeks beforehand, but he certainly understood the risk of such an impromptu rescue attempt in the midst of concentrated enemy forces. So did crew chief Ron Paschall and door gunner PFC Jose Astorga. There had been little reconnaissance of the area since up to 45,000 NVA attacked on 30 March from the west out of their sanctuaries in Laos and from across the Ben Hai river, only twelve miles north of them. As a general rule, only aviation units, along with a handful of Marine and Army ground advisers, were left to help the South Vietnamese military defend their country.

By 1972 nearly all the US ground troops had gone home for good. The situation changed almost hourly, and no one was sure how far south or east the NVA had progressed. To make matters worse, fighter jet air cover was unavailable from the Air Force, and therefore they would have to rely on a single Cobra helicopter gunship, or 'snake', for protection on the quick-snatch extraction. It was also getting late, and the weather was closing in. Still, they decided to try anyway. After all, any one of them could be in similar straits at any time, given the uncertainty of the moment.

Without hesitation, Kulland departed northwards at full power, heading towards the town of Dong Ha. 'Bilk' would vector him to the survivor's last known position from there. Capt Mike Rosebeary followed closely behind in the 'snake'. Kulland made a hard left turn and dropped to a scant 50ft of altitude to hug the Cua Viet river as it twisted west from Dong Ha. The crew began to hunt for the airman evading the enemy somewhere below. However, immediately after they had crossed the river, ground fire raked both helicopters. Rosebeary's ship was shot up so badly that the emergency panel lit up like a Christmas tree. As senior officer, he wisely ordered a retreat and headed for the coast, losing his engine along the way. Luckily, a 'Jolly Green Giant' helicopter, sent up from Da Nang to assist in the rescue, was there in minutes to pick up the two-man crew unhurt. Back in the lone Huey, Kulland had tried to turn and escape with Rosebeary, but his ship began trailing heavy smoke from hits on the engine. Astorga's M-60 machine gun jammed while he was attempting to suppress the fire and a round had exploded against his 'chicken plate', whilst another shattered a leg, knocking him unconscious.

Then they crashed hard. Astorga woke in a daze to find the crew chief Paschall pinned in the wreckage. Crawling to the front, he found the two pilots still strapped in their seats. Frink was conscious, but Kulland appeared to be dead. Frink then threw two survival vests to Astorga and indicated they may have to leave the others behind if they could not get Paschall out quickly. Astorga helped Frink out of the aircraft then crawled away with the vests while Frink tried to get to Paschall. After dropping the vests a safe distance away, Astorga crawled back to the helicopter to try and help rescue Paschall. Just then, the NVA rushed in firing madly. The Huey exploded, killing Frink and Paschall instantly. Weak from injury and loss of blood, the door gunner tried to crawl away again but was easily captured. He survived and was transported to Hanoi as one of America's last prisoners of war, coming home a few months later in the 1973 POW exchange.

# 6

# Pararescue and 'Nail'

The history of pararescue can be traced back to August 1943, when 21 people bailed out of a disabled C-46 over an uncharted jungle near the China-Burma border. So remote was the crash site that the only means of getting help to the survivors was by paradrop. Lt-Col Don Fleckinger and two medical corpsmen volunteered for the assignment. This paradrop of medical corpsmen was the seed from which the concept of pararescue was born. For a month these men, aided by natives, cared for the injured until the party was brought to safety. News commentator Eric Severeid was one of the men to survive this ordeal. He later wrote of the men who risked their lives to save his: 'Gallant is a precious word; they deserve it.' From this event the need for a highly trained rescue force was founded: the Pararescueman was brought into being.

Since that first rescue, many airmen, soldiers and civilians have had first-hand experience that, when trouble strikes, Pararescuemen are ready to come to their aid. Some of the most inspiring stories originate from the conflict in South-East Asia and involve heroic deeds performed by Pararescuemen. They risked their lives flying over hostile territory to find friendly forces needing aid. Daily, Pararescuemen volunteered to ride a helicopter rescue hoist cable into the Vietnamese jungle to aid wounded infantrymen and injured pilots whose aircraft had been shot down. The Air Force awarded nineteen Air Force Crosses to enlisted personnel during the South-East Asian conflict; ten of the nineteen were awarded to Pararescuemen.

The trademark of the PJ is his maroon beret with the ARRS flash adorning it, and this distinctive recognition symbol came to the Pararescuemen in early 1966 when Gen John P. McConnell, then Air Force Chief of Staff, approved the wearing of the maroon beret. The beret symbolises the blood sacrificed by Pararescuemen and their devotion to duty by aiding others in distress. In the Vietnam conflict all the PJs were volunteers, and they earned more decorations per head than any other group of USAF personnel. Airman 1st Class William

H. Pitsenbarger participated in over 300 rescue missions. He was killed during the war and was posthumously awarded the Air Force Cross. Chief Master Sergeant Wayne L. Fisk was awarded the Silver Star for his part in the abortive Son Tay rescue. Fisk, however, has a greater claim to fame, and a second Silver Star to his credit: as part of the *Mayaguez* rescue mission he was noted as the last man to be lifted off the island of Koh Tang, and therefore probably became the last American to engage in ground combat with communist forces in the Vietnam War.

A major development in pararescue was the combination of parachuting with scuba techniques, and, when ready to jump, the scuba-equipped Pararescueman carries as much as 170lb of equipment. One of the most dramatic events involving pararescue/scuba action came as a result of the early termination of the Gemini 8 space flight and the subsequent recovery of astronauts Armstrong and Scott. It is worth mentioning that Pararescuemen were among the first US combatants to parachute into Panama during Operation 'Just Cause' in 1989, where their combat medical expertise was heavily utilised during this short, intense operation. In fact, using specially modified vehicles dubbed 'RATT-Vs', they recovered and cared for the majority of the US casualties that occurred on the two Panamanian controlled airfields that were taken by the initial invasion forces. More recently, Pararescuemen have been tasked with rescue missions involving downed aircrew members and injured combatants during the United Nations operation 'Desert Storm'. This action, for the liberation of Kuwait, again proved the value of the Air Force Pararescueman. Among the missions performed by pararescue was the rescue of a downed F-14 navigator in a very hostile area, involving the destruction of enemy forces in very close proximity to the survivor (examined in detail in a later chapter). Pararescue also provided extensive support for airlift operations providing humanitarian relief to Kurdish refugees fleeing into northern Iraq. Most recently, Pararescuemen were involved in the struggle to capture Somali leader Mohammed Fhara Aidid. Assigned jointly with army Rangers, PJs were tasked to operate in a search and rescue (SAR) role on Army helicopters. After the initial assault began, two Army helicopters were shot down and PJs responded to the scene to assist survivors and treat the wounded.

The Pararescueman's missions and roles include: emergency medical treatment to save lives; search and rescue operations; the recovery of downed aircrews; NASA Space Shuttle Launch Rescue Support; and special tactics in support of interservice special operations.

## Pararescue Training

The formal training of a Pararescueman is a never-ending programme, and he continually strives to perfect procedures while constantly searching for new techniques. After selection and completion of six weeks of Basic Military Training, the Pararescue recruit spends the next seventeen months training at the following schools:

**Pararescue/Combat Control Indoctrination Course** (10 weeks, Lackland AFB, Texas). The mission of the I-Course is to recruit, train and select future Pararescuemen and Combat Controllers. At this school recruits participate in extensive physical conditioning with a great deal of swimming, running, weight-training and callisthenics. The course helps to prepare them for the rigours of training and the demands of these lifestyles. Other training accomplished at this course includes physiological training, dive physics, metric manipulations, medical terminology, dive terminology, the history of PJs and CCT and leadership laboratories.

**US Army Airborne Parachutist School** (3 weeks, Fort Benning, Georgia). Here the recruits learn the basic parachuting skills required to infiltrate an objective area by static line airdrop. This course includes ground operations week, tower week and jump week, where they make five actual parachute jumps. Personnel who complete this training are awarded the basic parachutist rating and are allowed to wear the coveted parachutist's wings.

**US Army Combat Divers' School** (4 weeks, Key West, Florida). Here the recruit becomes a combat diver and learns to use scuba to infiltrate areas surrounded by water undetected. This course provides training to depths of 130ft, stressing the development of maximum underwater mobility under various operating conditions.

**US Navy Underwater Egress Training** (1 day, Pensacola NAS, Florida). This course teaches the recruit how to escape safely from an aircraft that has ditched in the water. Instruction includes principles, procedures and techniques necessary to get out of a sinking aircraft. Training requires the personnel to experience water entry in a training device and perform underwater egress.

**US Air Force Basic Survival School** (2½ weeks, Fairchild AFB, Washington). This course teaches basic survival techniques for remote areas, using minimal equipment. It includes instruction of principles, procedures, equipment and techniques which enable individuals to survive, regardless of climatic conditions or unfriendly environments, and return home.

**US Army Military Freefall Parachutist School** (5 weeks, Yuma Proving Grounds, Arizona). This course instructs freefall parachuting (HALO) using the high-performance ram air canopy. The course provides wind tunnel training, in-air instruction focusing on student stability, aerial manoeuvres, air sense and parachute opening procedures. Each student receives a minimum of 30 freefall jumps, including two day and two night jumps with oxygen equipment and field gear.

**Special Operations Combat Medic Course** (22 weeks, Fort Bragg, North Carolina). This course teaches how to manage trauma patients prior to evacuation and provide emergency medical treatment. The course consists of two phases. Phase I comprises ten weeks of Emergency Medical Technician Basic (EMT-B) training, and Phase II consists of twelve weeks of instruction in minor field surgery, pharmacology, combat trauma management, advanced airway management and military evacuation procedures. Upon graduation, an EMT-Paramedic certification is awarded through the National Registry.

**Pararescue Recovery Specialist Course** (20 weeks, Kirtland AFB, New Mexico). This course qualifies airmen as pararescue recovery specialists for assignment to any pararescue unit worldwide. Training includes EMT-Paramedic certification, field, mountaineering, combat tactics, advanced parachuting and helicopter insertion/extraction qualifications. On completion of this course, each graduate is awarded the maroon beret.

## The Mayaguez Incident

On 12 May 1975, less than a month after taking control of Cambodia, the Khmer Rouge seized the USS *Mayaguez* and its crew near the island of Puolo Wai at the edge of the country's territorial waters. The ship was then moved to Koh Tang. Three days later President Gerald Ford ordered a team of Marines to rescue the crew from Koh Tang island. While the objects for the rescue mission—the crew of the *Mayaguez*—had been moved to the port city of Sihanoukville, the Khmer Rouge remained on the island and pinned the Marines down in a heavy fire-fight. Ford then ordered fourteen hours of bombing on the country's coast, and called for a further rescue to be made of the Marines, for which the ARRS would provide the air mobility using seven HH-53s and four HC-130s; the Air Force would provide A-7D 'Sandy' aircraft, in concert with other US forces.

Though the *Mayaguez* crew were released unharmed, fifteen of more than 200 Marines who stormed the island were killed and two helicopters were lost. During the operations, which lasted 18hr 28min, the ARRS crews flew nineteen sorties for a total of 70.2hrs. The HH-53s inserted 69 Marines on the USS *Holt* and 184 on Koh Tang island. The HH-53s then extracted 145 Marines and five downed USAF crewmen. Two ARRS personnel were WIA, but no ARRS personnel were KIA. The rotor masts of the two downed helicopters are still visible today above the surf just off the island. As mentioned earlier, Chief M/Sgt Wayne Fisk had the dubious honour of being the last American serviceman to engage communist forces as he ran towards his HH-53.

During 1998 a 200-strong US military team search team went back to Koh Tang to locate the remains of the fifteen soldiers killed during the *Mayaguez* incident—the United States' last direct armed confrontation with Indo-Chinese communists.

### 'Nail': Foward Air Controllers

The role of the 'Forward Air Controller–Airborne' (FAC/FAC-A) can be traced back to the First World War when balloons were utilised to hoist a 'spotter' to call ranges for artillery attacks on enemy positions. The role underwent many changes and many titles over the following two decades, but it was not until the Vietnam War that the true value of the FAC became evident, and he is today a vital component of any military operation. The slow, low-flying FAC—or 'Nail', as he was commonly known—was also a vital part of any rescue component, and his aerial presence became one of the necessities during the South-East Asian conflict. Prior to that time, the FAC had been more of an air liaison officer, assigned to a ground unit and directing aerial attacks by radio upon only those enemy targets which he could see from the ground. During the Korean War one T-6 'Mosquito' group did provide airborne fire control, flying 4,902 sorties.

During the Vietnam War the Forward Air Controllers came into more extensive use. By maintaining constant aerial surveillance over

## Cessna O-1 Bird Dog

The O-1 was a two-place light observation and liaison aircraft developed from the commercial Cessna Model 170 in 1949. Originally designated L-19, Bird Dogs were used by the US Air Force, Army and Marines for such tasks as artillery-spotting, front-line communications, medical evacuation and pilot training. In Vietnam O-1s were used by FACs for reconnaissance and combat rescue, and, being very small, the aircraft were not easy targets to hit from the ground. The FAC, often an experienced fighter pilot, was assigned to a specific geographical area so that he could readily identify enemy activity. If the FAC observed enemy ground targets he marked them with smoke rockets so that they could be easily attacked by fighter-bombers. The FAC then remained on the scene to report bombing results. A number of TO-1D Bird Dogs were returned to Cessna to be modified for combat duty, with underwing racks added as well as other improvements. The USAF ordered more than 3,200 Bird Dogs, most of which were built as L-19As between 1950 and 1959.

*Specifications:* Powerplant one Continental O-470 of 213hp; span 36ft (10.97m); length 25ft 10in (7.87m); height 9ft 2in (2.79m); weight 2,400lb (1,088kg); maximum speed 150mph (241kph); cruising speed 115mph (185kph); range 530 miles (853km); service ceiling 20,300ft (6,187m); armament generally none except smoke rockets; crew two.

a specific geographic area, the FAC was practically on the spot when needed; in fact, many Bird Dog FACs were Korean War veterans. They were almost always on hand to monitor enemy activity, and, should this require a response in the form of an air strike, the FAC would be there to call in the fighter-bombers. Moreover, his skills found much favour with the rescue forces. The FACs served as on-

## Cessna O-2 Skymaster

The O-2 is the military version of the Cessna Model 337 Super Skymaster and is distinguished by its twin tail booms and tandem-mounted engines, which feature a tractor/pusher propeller arrangement. Derived from the Cessna Model 336, the 337 went into production for the civilian market in 1965, and by late 1966 the USAF had selected a military variant, designated O-2, to supplement the O-1 Bird Dog forward air controller (FAC) aircraft operating in South-East Asia. Twin engines enabled the O-2 to absorb more ground fire and still return safely, endearing it to its crews.

The O-2 first flew in January 1967 and production deliveries began in March. Production ended in June 1970 after 532 had been built for the USAF. Two series were produced. The O-2A was equipped with wing pylons to carry rockets, flares and other light ordnance. In the FAC role it was used for identifying and marking enemy targets with smoke rockets, coordinating air strikes and reporting target damage. The O-2B was a psychological warfare aircraft equipped with loudspeakers and a leaflet dispenser and carried no ordnance.

*Specifications:* Powerplant two Continental 10-360s of 210hp each; span 38ft (11.58m); length 29ft 2in (8.89m); height 9ft 5in (2.87m); weight 4,900lb (2,222kg) loaded; maximum speed 199mph (320kph); cruising speed 144mph (232kph); range 1,060 miles (1,707km); service ceiling 19,300ft (5,880m); armament four wing pylons for rockets, flares, 7.62 minigun pods or other light ordnance; crew two.

## Cessna U-17A Skywagon

Basically a strengthened Cessna 180, the Skywagon was first flown in 1960. This powerful little aircraft was excellent for pilot training, especially for those destined for the similarly configured Bird Dog. The Skywagon was itself a useful addition to the FAC role.

*Specifications:* Powerplant one Teledyne Continental I0-520-D; span 35ft 10in; length 25ft 9in.

scene commanders until the heavily armed 'Sandys' arrived, and helped to locate downed crewmen, marking positions with smoke for the Sandys or pick-up helicopters to refer to and also directing any necessary ground-suppression fire.

The first of the flying FACs in the Vietnam conflict was the Cessna O-1 Bird Dog, which was assisted, and then replaced, by the unique 'push and pull' O-2 Skymaster (and to a lesser extent the U-17A) and later the jet powered OA-37 Dragonfly. During the early 1970s North American OV-10 Broncos from such bases as Ubon in Thailand began working with the rescue forces, replacing the older, slower and unarmed O-1s and O-2s as FAC aircraft. The OV-10s were equipped with 'Pave Nail' observation equipment that could locate survivors at night or in bad weather and aided the development of the rescue organisations' reliance on advanced technology instead of merely courage, firepower and tactics. The Fast-FAC technique was also employed during the conflict using jet-powered controllers such as two-seat F-100Fs to conduct operations.

## Cessna A/OA-37 Dragonfly

A light attack version of the T-37 basic trainer, the side-by-side two-seat A-37 Dragonfly first flew in prototype form on 22 October 1963. Some 39 T-37Bs were then similarly converted on the Cessna assembly lines to become A-37As. These aircraft featured armour-plated protection for the pilots and critical systems, an internally housed 7.62mm minigun, eight underwing stores points, wingtip fuel tanks, ground attack avionics and larger wheels and tyres. Stressed to 6G, a full production version was ordered as the A-37B, this variant introducing a fixed IFR probe and J85-GE-17A engines, with deliveries commencing in May 1968.

The A-37B could carry 5,680lb of stores, and around 130 aircraft were specifically optimised for forward air control work with a new avionics fit. These were designated OA-37B and used as such during the Vietnam War, examples being operated by the South Vietnamese Air Force during the conflict.

*Specifications:* Powerplant two General Electric J85-GE-17As; span 35ft 10in; length 29ft 3½in (excluding IFR probe); speed 525mph at 16,000ft; range 460 miles with full warload.

## Raven FACs

The Ravens were a group of élite pilots who flew 'low and slow' above the jungles in Laos, their mission being to support indigenous forces 'in-country' during their fight against the invading armies of North Vietnam. The Ravens were all volunteers who had previous experience as FACs in South Vietnam, and, owing to international treaties, were 'divorced' from the USAF, wearing only civilian clothes and operating out of generally small fields at different sites in Laos. Most Ravens knew little or nothing about what they were volunteering for, other than the fact that the work was classified, exciting and far removed from the bureaucratic battles and political rules of engagement in South Vietnam.

The Ravens used three different aircraft to accomplish their mission: the small, light O-1 observation aircraft, armed only with white phosphorous smoke rockets; the heavier, slightly faster U-17 (Cessna 185), with the same armament but a longer range and loiter time; and the 'Cadillac', the T-28. The last was heaven for the Ravens—bombs, napalm, high-explosive rockets and 50-calibre machine guns for strafing. Now they did not have to wait for jets when they had a fast-moving target. Some Ravens carried a 'back-seater', a local who trans-

---

### North American (Rockwell) OV-10 Bronco

The OV-10 was a twin-turboprop short take-off and landing aircraft conceived by the Marine Corps and developed under an Air Force, Navy and Marine Corps tri-service programme. The first production OV-10A was ordered in 1966 and its initial flight took place in August 1967. The Bronco's mission capabilities included observation, forward air control, helicopter escort, armed reconnaissance, gunfire spotting, utility and limited ground attack; however, the USAF acquired the Bronco primarily as a forward air control (FAC) aircraft. Adding to its versatility was a rear fuselage compartment with a capacity of 3,200lb of cargo, five combat-equipped troops or two litter patients and a medical attendant.

The first USAF OV-10As destined for combat arrived in Vietnam on 31 July 1968. A total of 157 OV-10As were delivered to the USAF before production ended in April 1969. After Vietnam the Bronco continued to serve as a primary FAC-A with both the USAF and latterly the US Marines; however, the 1991 Gulf War proved that the modern battlefield was not the place to be flying a lightly armed turboprop aircraft, especially in an environment of powerful AAA and shoulder-launched SAMs, and the aircraft were retired the mid-1990s.

*Specifications:* Powerplant two Garrett-Air Research T76s (-G-10 left, -G-12 right) of 715shp each; span 40ft (12.19m); length 41ft 7in (12.67m); height 15ft 1in (4.60m); weight 14,444lb (6,550kg); maximum speed 281mph (452kph); cruising speed 223mph (359kph); range 1,240 miles (1,996km); service ceiling 26,000ft (7,925m); armament four M60C 7.62mm machine guns in fuselage sponsons, plus 3,600lb (1,632kg) of mixed ordnance or gunpods carried externally.

lated, talked to ground troops and helped locate targets. Others were engaged essentially in deep interdiction missions aimed at stemming the flow of troops and supplies into neutral Laos. Some missions were basic visual reconnaissance sorties, looking for targets, and many were with 'troops in contact', providing life-saving tactical air strikes in support of ground troops being fired upon and being that crucial man on the spot to call in the rescue forces to recover an airman down under fire.

## Airborne Coordination: 'King' and 'Crown'

During the early years of the Vietnam War, the role of coordinating not only inbound and outbound strike packages but also the some-times complex combat rescue missions was undertaken by the HC-54 Skymaster and, between 1964 and 1965, the veteran Grumman HU-16B Albatross amphibian. By the mid-1960s a few HC-130 Hercules aircraft were becoming available, and, with their advanced tracking system used for the Apollo space flights and their greater capacity, the task of controlling rescues was undertaken by the 'King' ships.

A number of HC-130s were also converted to employ the Fulton STARS recovery system: operating out to a radius of 860 miles (1,384km), loitering for up to two hours and employing their AN/ARD-17 Cook Aerial Trackers originally designed to locate satellite capsules during re-entry from orbit, they were found to be equally useful in pinpointing faint signals from Personal Locator Beacons operated by downed aircrews. The HC-130s were also fitted with trailing drogue hoses to refuel the 'Jolly' helicopters in flight, and the type's ability to stay in touch with the helicopters meant that for the first time a stricken pilot had a genuine chance of being recovered. The conflict also saw the last operational use of the flying boat: the huge Martin Marlin saw out its service life undertaking coastal patrols and SAR duties from seaplane tenders in the South China Sea until 1967.

## Rescue from the Sea

The US Navy and Marine Corps have always conducted search and rescue operations for their own forces and others. Initially all rescue operations were undertaken either on land or by boat; however, in the late 1940s the helicopter was introduced to the military and quickly became a primary vehicle for conducting SAR operations. During the

**Top:** The HH-53 in flight. (USAF via Gary Madgwick)
**Above:** An HH-53 showing its IFR probe to good effect. (USAF via Gary Madgwick)
**Left:** The HH-53C. (Author)

**Left, top: O**ne of Boeing's 'Frogs', in its latest grey garb. (Author)

**Left, centre:** An S-61 Sea King (Author)

**Left, bottom:** The diminutive Kaman Seasprite. (Author)

**Above:** The rescue hoist sytem aboard the HH-1H. (Author)

**Right:** The Forest Penetrator has been standard equipment for the 'Pave Low' during and since the Vietnam War. (Author)

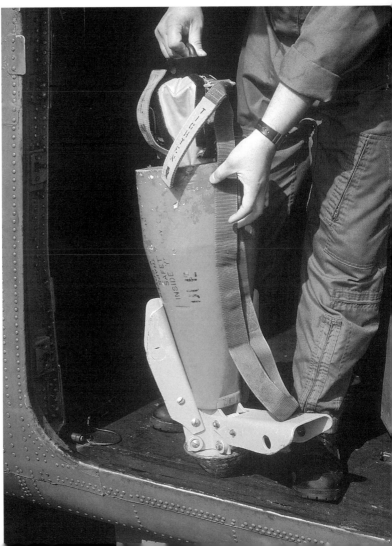

**Above:** Painted in a desert sand hue for Operation 'Eagle Claw', RH-53 Sea Stallions line up along the deck of the USS Nimitz. Only one of the Stallions that began the mission survived to tell the tale. (US Navy via Gary Madgwick)
**Below:** The immense power of the 'Pave Low' is evident from this shot. (Author)
**Right:** An MH-53J powers in at low level. (Sikorsky)

**Left, upper:** An AC-130 is prepared for a mission. (Lockheed)

**Left, lower:** The 'hump back' of the HC-130, carrying the Cook Tracker. (Author)

**Right, upper:** Soldiers carry a wounded comrade towards a waiting Scout helicopter for evacuation to a field hospital. (AAC Museum)

**Right, lower:** On arrival at the hospital, medics are quickly on hand to get the casualty attended, whilst the crew of the Scout prepare for another trip to the front line. (AAC Museum)

**Below:** The current 'life saver' on the Falklands is the RAF rescue Sea King from No 78 Squadron, adopting an all-over tactical grey colour scheme, rather than the conspicuous bright yellow of the UK-based machines. (RAF)

**Above left:** A pair of 'Firehawks' over the desert. (Via Author)
**Left:** The art of rescue. A HH-60 picks up a 'downed' airman during a training exercise. (Sikorsky)
**Above:** A 'Pave Low' in desert garb. (USAF via Gary Madgwick)
**Below:** The Bendix nose radar of the HH-60. (Author)

**Above:** A fish-eye view inside the HH-60's cockpit. (Via Gary Madgwick)
**Below:** A 771 NAS SAR Sea King recovers a civilian casualty. (Royal Navy)

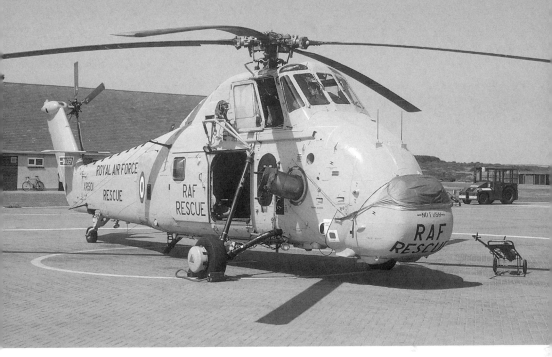

**Above:** The RAF's venerable Wessex, now retired from service in the United Kingdom. (Author)
**Below:** The Norwegian SAR Sea King has an RDR-1300C nose radar developed by Bendix King. (Westland)

**Above:** Snow-covered peaks highlight an Italian AB-412. (Via Gary Madgwick)
**Below:** A radar-equipped HH-3F from the US Coast Guard, pictured in 1980. (Author)

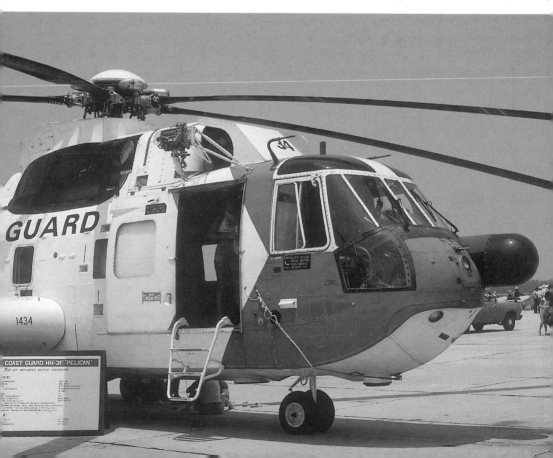

**Above:** A colourful Canadian CH-113 from No 424 Squadron. (Author)
**Below:** A bright yellow Sea King HAR.3 of the Royal Air Force. (Author)

**Left, top:** A rather drab Kawasaki KV-107. (Via author)

**Left, centre:** An example of the US Coast Guard HH-65 Dolphin. (Author)

**Left, bottom:** A Cherry Point-based CH-46 demonstrating rescue techniques. (Author)

**Right, upper:** Based at Aviano in Italy, an OA-10 waits for its next foray over the Balkans. (Author)

**Right, lower:** A Royal Navy Lynx demonstrating its SAR capabilities. (Westland)

**Left:** The Royal Navy's latest helicopter, the EH-101 Merlin. (Westland)
**Below:** Canada's EH-101 Cormorant. (Westland)

Vietnam War the importance of having personnel specifically trained to conduct SAR missions was realised, SAR crews were unofficially formed and swimmers and corpsmen were incorporated into aircrews to improve recovery and provide immediate medical aid. The US Navy also provided 'high drink' capabilities, refuelling hovering rescue helicopters from Navy vessels in the Gulf of Tonkin.

## Piasecki's Retrievers

The Navy helicopter pilots were by their very nature trained in rescue techniques, and therefore their approach differed from that of the USAF in many ways. Where the Air Force relied on packages with massive firepower support, the Navy's view was 'fast-in, fast-out', whether fighter protection could be offered or not. In the early phases of the war, plane-guard helicopters such as the Piasecki HUP were operated from ships and carriers in the Gulf of Tonkin, flying utility and rescue missions. The Piasecki HUP-2 was the result of a 1945 request by the US Navy for a helicopter that would be able to perform search and rescue missions within a 100-mile radius of its home ship. Designed primarily to fly from smaller shipboard platforms, the HUP could, of course, also operate from large aircraft carriers and from shore stations.

The Piasecki Helicopter Corporation, located near Philadelphia, was one of the two aircraft manufacturers selected by the Navy to build prototypes. Piasecki's proposal included a new tandem-rotor design for its XHJP-1, using large rotor overlap to decrease its length. After a 'fly off' competition with the Sikorsky proposal, the Navy selected the Piasecki design for production. The XHJP-1 was then redesignated HUP-1, the 'U' representing 'Utility'. The HUP was powered by the Continental R-975 air-cooled radial engine—the same engine that powered many Second World War tanks and therefore known colloquially as the 'tank' engine.

The HUP's construction was all-metal, excepting the wooden rotor blades and fabric-covered rear half of the pylon extending aft. Large intakes at the base of the pylon took in cooling air ducted to the engine, after which the air was ducted out via a bottom fuselage exit. Early in production an autopilot and dipping sonar were incorporated into the design, making the HUP the Navy's first anti-submarine warfare helicopter. ASW technology was in its infancy at the time, and in 1952 production shifted to non-ASW capable HUP-2s,

97

or 'Retrievers' as they were now nicknamed.

Thirty-two HUP-1s had been delivered prior to January 1952, the first fleet squadron utilising them being Helicopter Utility Squadron 2 (HU-2). The Navy ordered 70 H-25As for the Army in 1951, with the 'paper' designation HUP-3. The Army would use these 'Flying Mules' as troop and cargo helicopters, pending receipt of the larger Piasecki H-21s then being developed. Nineteen other HUPs were added to Navy contracts, to be later transferred to France and Canada. Production deliveries continued through 1952 and 1953.

Both Navy and Marine Corps air stations and reserve units began using HUPs for search and rescue, as well as for utility missions. The initial HUP-2 ASW versions were delivered in late spring 1953, some going to Helicopter Anti-Submarine Squadron 2 (HS-2). HUPs were chronically underpowered, and the ASW versions were soon stripped of their submarine detection gear and relegated strictly to utility and SAR missions. Deliveries concluded in 1954, after a production run of 336.

The HUP stayed in service throughout the 1950s and is best known for its service as plane-guard, flying from aircraft carriers. The standard crew for these missions was one pilot (in the left seat) and one aircrewman to assist in rescues. A single HUP would maintain position off the carrier's starboard side at flight deck level during day VFR operations, often flying sideways to enable the pilot to watch the action. The last HUPs were phased out of service in 1964.

The relatively small Kaman UH-2B Seasprite could also be found aboard Navy ships during the war, and although these helicopters were considered too 'short-legged' and vulnerable for combat recov-

---

### Sikorsky S-61/H-3 Sea King

As a multi-purpose helicopter, the H-3 remains an excellent twin-engine, all-weather rotary vehicle. The first version of this workhorse helicopter was flown more than twenty years ago, and currently the Sea King is being replaced by another Sikorsky design, the SH-60F Seahawk, in the anti-submarine warfare role. The transition will last into the late 1990s, and upon completion the Sea King fleet will then be converted for a dedicated search and rescue mission.

*Specifications:* Powerplant two General Electric T58-GE-10 turboshaft engines; length 73ft (21.9m); fuselage length 54ft 9in (16.5m); height 17ft (5.1m); empty weight 11,865lb (5,339kg); maximum take-off weight 21,000lb (9,450kg); range 542nm (997km); ceiling 14,700ft (4,410m); cruising speed 136mph (217.6kph); armament two Mk 46 torpedoes; crew four; first flight March 1959; operational June 1961.

---

ery situations, they still managed to perform creditable rescue missions up until the final withdrawal of American forces. The SH-3 Sea King, like the USAF's 'Jolly Green Giants' proved a much more effective rescue tool, especially the helicopters from Navy squadron HS-6. Like many of the naval units, HS-6 modified a number of their Sea Kings for the rescue role, designating them HH-3A. As part of this ever-risky recovery business, a Navy gunner was killed during 1967 attempting a rescue; and on another occasion Vietnamese troops riddled a Sea King with fire, sending it crashing to the ground with the loss of all on board.

The US Marines were also involved some highly acclaimed acts of heroism in the SAR role, using their elderly UH-34Ds, but the undoubted workhorses were the CH-46 Sea Knight—which, like many of the American helicopters, flew a variety of roles, including vital medical evacuation flights—and the UH-1D Huey. The Vietnam conflict also introduced the French Aéronavale to helicopter combat operations, and the tandem rotors of the Piasecki HUPs of Escadrille 58S were a familiar sight on their plane-guard duties.

## Marine Corps HUS/U/H-34D 'Dog'

This helicopter was a success from the day the first one rolled off the production line. Relative to its predecessors, the HUS/U/H-34's 'Dog''s performance justified its looks. It was responsive, agile, well-powered and forgiving, and it required little maintenance per hour of flight time. For its time it was the ideal helicopter in reliability and performance.

Prior to the commitment of helicopters to combat in Vietnam there was considerable wonder among the aircrews concerning the ability of these aircraft to survive direct enemy fire, as there was scant practical experience in this matter. The initial commitment of H-34s to assault and medevac operations proved that helicopters were more difficult to hit than imagined and that they could absorb a lot of damage—and still fly home. That so many damaged H-34s made it back to base was not so much a criticism of the VC gunners but a testament to the aircraft and its fliers. In Vietnam there was no mission to which the H-34 was not assigned, and no matter what the 'missions or conditions' the aircraft and crews found some way to get the job done. Sorties in the mountains west of the coastal plain were especially challenging since rotor and engine performance deteriorated quickly with altitude. Under these conditions an H-34 with any appreciable payload was operating at the very edge of the envelope.

For many reasons, the most rewarding mission for the aircrews was probably medevac. It provided a life-saving service to fellow Marines, often when the LZs were 'hot'. There were a lot of nuances to performing this mission correctly: land with the helicopter between the medevac and the source of enemy fire so as to shield those carrying the casualties; land as close to the medevac as possible to reduce the carrying task and the exposure of the 'grunts' to the VC; and, in the event of enemy fire, call in the escorting gunship to blow up the general part of the world whence the fire came. Flying the UH-34 'Dog' in Vietnam changed the meaning of the phrase 'dog days'. The machines were a joy to fly, and H-34 pilots and aircrews hold a special place in their hearts for them.

### Boeing Vertol CH-46 Sea Knight: The 'Frog'

The replacement for the UH-34D was the Boeing Vertol CH-46, nicknamed 'Frog' on account of its posture and appearance on the ground As the new primary assault helicopter it brought a greatly increased capacity for carrying passengers and cargo while retaining all of the UH-34's virtues. While the 'Frog' distinguished itself throughout its service in Vietnam, the battles around Khe Sanh and its outposts were the high points of its career. In generally bad weather and from bases near the coastline, CH-46s shuttled throughout the mountainous Khe Sanh area. They constantly moved medevacs, people and supplies as the tactical situation required, often under IFR conditions.

The United States' involvement in South-East Asia ended with Operation 'Frequent Wind', the evacuation of Americans and foreign nationals from Saigon, with the HH-53s again being employed to undertake the evacuation. The Saigon government finally surrendered on 30 April 1975.

# 7

# American Embarrassment and the Future of Combat SAR

### Operation 'Eagle Claw'

If one could draw a line in the sand to denote where the old theories of combat rescue and, indeed, of covert intervention met their 'Waterloo', the eye must inevitably be drawn to the events of the late 1970s in the Middle East. A bloody revolution toppled the pro-Western Shah of Iran, and brought into power a fanatical fundamentalist Islamic government, whose inception swept a fierce wave of anti-American fever across the nation. This fever became more impassioned and intense when the United States granted asylum to the deposed Shah, whose regime it had vigorously supported. Passions ran high, culminating in, perhaps, the most infamous of the many anti-American protests that took place when on 6 November 1979 militant Islamic students seized the American Embassy and Public Affairs Building in Tehran, taking 66 American citizens hostage in the process.

Shock-waves reverberated around the halls of power on Capitol Hill, and, in an uncharacteristic move, a determination was made by the President, Jimmy Carter, to form a special joint task force, cloaked beneath a thick veil of secrecy, to investigate the possibilities of exercising a 'military option' to extricate the hostages from the clutches on the militants should diplomatic efforts prove fruitless. The events that followed became a salutary lesson to the American armed services, and proved to be a watershed for its 'special operations' forces, whose future roles in combat rescue and clandestine operations would undergo vehement scrutiny in the light of what became an ill-fated hostage rescue attempt.

On 8 January 1980 President Carter informed Congress that 'any military action to recover the hostages would lead to almost certain failure, and cost many American lives.' This apparent distancing of any military solution was at odds with what was in fact happening in the background, as the planning stages of a rescue mission, known as Operation 'Ricebowl', were already complete, and preparations for the actual recovery itself, established as Operation 'Eagle Claw' were well under way. The façade of diplomatic initiatives continued until 11 April, when it became clear that there was little left to be gained by peaceful means.

The ground forces chosen to conduct the 'Eagle Claw' operation were the Army's Delta Force, a small but élite band drawn from the ranks of the famous Green Berets, based at Fort Bragg in North Carolina and operating roughly along the same lines as the British SAS. The brainchild of Col Charles Beckwith, Delta Force had been established as a result of the poor showing of the American special forces during the Vietnam War and carried the task of using imaginative, low-profile, clandestine missions against terrorist organisations posing a threat the security of the United States. Unfortunately, however, the force was a relatively new organisation, untried and basically unknown to many senior officers or politicians.

Many believed that President Carter would be unwilling to exercise the military option and much of the initial operational planning reflected a sincere lack of urgency, and therefore valuable time was wasted dealing with many implausible suggestions. To counter this, Delta Force was made responsible directly to the Joint Chiefs of Staff, although this had an adverse effect in that the operational decisions were now split among several commanders, none of whom had overall authority. There was also a serious shortage of intelligence, mostly about the embassy buildings, the surrounding area and, most importantly, the number and disposition of the guarding troops as well as the actual location of the hostages themselves.

The leading option was to insert Delta Force by truck from Turkey, but this was made impossible because of the political uncertainty of using Turkey as a base. The injury toll expected by parachuting the force directly into Iran by night ruled out that option as well. The choice was, therefore, narrowed to the use of helicopters. But which ones? Eventually the Navy's Sikorsky tri-engined RH-53D Sea Stallion was selected, mainly because of its lift capability—30 people when fully fuelled and 50 people when lightly fuelled—and its useful range and because it had a shape that would not compromise the operation's security by being a non-standard silhouette in an aircraft carrier's complement. Eight RH-53s were therefore stripped of their usual minesweeping gear and given additional fuel tanks and new navigational equipment.

Unfortunately the Navy pilots originally assigned to Delta Force were found not to have the neccessary flying attributes required for the mission, as the operation called for certain specialist skills that were unavailable from the service. They were therefore replaced by more capable Marine pilots under the command of Lt-Col Ed Sieffert, their introduction raising a number of questions as to whether the move had actually been politically motivated to ensure that all three services were represented in the 'Eagle Claw' operation. However, the performance of the Marine pilots during practice low-level night-flying sessions with lights out over the deserts around Nellis and Yuma soon dispelled any such considerations.

Even though the huge RH-53s had a creditable range, they could not lift the troops straight from the chosen land site at Masirah, a small island off the coast of Oman, or from a closely based carrier directly into the target area. Thus instead of flying all the way to Tehran by helicopter, Delta Force would now arrive in three MC-130 'Combat Talon 1' Hercules, from the 1st, 7th and 8th SOS, at a predetermined spot in the Iranian desert, some 305 miles from the capital (a point to be known as 'Desert One') whilst the six helicopters would arrive slightly later at the same position from the aircraft carrier USS *Nimitz*. At the Desert One site the helicopters would be refuelled from three 'Fatcow' EC-130 Hercules from the 7th ACCS, carrying extra fuel internally; Delta Force would embark in the RH-53s, be flown to a secluded wadi 50 miles from Tehran, arriving an hour before dawn, and dig in, whilst the Sea Stallions also took cover at a separate site near to a second RV point, 'Desert Two'. Earlier consideration was given to refuel the helicopters from large air-dropped rubber blivets, but this proved impractical for a variety of reasons. Having then been inserted at the appointed position, Delta Force would lie low until dusk, when they would enter the embassy buildings, free the hostages and move them to Tehran's football stadium, from where the RH-53s would be called in to evacuate them to Manzariyeh, or 'Desert Three', a disused airfield near Qom, which was to be secured by a company of US Rangers.

The eight RH-53s, now resplendent is an overall desert sand colour scheme, were airlifted to Diego Garcia in the Indian Ocean, from where they joined the USS *Kitty Hawk*, embarking aboard *Nimitz* in late January 1980. Other forces were also pre-positioned, and the final go-ahead for the operation was given by President Carter on 16 April, with Col Beckwith and Delta Force flying from Pope AFB in the United States to Frankfurt in Germany before transiting on to Wadi Kena, a disused Soviet-built airfield in Egypt and the command post for the operation on the 21st. The 'Eagle Claw' operation also had available to it the aircraft on board both the USS *Nimitz* and *Coral Sea*, and these included F-14 Tomcats, A-6 Intruders and A-7 Corsairs, as well as a pair of land-based AC-130E Spectre gunships, one of whose tasks it was to thwart the use of the Iranian F-4 Phantoms from Mehrabad International Airport.

At 1640hrs on the 24th the now 132-man team boarded the three MC-130s; this number consisted of 93 personnel from Delta Force to move into the embassy, thirteen assigned to rescue the hostages from the Foreign Affairs Building, twelve drivers, twelve road watchers and two Iranian generals. With the Delta Force operatives now dressed in Levis, black jackets and unpolished boots, the first 'Combat Talon' left Masirah at 1800hrs, an hour ahead of the rest of the force, crossing into Iran at 400ft off the coast of Chas Bahar and arriving on schedule at 2200hrs at the appointed 'Desert One' site. Switching on a beacon left by an earlier survey team, they deployed their road watchers. Before the MC-130 could leave, however, an Iranian bus arrived and was quickly put under guard, and shortly afterwards an Iranian truck ignored orders to stop and was finally halted by a round from an M27 anti-tank rocket. All five following Hercules arrived on schedule at 2300hrs, and as auxiliary power units were not available the big transports were unable to shut down their engines, so had to sit for the duration with their propellers turning.

The eight RH-53s launched successfully from *Nimitz* at approximately 1930hrs. However, en route the No 6 aircraft force-landed in the desert as an imminent rotor blade failure was feared. Accompanied in by aircraft No 8, No 6 was then abandoned, its crew boarding No 8 to continue the mission. A second RH-53, No 5, was forced to turn back after losing part of its flight control system following a cooling system failure; as will be described later, this was the only helicopter to survive the mission. The helicopters were scheduled to arrive at Desert One around 30 minutes after the last Hercules had touched down. However, the first of the Sea Stallions actually arrived 60 minutes later at 0030hrs, and the other five arrived over the next 30 minutes from all points of the compass. During their ingress the Marine pilots had encountered severe sandstorms, dust clouds and disorientation, and they were not helped by having to rely on an unfamiliar Palletised Navigation System in place of their more familiar Omega set-up, and lengthy, concentrated night flying using full-face ANVIS night vision goggles. Beckwith expected to greet formation leader Col Sieffert but was met instead by Maj James Schaffer, a vastly experienced pilot, who was in a state of shock, physically and mentally drained from his experiences getting to the Desert One site and unable to consider going on. Nevertheless, the helicopters were refuelled for the next leg, although one was found to have a serious hydraulic fault which was deemed irreparable. As it had been previously decided that a minimum of six RH-53s were necessary to complete the rescue, the mission was aborted.

Again, the plan called for the RH-53s to be abandoned at Manzariyeh. However, it was decided not to relinquish them at Desert One but fly them back to *Nimitz* after refuelling. Moreover, by now the Hercules were getting short of fuel, having sat on the ground for over three hours with their engines running. The first of the RH-53s, piloted by Maj Schaffer, also now needed additional fuel and therefore lifted off to take up position for a second top-up for the return journey to the carrier, creating a large dust cloud as it banked and passed over one of the EC-130 tankers. During this manoeuvre one of the Stallion's main rotor blades sliced through the tail of the Hercules as it crossed, causing a major explosion which consumed both aircraft. Detonating ammunition made it impossible to recover the bodies of the five airmen from the EC-130 and three from the RH-53, and several of the other helicopters were damaged by exploding ammunition, as were a number of their aircrew. The remainder of the force was therefore evacuated aboard the MC-130s, and together with the two surviving EC-130s left Desert One at 0256hrs, abandoning the rest of the helicopters. The wounded were eventually flown to Ramstein in Germany, whilst the remaining forces headed back to their home bases.

It was an audacious plan on a very large scale, and one that could have worked, albeit relying on a huge slice of good fortune since it was dependent on many factors having to work in the Americans' favour. Post-mission analysis showed the serviceability of the RH-53s to be atrocious, and attributed this to the *Nimitz* maintenance per-

## Sikorsky RH-53 Sea Stallion

This RH-53 was the specialised minesweeping version of the Sea Stallion assigned to US Navy Helicopter Mine Countermeasures (HM) squadrons. It has now been replaced by the MH-53E Sea Dragon, which is outfitted with enlarged fuel sponsons, is able to provide long-range fleet support and can tirelessly search the world's strategic waterways, detecting every known type of mine. The three-engined MH-53E is the most powerful helicopter on the US military inventory and is cleared up to 73,500lb with external loads.

*Specifications:* Length overall 99ft 0½in (30.19m); length overall (folded) 60ft 6in (18.44m); width overall (folded) 27ft 5in (8.36m); fuselage width 8ft 10in (2.69m); height overall 28ft 4in (8.63m); height overall (folded) 18ft 7in (5.66m); main rotor diameter (blade tip circle) 79ft 0in (24.08m); tail rotor diameter (blade tip circle) 20ft 0in (6.10m); cabin length (internal) 30ft 0in (9.14m); cabin width (internal) 7ft 6in (2.29m); cabin height (internal) 6ft 6in (1.98m).

sonnel's lack of experience. Although the RH-53s had an IFR capability, the EC-130 tankers did not, limiting their effective range and giving rise to the 'Fatcow' refuelling at Desert One, and thereby contributing to the over-contrived schedules required to get Delta Force into position. Too much was entrusted to chance, and not enough consideration was given to bad weather, unserviceability or the possibility of Iranian intervention. Poor communications and the use of non-specialist aircraft such as the RH-53, which had to be 're-roled' for special operations with non-familiar navigation equipment, were also cited as major factors. Likewise, too many elements of the US armed forces were involved, many of whom did not have adequate training or sufficient experience in vital areas to hope to pull off such a daring mission.

Desperate times breed desperate measures, especially after the first abortive rescue mission in the Iranian desert had met with such disaster. It is now known that the United States planned a second rescue attempt, Operation 'Credible Sport', and for this the US military made radical modifications to three C-130 Hercules to enable them to take off and land almost like a helicopter. This was one of the more novel ideas for retrieving the hostages from the football stadium and called for the fitting of the C-130s with powerful retro and take-off rockets. Three aircraft so configured (74-1683, 74-1686 and 74-2065) were referred to as 'Eagle Claw C-130Ys' ('Yanks'). They were each fitted with an IFR receptacle, tailplane and tailfin extensions and a new radome carrying unidentified avionics. However, the plans were abandoned when one of the aircraft, 74-1683, was destroyed during STOL landing trials when the computer-controlled retro-rockets fired too early, causing a catastrophic fire. At the time of the project, 53 Americans were still being held hostage in Tehran. Following the failure, the remaining two aircraft were stripped of their non-standard equipment; one is now on display at Warner Robins Museum, whilst the other was returned to active service.

It was a desperate response to a very desperate situation and documents relating to that response, classified for the last sixteen years, describe how hundreds of Navy and Air Force service members worked with Lockheed aircraft engineers to festoon the old C-130 workhorse with rockets, fill it with new electronics and reconfigure the fuselage into that of a 'hot rod'. The aircraft was equipped with lift rockets slanting downwards, slow-down rockets facing forwards, missile motors facing backwards and still more rockets to stabilise the aeroplane as it touched down. Delta Force commandos would bring rescued hostages to the stadium, then everybody would brace themselves for a leap to liberty. It was an extreme measure when it is borne in mind that 150 people would have been sitting in this contraption as it blasted off, like a rocket, to exit the stadium. The first modified aircraft, created in just a couple of months, crashed on the runway after a rocket went off prematurely and ripped off one of the mainplanes. Engineers never had to use the second modified aircraft on which they were working: for good or ill, before it could be tried, Iran announced plans to free the hostages. 'Credible Sport' stayed in the test phase, but, by any measure, the technology is obsolete now.

### The 'Eagle Claw Effect'

In the aftermath of the Desert One débâcle, the US Government set up the Holloway Commission to review the events and make recommendations as to the future requirements for the military's Special Operations. Their considerations were far-ranging, and in respect of the airborne function of the special forces specific directions were given, resulting in a considerably more effective operational force. The main result was the amalgamation of the USAF's ARRS units into Special Operations Aviation units, which would be given specialist equipment to undertake their work and would in future regularly work alongside Army, Navy, Marine Corps and other assets and establish Common Standard Operational Procedures (CSOPs) to undertake joint-force operations and combat rescue missions.

One of the specific recommendations made by the Commission was the development of an all-weather, night capable, low-level, infil/exfil penetration aircraft, capable of being air-refuelled and of being fitted with such equipment that would permit it to enter hostile airspace in order to support clandestine missions, as well as being used in the CSAR role. The Air Force already had the HH-53 'Super Jolly' in service, together with a small number of CH-53 'Pave Knife' models used by the special operations forces—which had already proved their worth in Operation 'Frequent Wind'. The Navy had their own RH-53s, and the Army their 'Big Windy' CH-47 Chinooks.

Following the extensive evaluation of an advanced avionics package for night/adverse weather and SAR under the aegis of Project 'Pave Low', one HH-53B was tested in 1969 with a night/all-weather rescue system known as 'Pave Low I', which did not prove successful. The system was then fitted into a modified HH-53B, thereby converting it to YHH-53H (66-14433) standard, and this served as a 'proof-of-concept' vehicle for HH-53H system, now dubbed 'Pave Low II'. The USAF then commissioned a production version of this improved HH-53B variant as the HH-53H 'Super Jolly'. The order called for two CH-53Cs and eight HH-53B/Cs to be converted for the NAW/SAR role and incorporate an uprated 'Pave Low III' sensor suite including an APQ-158 TF/TA (terrain following/terrain avoidance) radar, an AAQ-10 FLIR, a much improved Doppler navigational capability tied into an INS with colour moving map display, and provision for pilot night vision goggles (NVG). The HH-53H modification was found to increase the maintenance demands of the type, a problem rectified in the subsequent J model.

In 1988 these aircraft were redesignated MH-53H after being further modified under the 'Constant Green' programme, giving them additional capabilities for inserting or extracting Special Forces teams. The USAF, however, was not altogether happy with its MH/HH-53Hs and therefore decided to upgrade all its remaining 31 'heavy-lifters' to a new MH-53J 'Pave Low III Enhanced' variant by converting 24 HH-53Bs and seven HH-53Cs as well as further upgrading its ten existing MH-53Hs. These aircraft would then be released for service, under the authority of the Air Force's Special Operations Command, for clandestine, CSAR and counter-insurgency missions.

The HH-53 is a conventional, long-range helicopter with twin turboshaft engines and self-lubricating, all-metal main and tail rotors. A large horizontal stabiliser is on the starboard side of the rotor pylon. The tricycle landing gear has twin wheels on each unit, with the main units retracting into the rear of the sponsons on each side of the fuselage. The helicopter is equipped with an inflight refuelling probe, two 315 US gallon (1,192-litre) self-sealing bladder-type fuel tanks and two 450 US gallon (1,703-litre) external auxiliary fuel tanks.

### The MH-53H/J 'Pave Low II/III' and 'Enhanced'

As mentioned, in order to make the CH-53, HH-53 and MH-53 more capable, additional sensors and avionics were added, producing an external shape that is not particularly pleasing aesthetically. The converted helicopters began to be delivered from 1987 and were equipped with the more powerful twin T64-GE-415 turboshaft engines—rated at 4,360shp and driving a five-bladed 72ft 3in (22.02m) main rotor, so that the aircraft's performance would not be degraded by the increase in weight from the avionics—and retro-fitted with a folding tail, folding main rotors and additional armour. (The MH-53J is intended to launch from a variety of environments, including ships' decks, and the main reason for the folding tail and rotors is to aid stowage aboard aircraft carriers and assault ships.)

The multi-mode AN/APQ-158 TF/TA radar is in an offset thimble fairing on the left side of the nose and can be coupled to the autopilot system. This permits dangerous NOTE (nap-of-the-earth) profiles at speeds in excess of 172kts at 150ft and in visibility of less than a quarter of a mile; or at 100ft or below over water or in desert conditions. Beneath the nose a Texas Instruments AN/AAQ-10 stabilised FLIR can be found in a rotatable ball turret—the aircraft's window into the night or through murky conditions—and this displays its imagery on the colour multi-function displays (MFDs) in the cockpit. This low-light sensor is complemented by the crew routinely wearing NVGs (the MH-53H was the first version to be fully cleared for nocturnal operations with the crew employing NVGs). Also installed is a high-capacity mission computer, secure voice and satellite communications, a Navstar GPS receiver, a twin inertial system with Doppler navigation equipment and a computer-generated projected map display.

For self-protection the 'Pave Low' carries twin Loral AN/ALQ-157 IRCMs which are mounted on the external fuel tank sponsons directly below the engine exhausts, as well as a missile launch warning sensor. Copious amounts of chaff and flares are also carried, launched from dispenser boxes located at the front and rear and on the under-sides of the aircraft. Pilot protection has also been considered, with titanium seats for the crew and 1,000lb of armour plate added for general protection.

The 'Pave Low', still widely known by its Vietnam-era nickname 'Super Jolly', is the USAF's largest and most powerful helicopter. A fixed and extendible IFR probe is located on the right side of the nose, and the aircraft's unrefuelled range has been further extended by the addition of two externally mounted 541-gallon fuel tanks. The MH-53J carries a crew of six, two officers and four enlisted men. The pilot/aircraft commander occupies the right-hand seat and his co-pilot the left, with a flight engineer occupying a seat to their rear. A second flight engineer sits in the main cabin; he has authority over that area and also acts as a 'right gunner/scanner' and takes charge of the rescue hoist. The remaining duo are aerial gunners, also acting as 'left scanner' and 'rear scanner', responsible for two of the three General Electric GE GAU-2A/B 7.62mm miniguns mounted on shock-absorbing pedestals on the inside of the rear ramp and at the cabin windows. Ammunition is fed into the weapons from boxes fixed to the cabin floor, each supplying the 'brass' to satisfy the guns' appe-tites of 4,000 rounds per minute. The 'Pave Low' crews are, however, at pains to point out that the 7.62s are for self-protection only, leaving the 'gunship' duties to the AC-130, although these 'shooters' can be exchanged for more aggressive 12.7mm units complete with armour-piercing rounds!

The 'Pave Low' crews have the benefit of the latest SOFPARS—Special Operations Force Planning and Rehearsal System—which enables them to input mission data into a powerful computer and 'fly' the sortie on a television screen. SOFPARS will indicate any known threats, or likely threat areas, displays the terrain and indicates waypoints etc. In a combat rescue the 'Pave Low' would leave its 'Com-bat Shadow' support at a suitable ground location and move in to recover any survivors. The Hercules would be sitting with engines running and with its rear ramp open, awaiting the re-arrival of the helicopter. Inbound, the 'Pave Low' would land with its rear ramp down also, back to back with the 'Shadow' to enable the personnel to be transferred quickly aboard the fast moving Hercules. Both aircraft would then make a hasty egress, covered by supporting fighters.

During Operation 'Just Cause' in Panama, the MH-53J 'Pave Low III' dropped US Navy SEAL commandos who assaulted Panama City's Patilla Airport to destroy a Lear Jet which might otherwise have been used to assist the escape of Panamanian leader Manuel Noriega. In March 1990 MH-53Js were transferred to USAF Special Operations Command, and during 'Desert Storm' they provided navigation and support for the US Army AH-64 Apaches which assaulted Iraqi radar defence sites during the first attack of the war. During the war with Iraq, special operations MH-53Js inserted American and British commandos behind the lines, including some who scouted for Iraqi 'Scud' missile sites. Current missions assigned to the MH-53J reflect the increased emphasis on special operations in the USAF Special Operations Command. AFSOC employs the aircraft to penetrate enemy territory in support of Special Forces, Delta Force and SEAL teams operating in denied areas, or for combat rescue of friendly personnel. MH-53Js are also routinely made available for peacetime SAR emergencies, thereby operating in both the military and civilian worlds.

### Spectre Support: The AC-130 Gunship

It was September 1967 when the first of Lockheed's Spectre Gunships—aptly code-named 'Surprise Package'—undertook missions in Vietnam. Following in the footsteps of the AC-47 'Spooky' and the AC-119 'Stinger', the AC-130A 'Spectre' Hercules was designed to provide a heavy, concentrated and continuous stream of firepower on to a target. The AC-130A Hercules was equipped with four side-firing General Electric 7.62 miniguns and four GE M61A1 Vulcan cannon. To assist the crew in locating targets, the AC-130A also carried a Starlight Scope, an infra-red sensor, a target tracking computer and a 20kW searchlight. Other sensors, such as the Texas Instruments AN/AAD-4 FLIR, a new fire control computer and a moving target indicator (MTI), were added later, as well as an ASD-5 'Black Crow' which was able to detect truck ignition motors. The next incarnation, the AC-130E, introduced heavier firepower in the form of a 40mm Bofors cannon and an all-purpose 105mm Army howitzer, together with better sensors, all of which were again updated in the AC-130H model. The current variant is the even more fearsome AC-130U.

The AC-130 gunship found its feet during the Vietnam War. However, its awesome firepower has made it an essential item on the list of any combat SAR planner, if available: the AC-130 is a highly special-ised aircraft and was therefore produced only in small numbers. It is thus a highly prized asset. One of its number, 'Spirit 03', was lost during the Gulf War whilst supporting US Marines near the town of Khafji.

### MC-130 'Combat Talon I' and Robert Fulton's 'Skyhook'

The infiltration of agents behind enemy lines during the Second World War could be accomplished without undue technical difficulty, thanks to the use of parachutes. Thousands of individuals descended upon occupied Europe through 'Joe holes' in Royal Air Force Halifaxes and US Army Air Forces B-24s, or from the side doors of C-47s. The extraction of personnel, however, proved a far more challenging task. Usually, individuals had to exfiltrate enemy territory by hazardous land routes. Sometimes they could be flown out by light aircraft, like the British Lysander, that landed at night on makeshift airstrips.

An innovative extraction method, reportedly used by the British towards the end of the war, involved the use of a modified version of a mail pick-up system that had been invented by Lytle S. Brown dur-ing the 1920s and perfected before Pearl Harbor by All American Aviation. The All American system used two steel poles, set 54ft apart, with a transfer line strung between them. An aircraft approached the ground station in a gentle glide at 90mph while a flight mechanic paid out a 50ft steel cable. As the aircraft pulled up, a four-finger grapple at the end of the cable engaged the transfer rope, shock ab-sorbers cushioned the impact and then the flight mechanic winched the mail pouch on board. In July 1943 the need to rescue airmen from difficult terrain led to tests of this system by the Army Air Forces. However, early results, using instrumented containers, were not prom-ising.

The instruments recorded accelerations in excess of 17G following the pick-up, a force far in excess of what the human body could toler-ate. Changes in the transfer line and modifications to the parachute harness, however, brought this down to a more acceptable 7G. The first live test, with a sheep, failed when the harness twisted and stran-gled the animal. In subsequent tests other sheep fared better. Lt Alex Doster, a paratrooper, volunteered for the first human pick-up, made on 5 September 1943. After a Stinson had engaged the transfer rope at 125mph Doster first was yanked vertically off the ground, then he soared off behind the aircraft. It took less than three minutes to retrieve him. The Air Force continued to improve the system, even developing a package containing telescoping poles, a transfer line and a harness that could be dropped by air. The first operational use of the system came in February 1944 when a C-47 snagged a glider in a remote location in Burma and returned it to India. Although the Air Force never used it to pick up individuals, the British apparently did use it to retrieve agents.

## CIA Involvement

During the Korean War the CIA became interested in the All American system. In the spring and summer of 1952 the organisation attempted to establish a resistance network in Manchuria. Civil Air Transport (CAT), its proprietary airline, dropped agents and supplies into Kirin province as part of a project known to the pilots as Operation 'Tropic'. The All American system seemed to answer the problem of how to bring people out of Manchuria. In the autumn of 1952 CAT pilots in Japan made a number of static pick-ups, then successfully retrieved mechanic Ronald E. Lewis.

A remarkable inventor, Robert Edison Fulton Jr, had observed a demonstration of the All American system in London after the Second World War, and he believed that he could do improve matters. Using a weather balloon, a nylon line and 10–15lb weights, Fulton made numerous pick-up attempts as he sought to develop a reliable procedure. Based at El Centro, California, he conducted numerous flights over the desert, using a Navy P2V for the pick-ups. He gradually increased the weight of the pick-up until the line began to break. A braided nylon line with a test strength of 4,000lb solved the problem. More vexing were the difficulties that were experienced with the locking device, or sky anchor, that secured the line to the aircraft. Fulton eventually resolved this problem, which he considered the most demanding part of the entire developmental process.

## The 'Skyhook System'

By 1958 the Fulton aerial retrieval system, or 'Skyhook', had taken its final shape. A package that easily could be dropped from an aircraft contained the necessary ground equipment for a pick-up. It featured a harness, for cargo or person, that was attached to a 500ft, high-strength, braided nylon line. A portable helium bottle inflated a dirigible-shaped balloon, raising the line to its full height. The pick-up aircraft sported two tubular steel 'horns' protruding from its nose, 30ft long and spread at a 70-degree angle. The aircraft would fly into the line, aiming at a bright mylar marker placed at the 425ft level. As the line was caught between the forks on the nose of the aircraft, the balloon was released and at the same time the spring-loaded trigger mechanism (sky anchor) secured the line to the aircraft. As the line streamed under the fuselage it was snared by the pick-up crew, using a J-hook. It was then attached to a powered winch and pulled on board.

Fulton first used instrumented dummies as he prepared for a live pick-up. He next used a pig, as pigs have nervous systems similar to those of humans. Lifted off the ground, the pig began to spin as it flew through the air at 125mph. It arrived on board undamaged but in a disoriented state; once it had recovered, it attacked the crew! The first human pick-up took place on 12 August 1958 when S/Sgt Levi W. Woods USMC was winched on board the P2V. Because of the geometry involved, the person being picked up experienced less of a shock than during a parachute opening. After the initial contact, which was described by one individual as similar to 'a kick in the pants', the person rose vertically at a slow rate to about 100ft, then began to streamline behind the aircraft. The extension of arms and legs prevented the oscillation that had affected the pig as the individual was winched on board. The process took about six minutes.

In August 1960 Capt Edward A. Rodgers, commander of the Naval Air Development Unit, flew a Skyhook-equipped P2V to Point Barrow, Alaska, to conduct pick-up tests under the direction of Dr Max Brewer, head of the Navy's Arctic Research Laboratory. With Fulton on board to monitor the equipment, the P2V picked up mail from Floating Ice Island T-3, retrieved artefacts, including mastodon tusks, from an archaeological party on the tundra and secured geological samples from Peters Lake Camp. The high point of the trials came when the P2V dropped a rescue package near the icebreaker USS *Burton Island*. Retrieved by a ship's boat, the package was brought on deck, the balloon inflated and the pick-up accomplished.

While the Skyhook system provided an important asset for all manner of intelligence operations, its utility as a long-range pickup system was somewhat undermined during the 1960s by the development of an aerial refuelling capability for helicopters. Even so, it appears likely that Fulton's Skyhook did find employment in a number of special-ised clandestine operations following its trials, although its subsequent use by CIA and the military services remains shrouded in secrecy.

### 'Skyhook' in Service

As noted elsewhere, in order to utilise the opportunities offered by the 'Skyhook' a specialised variant of the ever-useful Lockheed Hercules, the C-130-I, was developed. The aircraft was later desig-nated the MC-130E 'Combat Talon', and the programme included the installation of the complete Fulton STARS recovery system. This involved a much modified nose section with a curiously shaped radome, so designed as to accommodate the 'cat's whiskers' array used for snagging the helium balloon line, with the underside of the radome 'notched' so as to guide the cable in the slipstream. The aircraft also had deflection lines fitted from the nose to the wing tip to ensure that, should the line not be caught cleanly in the 'whiskers' or should some other airborne malfunction occur during the latter recovery phase, the line and/or airman would not become entangled in the propellers or engines.

These aircraft are also equipped with an in-flight refuelling system, terrain-following and terrain-avoidance radar, an inertial and global positioning satellite navigation system and a high-speed aerial deliv-ery system. The special navigation and aerial delivery systems are used to locate small drop zones and deliver people or equipment with greater accuracy and at higher speeds than is possible with a standard C-130. The aircraft is able to penetrate hostile airspace at low altitudes, and crews are specially trained in night and adverse weather operations. The MC-130H features highly automated controls and displays to reduce crew size and workload. The cockpit and cargo areas are com-patible with NVGs.

The integrated control and display subsystem combines basic air-craft flight, tactical and mission sensor data in a comprehensive set of display formats that assists each operator in performing his task. The pilot's and co-pilot's displays on the cockpit instrument panel and the navigator/electronic warfare operator's console, on the aft portion of the flight deck, each have two video displays and a data-entry key-board. The electronic warfare operator has one video display dedi-cated to EW data. The primary pilot's and co-pilot's display formats include basic flight instrumentation and situational data, the display

---

## Lockheed MC-130E Hercules

Over the years the original C-130-Is have been upgraded a number of times with a variety of new systems to improve the aircraft's survivability. The designation MC-130E was officially adopted in the late 1970s, but other designations, such as 'Skyhook EC-130', 'C-130H(CT)' and 'HC-130E', have also been utilised An inflight refuelling receptacle was added, as were avionics upgrades, and a system to allow for precision airdrops of special forces teams or equipment.

Three distinct versions of the MC-130E Hercules exist, 'Rivet Clamp', 'Rivet Swap' and 'Rivet Yank'. Nine aircraft are of the 'Rivet Clamp' version (64-0523, -0551, -0555, -0559, -0561, -0562, -0566, -0567 and -0568), fitted with the Fulton recovery yoke together with an infra-red detection system, chaff/flare dispensers and a tailcone-mounted radar warning receiver. In addition these aircraft retain the T56-A-7 engines. Three aircraft (62-1843, 63-7785 and 64-0565) are identified as 'Rivet Yank' and are similarly configured to the 'Rivet Clamp' but lack the Fulton system and are powered by four T56-A-15 engines. Just two aircraft (64-0571 and -0572) are designated 'Rivet Swap': these are powered by T56-A-7 engines and appear to be systems evaluation aircraft as they lack the external defensive equipment and have no internal ECM consoles.

*Specifications:* Powerplant four Allison T56-A-15 turboprop engines of 4,910shp each; length 100ft 10in (30.7m); height 38ft 6in (11.7m); span 132ft 7in (40.4m); speed 300mph (480kph); ceiling 33,000ft (10,000m); range 3,110 miles (2,700nm)—unlimited with air refuelling; maximum take-off weight 155,000lb (69,750kg); load 53 troops or 26 paratroopers; crew 5 officers (2 pilots, 2 navigators, 1 electronic warfare officer) and 4 enlisted men (1 flight engineer, 2 loadmasters, 1 communications specialist).

---

formats being available with symbology alone or with symbology overlaid with sensor video. The navigator uses radar ground map displays, a forward-looking infra-red display, tabular mission management displays and equipment status information. The EWO's displays are used to supplement the navigator's displays in certain critical phases. On a BAI mission, for maximum psychological impact on enemy troops the MC-130E can fly to a radius of some 760 miles (1,223km) and drop one 15,000lb (6,803kg) BLU-82 bomb followed by a drop of up to 2,000lb (907kg) of psychological warfare leaflets.

## MC-130H 'Combat Talon II': Go Anywhere

The increasing importance of special operations resulted in the development of the MC-130H 'Combat Talon II' as a replacement for the 'task-saturated' MC-130E 'Combat Talon I'. A revised nose cone houses an AN/APQ-170 multi-mode radar to enhance low-level navigation, terrain-following and terrain-avoidance equipment, while defensive systems include infra-red detection, chaff/flare dispensers, a tailcone-mounted radar warning receiver and a missile launch warning receiver. For its primary purpose of inserting, extracting and sup-

116

porting special operations forces from behind enemy lines, the MC-130H employs terrain-following radar, special avionics and low-level flight techniques, and although it can be refuelled in flight it is well able to fly to a radius of about 600 miles (966km) unrefuelled on a medium-lo profile with up to one-third of its run-in at 300ft (92m). Typically a team of three to seven Special Forces, SEAL, Delta Force or allied special operations commandos would be carried. Twenty-four aircraft have been funded: 83-1212, 84-0475 and -0476, 85-0011 and -0012, 86-1699, 87-0023 and -0024, 87-0125 to -0127, 88-0191 to -0195, 88-0264, 88-1803, 89-0280 to -0283 and 90-0161 and -0162.

The 'Combat Talon II' also carries the AN/APQ-170 Adverse Weather Aerial Delivery System (AWADS) radar, developed to meet the special operational requirements of the US Air Force. This dual-band multi-mode radar provides MC-130H aircraft with advanced navigation capabilities that ensure mission success. It provides the 'Combat Talon II' fleet with the one of the most advanced terrain-following and terrain-avoidance navigation capabilities in service. 'We can literally pick holes through the terrain like thread through the eye of a needle,' comments Capt Mark Ramsay, a 'Talon' pilot with the Mildenhall-based 7th Special Operations Squadron. 'The Talon has a glass cockpit, with MFDs replacing the more traditional flight instruments, and these displays can be overlaid with radar and FLIR information.'

The complex MC-130 'Talon II' was a product of IBM Federal Systems and E-Systems, specialising in the avionics. For accuracy in its mission, the aircraft has a dual INS and GPS, which is updated by an AN/ARN-92 LORAN-C. Bad weather and night operations are aided by the FLIR fitted in a ball turret beneath the curiously shaped 'duckbill' radome, and self-protection is enhanced by copious chaff and flare launchers, two AN/AAQ-8 IR jammer pods, an AN/AAQ-15R detection system and ALR-44/ALR-69 missile launch warning receiver, and NVG cockpit-compatible lighting. 'Crew cooperation is a high priority,' continues Mark Ramsay, 'and the VDTs give the crewmen an unrivalled ability to see the situation ahead. The navigator controls the FLIR, TFR radar and mission management, whilst the Electronic Warfare Officer uses his VDTs to control the passive and active sensors and jamming equipment, and works closely with the navigator at all phases.'

## HC-130 'Combat Shadow': Force Extender

On a rescue or combat rescue mission, the extended-range HC-130H/N/P Hercules 'flying gas stations' are designed to operate up to a radius of 860 miles (1,384km) and loiter for up to two hours with a 45-minute fuel reserve in order to direct rescue operations, air-drop rescue kits and survival equipment and refuel rescue helicopters. Helicopters such as the 'Pave Low' and 'Pave Hawk' rely on the 'Shadows' to give them their 'long legs', and they are also able to undertake portions of a rescue mission that the helicopters may be unable to achieve swiftly. The Hercules fly high and fast whereas the helicopters are low and slow, so that they can get Pararescuemen quickly to the scene of the incident.

If, for example, an aircraft has come down in the sea 400 miles from the US coast, an HC-130 could leave ahead of the 'Jolly' team, locate the survivors and air-drop them a boat and medical equipment to assist them until the slower helicopters arrive. They would then orbit the area and coordinate the rescue situation until the helicopters arrive, refuelling them for the return journey. Like the MC-130Es, a number of the HC-130H aircraft were also converted to employ the Fulton STARS recovery system to snatch people or payloads from the ground.

The HC-130H and HC-130N Hercules aircraft can also employ their Cook Aerial Trackers. The powerful 'Cook Tracker' (AN/ARD-17) was originally designed to locate satellite capsules during re-entry from orbit but was found to be equally useful in pinpointing faint signals from Personal Locator Beacons, and to that end the aircraft is equipped with rescue kits and inflatable liferafts for long-range recovery missions. The first version of the C-130H obtained for the Air Force was the HC-130H, of which 43 were ordered in 1964 and 1965 for the air rescue and recovery role, and these aircraft are instantly distinguishable by their giant tracking radar housed in a radome atop the forward fuselage and the Fulton recovery system mounted on a modified nose cone. Chaff and flare launchers are carried for self-defence, and the rear ramps have been modified to carry high-powered flares for illuminating drop or rescue sights at night. A further two former Coast Guard HC-130Hs have been transferred to Air Force charge, although these have yet to become operational. HC-130Hs are numbered 64-14852 to -14866, 65-0962 to -0987, 65-0989 and -0990, 67-7185 and 72-1302.

The similarly equipped HC-130N was also primarily fielded for rescue work and for the recovery of re-entering space satellite capsules. The HC-130P employs underwing refuelling drogue pods developed earlier for the US Marines' KC-130F Hercules tankers. Fifteen H models were constructed to HC-130N standard for the air rescue role with a pair of underwing flight refuelling pods but without the Fulton recovery system, these being 69-5819 to -5833. Twenty H models were built to HC-130P configuration with the addition of a pair of underwing flight-refuelling pods and retaining the Fulton system, these being 65-0988, 65-0991 to -0994 and 66-0211 to -0225. Finally, twelve HC-130Hs were converted to HC-130P standard with the addition of underwing air refuelling pods: 64-14853 and -14854, 64-14856, 64-14858, 64-14860, 64-14863 to -14865, 65-0971, 65-0973, 65-0975 and 65-0987.

Although the primary mission of the HC-130 fleet is to support the 'Pave Low' or 'Pave Hawk' helicopters, it has a secondary role roughly similar to that of the MC-130—air dropping special teams, cargo loads, rubber raiding craft and Zodiac boats, flying at low level in hostile territory, mostly under the cover of darkness. The aircraft would normally pass fuel at around 115kts, which is close the Hercules' stall speed, and very slow for a huge aircraft. During 'Desert Storm' some aircraft went as low as 100ft with hoses out in the darkness to refuel 'Pave Lows'—'really wild flying'. Inside the forward portion of the cargo hold are seats and low-aspect windows to enable the 'left and right scanners' to search during a rescue mission, and also at their fingertips are the controls for the 'Cook Tracker' radar system.

In early 1996 the USAF changed the designation of some of its HC-130N/P 'Combat Shadow' tanker aircraft to MC-130P, the change affecting the 28 aircraft assigned to AFSOC. Other HC-130s, including those flown by Air Combat Command rescue units, retained their earlier designations. The 'H' now specifies a search and rescue mission, while 'M' aircraft have a specific mission, which is to refuel Air Force and Army special operations helicopters. AFSOC's 'Combat Shadows' are undergoing modifications that will further distinguish them from HC-130s under the Special Operations Force Improvement (SOFI) programme. The modifications include the addition of improved navigation, communications and threat detection and countermeasures systems. Other SOFI upgrades include the installation of a forward-looking infra-red (FLIR) sensor for night navigation;

## Lockheed MC-130P 'Combat Shadow'

The MC-130P 'Combat Shadow' flies clandestine or low-visibility, low-level missions into politically sensitive or hostile territory to provide air refuelling for special operations helicopters, and primarily flies its single- or multi-ship missions at night to reduce detection and interception by airborne threats. Secondary mission capabilities include air-dropping small special operations teams, small bundles and Zodiac and combat rubber raiding craft, as well as night vision goggle take-offs and landings, tactical airborne radar approaches and in-flight refuelling as a receiver. To enhance the probability of mission success and survivability near populated areas, crews employ tactics that require no external lighting or communications and avoid radar and weapons detection.

*Specifications:* Powerplant four Allison T56-A-15 turboprop engines each of 4,910shp; span 132ft 7in (40.4m); length: 98ft 9in (30.09m); height 38ft 6in (11.7m); maximum take-off weight 155,000lb (69,750kg); speed 289mph (464kph) at sea level; ceiling 33,000ft (10,000m); range over 4,000 miles (6,440km); crew 4officers (pilot, co-pilot, primary navigator, secondary navigator) and 4 enlisted men (flight engineer, communications systems operator and two loadmasters).

integrated inertial navigation and GPS systems; a night vision goggle-compatible head-up display and interior and exterior lighting; chaff and data-burst communications; and an in-flight refuelling capability for the aircraft (making it a receiver, as well as a dispenser, of fuel).

## HH-1H Rescue Huey

For 'local' base and area rescue, the USAF turned to yet another version of the 'Huey', the HH-1H. Camouflaged in triple-green, it provided sterling service with its rescue hoist always at the ready to recover any airman within its range.

## C-9A: AMC's Flying Hospital

The C-9 Nightingale, a modified version of the McDonnell Douglas DC-9, is a twin-engine, 'T'-tailed, medium range, swept wing jet aircraft used primarily for Air Mobility Command's aeromedical evacuation mission. The Nightingale is the only aircraft on the inventory specifically designed for the movement of litter and ambulatory patients, and carries a crew of eight comprising a pilot, co-pilot, flight mechanic, two flight nurses and three aeromedical technicians. The C-9A has the airlift capability to carry 40 litter patients, 40 ambulatory and four litter patients or various other combinations, providing the flexibility for AMC's worldwide aeromedical evacuation role. Operated by the 375th Airlift Wing at Scott Air Force Base, Illinois, C-9As are also assigned to the 374th Airlift Wing at Yokota Air Base,

Japan, for use in the Pacific theatre and to the 435th Airlift Wing at Rhein-Main Air Base, Germany, for use in the European and Middle East theatres. A hydraulically operated folding ramp allows efficient loading and unloading of litter patients and special medical equipment.

The aircraft has ceiling receptacles for securing intravenous bottles; a special care area with a separate ventilation system for patients requiring isolation or intensive care; eleven vacuum and therapeutic oxygen outlets, positioned in sidewall service panels at litter tier locations; a 28 VDC outlet in the special care area; and twenty-two 115 VAC-60 Hertz electrical outlets located throughout the cabin which permit the use of cardiac monitors and respirators. There is also a medical refrigerator for preserving whole blood and biological drugs; a medical supply work area with sink, medicine storage section and work table, fore-and-aft galleys and lavatories; aft-facing commercial airline-type seats for ambulatory patients; a station for a medical crew director that includes a desk communication panel and a control panel to monitor cabin temperature, and therapeutic oxygen and vacuum systems; and an auxiliary power unit which provides electrical power for uninterrupted cabin air conditioning, quick servicing during stops and self-starting for the twin jet engines.

# 8

# Fires at Fitzroy: The Falklands

*'My overriding memory is the smell of burning bodies and smouldering flesh. It permeated the very fabric of the Sea King's rear cabin, and for the remainder of the campaign we had to fly with the doors open.'*—Thoughts from Aircrewman (now Lt-Cdr) Clive Wilson RN on the tragedy that befell the Royal Fleet Auxiliary vessel *Sir Galahad* during the Falklands War of 1982.

The dark and dire day was 4 June 1982. The LSLs RFA *Sir Galahad* and *Sir Tristram* had moved into Fitzroy Bay to offload troops. The latter had almost completed her task, whereas the *Sir Galahad* had a large contingent from the 1st Battalion Welsh Guards still on board. The ship, now a 'sitting duck', was attacked by Argentinian Skyhawk bombers which had evaded the radar picket ships and Sea Harrier CAP, and was grievously and mortally damaged with 500lb bombs. She immediately caught fire with many of the Guardsmen still below decks, and the tragedy was exacerbated by virtue of the bombs penetrating one of the holds which was full of ammunition: mortars and shells exploded in the ensuing fire.

The reasons why the ships were in that position without the necessary Rapier air defence systems being fully operational have remained a matter of debate and are beyond the scope of this book. However, there was a further Skyhawk raid that evening, and with the Rapiers then fully operational it was reported that four out of the five attackers were brought down. The Navy also had other 'over-the-horizon' problems resulting from the lack of a dedicated airborne early warning platform, a luxury that had been dispensed with years earlier with the retirement of the Fairey Gannet AEW from the ultimate Fleet Air Arm carrier HMS *Ark Royal*. Because the British armed forces were trained for a war over Europe where they would form part of an integrated force, at that stage there was no relevance for a sea-going AEW platform as the task would be undertaken by other operators, most probably the United States. Reliance was therefore placed on outlying radar picket ships and Sea Harriers on combat air patrol to provide sufficient early warning of incoming attacks. However, as with the aforementioned raid, the loss of both military and civil shipping to low-flying Exocet missiles proved that this arrangement was woefully inadequate. (Towards the end of the conflict a pair of Sea King helicopters were hastily outfitted with an underslung airborne radar and despatched to the fleet, but they arrived well after the Argentine surrender. The newly established 849 Naval Air Squadron, specialising in AEW, has since become an integral part of fleet protection.)

At the time of the Falklands War Sea King Mk 5s were operated by 820 Naval Air Squadron aboard HMS *Invincible*, 826 NAS on HMS *Hermes* and aboard the RFA *Fort Austin*. Mk 2s were operated by 826 NAS from the RFAs *Fort Grange* and *Olmeda* and other ships, whilst 846 NAS flew Mk 4s from various ships and land bases. 820 and 826 NAS were mainly tasked with anti-submarine screening, although both were also involved in rescue tasks, most notably the unsuccessful search for the pilots of two Sea Harrier FRS.1s that had collided in thick fog on 6 May, and the plucking of an RAF Harrier GR.3 pilot, Sqn Ldr Jerry Pook, out of the 'drink' on 3 May after he had ejected 30 miles from *Hermes* just before darkness fell. To avoid being detected by hostile Argentine aircraft, Pook had deliberately switched off his rescue beacon transmitter, but he was found by virtue of his small helmet light after the Sea Kings had undertaken several hours of painstaking search pattern flying.

846 Naval Air Squadron worked between HMS *Fearless* and *Hermes* and the RFAs *Engadine*, *Fort Austin* and *Sir Galahad*, as well as the merchant ships *Canberra*, *Norland* and *Elk*, and their aircraft were involved in the rescue of crewmen from HMS *Sheffield*, a Type 42 destroyer struck amidships on 4 May by the now infamous Aérospatiale Exocet sea-skimming missile, launched from a low-flying Argentinian Super Etendard. 820 and 846 NAS also undertook the rescue of injured seamen from HMS *Coventry*, the second British warship to fall victim to the Exocet. During this rescue one of the aircraft, piloted by Lt-Cdr Thornewill, winched down Aircrewman CPO Alf Tupper on to one of the floating liferafts; Tupper then unhooked himself and swam from raft to raft helping the injured and guiding in the waves of rescue helicopters. Not wearing a lift preserver himself, he was credited with 'materially saving between 40 and 50 lives', for which he later received the Distinguished Service Medal

Lt-Cdr Wilson's unit, 825 NAS, was hastily recommissioned at RNAS Culdrose in order to provide an additional utility unit for the forthcoming campaign. Lt-Cdr Hugh Clark, then the OC 706 NAS, the Sea King Advanced Flying Training Squadron (AFTS), was invited to re-form the squadron, which he did on 7 May within four days of asking, calling on ten aircraft, mostly from 706 NAS and with others arriving from 814, 819 and 824 NAS. Thirty-six pilots and aircrewmen were also gathered, most of these being instructors from the unit and therefore vastly experienced aviators. Most of the aircraft were Sea King Mk 2s, which had their ASW gear stripped out to give them a troop-carrying capacity of between 16 and 24 according to the range requirements, with an alternative stretcher accommodation for the casevac role. The unit left for the South Atlantic aboard the *Queen Elizabeth 2*, *Atlantic Causeway* and RFA *Engadine*. Outbound the aircraft received a coat of paint similar to the Sea King Commandos' olive drab, although this was removed during the voyage home. Their role once on station at San Carlos was almost entirely that of transport. Several of the aircraft were hit by gunfire but there were no casualties.

When the RFA *Sir Galahad* moved into Fitzroy Bay, three of 825 NAS's aircraft were engaged in the offloading of the Rapier AAM units, including one helicopter flown by the unit's OC, Hugh Clark, with his P2 Sub-Lt Brian Evans and Aircrewman CPO David Jackson. Clark later recalled that, although the rescue situation was a horrific task, it seemed to him to be an orderly event, far less complicated than the civilian rescues such as the *Lovat* and *Merc Enterprise* incidents in which he had been involved years earlier. However, Clark's part in the rescue will be forever etched in the memory of those who witnessed the brave actions of him and his crew. Television images showed his Sea King hovering just 20ft away from the stern of the blazing ship, using the 'Sir Galahad' lettering as a visual reference, battling through the pall of smoke not only to pick up survivors from the sea but also to use the helicopter's downwash to 'blow' the inflated liferafts loaded with badly burned soldiers towards the shore and away from the stricken vessel. Clark was later to receive the Distinguished Service Cross for his part in the rescue, which cited 'action with a total disregard for his own safety', in the good company of Lt Phil Sheldon and Lt John Broughton, who were awarded the Queen's Gallantry Medal.

Lt-Cdr Clive Wilson continues: 'I recall it was a clear blue sky, and a pretty cold atmosphere, and part of another 10-hour multi-tasked day. We had just taken off another of the Rapier kits from *Galahad*, when we received an order to go to Goose Green to ferry troops. Having accomplished the first trip we were low on gas, so moved to *Tristram* to refuel before heading back to Goose Green. As we crossed behind the Sound we could see smoke rising from the area, but with so many ships in the sector, and many having "dirty smoky" engines, we thought nothing of it. We set down on *Tristram* to hot-refuel, and at about the mid-point the pilot called, "*Galahad*'s hit—we're going", at which point the fuel hose was dropped and away we went.

'As we crossed we instantly saw the smoke and flames, and from half a mile away the exploding ammunition was very visible. We joined up with two other Sea Kings, including the Boss's, and slotted into a well-ordered rescue pattern. We moved right up to the forecastle of *Galahad* and began lifting the badly injured. Most of the Guardsmen were going over the side and down the nets into the water and life-boats, but the worst affected were being marshalled to the helicop-ters. We took on casualties three at a time, in order to give them plenty of space with their injuries; and with some guys really badly dam-aged—legs and arms blown off and with smouldering flesh all around—it was impossible to take more aboard. We flew them direct to the field hospital, and went back for others. I remember thinking how "quiet" it all was, and in spite of the explosions and the injured there was no panic. It was very surreal, and basically there was no time to dwell on it—you just got on and did the job.

'I also distinctly remember watching the mortar rounds going off as we were hovering about 7–8 feet above the forecastle. This position made it easier for us to get the injured aboard and easier for the pilot to hover. I was telling him where the rounds were going, and he said to be sure to tell him if one was coming our way—which in reality would have made little difference as we were in not position to try to evade it! It was our Sea King that picked up Simon Weston, the cel-ebrated Guardsman: he was so badly burned that he needed to be strapped to a pallet for removal. To be honest, at the time he didn't look too bad, but about two hours later we had to move him to Ajax Bay, and by then he looked very, very ill, and we have always kept a keen eye on his progress ever since. We took many other wounded over to Ajax. Guys were on drips, and we had a cabin crowded with medics keeping their charges comfortable. But the overriding factor was the distinctive smell—very disturbing.'

During the *Sir Galahad* rescue Lt John Miller and PO Aircrewman Al Ashdown, flying Sea King 'Victor Zulu', were also tasked with off-loading Rapier AA weapons from the ship and were a mere 200yds distant when the attack went in. They hovered out of sight behind high ground, set down their load and moved in to lift the casualties from the foredeck and take them ashore in sticks of five, flying amongst smoke and exploding ammunition. They were later Mentioned in Dispatches. Other aircraft which played their part in the rescue were the Naval Commando Wessexes. In all 146 Welsh Guardsmen were injured, with 63 fatalities.

## Army Casevac

Often overlooked because of the more 'visible' work of the Sea Harriers, RAF Harriers and the larger helicopters such as the Wessex, Lynx, Sea King and the one and only surviving Chinook is the critical role undertaken in the Falklands by the Army Air Corps' small fleet of Westland AH-1 Scout helicopters. These not only provided armed support for the troops on the ground, but undertook vital and dangerous casevac missions to recover wounded soldiers, often at night and in bad weather and sometimes under fire. Also in action were the Army's more powerful Gazelle helicopters, many of which were pressed into service in the casevac role.

---

### Westland Scout AH-1

Designed in 1956 as an advanced light utility helicopter with a turbine powerplant, this helicopter was adopted by the Army and the Royal Marines as the AH-1 Scout and by the Royal Navy as the Wasp HAS.1 for duties around the globe. The Scout could carry a crew of two, with a folding rear seat to accommodate three passengers or a stretcher. Later in its long service life it was armed with anti-tank AS.11 optically tracked wire guided missiles and a roof-mounted Ferranti AF120 gyro-stabilised sighting system, used with some success during the Falklands War. Most notably, it was in its Wasp guise that the helicopter caught the headlines, when one of the aircraft from 829 NAS/HMS *Endurance* Flight (XS527) damaged the Argentinian submarine *Santa Fe* in Grytviken harbour, South Georgia, on 25 April 1982 with an AS.12 anti-shipping missile.

*Specifications:* Powerplant one Rolls-Royce Nimbus Mk 101 or 102 turboshaft rated at 1,050shp (derated to 885shp); maximum speed 131mph (211kph); maximum ceiling 13,400ft (4,084m); range 314 miles (505km) with 1,240lb (562kg) internal fuel and 4 persons on board.

---

The Scouts carried stretchers and 'pods', pre-shaped 'coffin-like' containers that could be attached to the skids and were large enough to accommodate a single casualty and protect him from the wind and weather. Their small rear cabins could carry two or three people, the front seats being occupied by a single pilot and his air gunner. One incident occured in the night of 13 June when Capt Sam Drennan and his co-pilot/gunner Cpl Jay Rigg were tasked with recovering wounded Scots Guardsmen from Mount Tumbledown and flying them to the medical dressing station near Fitzroy. In the course of the next few hours Drennan's Scout brought out sixteen Guardsmen and Gurkhas from the 1/7th Rifles, including Lt Bob Lawrence, who had a bullet lodged in his skull, and a young soldier who had been badly shot up, had become separated from his platoon and had spent hours in the field before he was found. Both of these rescues were undertaken in the face of Argentinian small-arms fire and mortar rounds. Drennan was later to receive the DFC. The recovery from Sapper Hill of a Welsh Guardsman who was found to have a perforated ulcer was also undertaken by Drennan during a pitch black night with no moon and in a blizzard. He and AG WO Mick Sharp made three attempts to get into the area before they were successful. The wind was so strong that the Scout was hover-taxied over Sapper Hill in order to attempt a take off from the top. At some point during this time the Scout was hit by a hefty bump of turbulence which knocked out the artificial horizon, leaving Drennan blind. However, sighting the lights of Fitzroy in the blurred distance, he brought his aircraft and casualty to a safe recovery.

With the ending of hostilities, a new military airfield, RAF Stanley, was created to house a deterrent force of fighters, along with logistic and tanker support to ensure the continuing protection of the islands. Sea King search and rescue helicopters were added to the garrison, No 78 Squadron being assigned to the remote outpost.

# 9

# From Cold War to Gulf War: The Face of Rescue for the Decade

In United States military circles, combat search and rescue (CSAR) is a now a totally specialised task performed by specially trained and equipped rescue forces to effect the recovery of distressed personnel during wartime or contingency operations. To accomplish this, a search and rescue task force (SARTF) is established and, depending on the mission in hand, this may be a sizeable force or simply a single rescue helicopter. Although rescue helicopters may operate independently, certain scenarios dictate the use of a larger SARTF. The rescue task force will normally now include A-10 'Sandys', a rescue combat air patrol (RESCAP), HC-130N tankers, recovery vehicles, AWACS, airborne forward air controllers (AFAC), pararescue personnel (PJs) and AC-130 Spectre gunships.

The 'Sandy' is a specially qualified and dedicated A-10 pilot trained in search procedures, survivor location and authentication techniques, and in helicopter support tactics. The 'Sandy' mission is extremely complex and very demanding, and careful consideration is given to the pilot's skill and experience level when designating a 'Hog' pilot as being 'Sandy'-qualified. The lead pilot, or 'Sandy 1', will act as the on-scene commander (OSC) for CSAR missions, is in overall control of the situation and coordinates communications with the SARTF and the survivor. 'Sandy 2' is his wingman and 'book-keeper' and assists in the coordinating process. Each pilot in a normal four-ship 'Sandy' flight is specially trained for his individual role. 'Sandy 3' and 'Sandy 4' are trained to be responsible for rescue helicopter escort into the pick-up area. All USAF CSAR efforts are now controlled by the USAF Rescue Co-ordination Center (RCC) in coordination with an on-scene Joint Search and Rescue Center (JSRC).

The RCC obtains survivor authentication information from individual unit intelligence sections for use during actual combat recoveries. Throughout the CSAR mission, the RCC monitors the status of all the employed assets. 'Sandy 1', the OSC, is designated by the senior controlling agency to coordinate efforts at the rescue site. Any aircraft commander may assume OSC responsibilities upon observing or contacting a distressed aircraft, a bail-out or survivors on the ground. It is preferable to use an OA-10 airborne FAC in this role until relieved by a qualified 'Sandy' pilot. However, if a 'Sandy'-qualified A-10 pilot is on station, the FAC will pass on-scene command to the 'Sandy'-qualified flight. The FAC will then normally remain on station to support the CSAR.

Voice radio contact with the survivor is highly desirable, although not mandatory. If the survivor has a personal survival radio (or if an electronic search is conducted on the assumption that he does), the recovery task force may have to use UHF radio transmissions for at least a portion of the mission. However, everyone can monitor UHF transmissions, including the enemy. If the survivor has a specially designed PRC-112 survival radio, finding him can be accomplished with the minimum communication using special locating equipment carried aboard some A-10s. No fighter pilot plans to get shot down behind enemy lines and no special forces teams plan to be isolated without an escape route. Planning for a CSAR is therefore a reaction to circumstances rather than a deliberate act.

The SARTF is organised beforehand to deal with this time-sensitive contingency. Roles and missions are carefully designated and participants are constantly trained to perform them. The Airborne Mission Commander (AMC) role can be divided into two phases: in the first he is the airborne coordinator and organiser of assets for the mission, and in the second the manager and director of these forces. The AMC can be located aboard the rescue HC-130, at the Airborne Battlefield Command and Control Center (ABCCC), aboard an AWACS, embarked aboard naval assets or located as dictated by the RCC. When the AMC is on board the HC-130, the call would be designated 'King'.

The AMC will respond to any distressed aircraft. If the aircraft is still flying, he will locate an escort for the damaged aircraft, alert ground personnel and collaborate with all necessary agencies to ensure a safe arrival and landing for it; if an aircraft is missing, he will organise the search and coordinate additional support. The AMC will also continue to coordinate the search until the evaders have been located or until the search is abandoned. Once the survivor has been located, the AMC will continue to coordinate the forces needed for a successful pick-up and appoint an OSC. This can be a fighter (a 'Sandy'-qualified A-10 being preferred), an A-FAC or any other aircraft that has pinpointed the survivor. The AMC and OSC will decide if an immediate pick-up is possible. If the evaders are located in a relatively secure or friendly area, the AMC will attempt to arrange for the nearest helicopter or ground party to effect the pick-up; if they are in a hostile area, the AMC and the OSC will determine what forces are necessary to neutralise the threat. Finally, the AMC will organise a SARTF via the RCC network. Once the 'Sandys' arrive on the scene, 'Sandy 1' will accept OSC responsibility and work with the AMC, the AFAC and other forces to ensure a successful pick-up.

'Sandys' can be launched or diverted from another mission, and thankfully the A-10 can carry most, if not all, of the ordnance required in CSAR operations (for example, rockets, CBUs, GP bombs and PGMs). Moreover, the 30mm cannon is an excellent weapon for precise stand-off suppression or for marking targets for supporting attack aircraft, not to mention scaring the daylights out of any enemy troops!. Whenever possible, 'Sandy' ordnance loads are tailored to each individual CSAR mission. Fighter aircraft, other than designated 'Sandy' aircraft, may assist CSAR forces by suppressing ground threats and cutting lines of communication (LOCs). The use of these forces can significantly increase the chances of success for the mission. Dedicated combat air patrol (CAP) fighters can also be assigned to the rescue effort if required. There are now two primary recovery vehicles used in USAF CSAR operations, the HH-60G 'Pave Hawk'—the primary rescue vehicle—and the MH-53J 'Pave Low III'.

If available, AWACS 'magic' can significantly increase the effectiveness of the rescue force. Its long range, mobility, look-down radar, surveillance coverage and communications capabilities are useful assets in CSAR operations. As an extension of its normal command and control duties, the AWACS can function as a CSAR coordinator unless relieved by a dedicated AMC. The availability of a FAC also gives the rescue force several significant advantages. He may be able to locate and authenticate the survivors before the arrival of the CSAR forces if the survivor is in the area which the FAC is controlling; he may be able to provide a current and accurate assessment of the threat in the recovery area; and he can also control any available diversionary and suppressive attack flights, can direct battle-damaged aircraft to a nearby safe bail-out area and will assume initial on-scene command of the rescue effort.

A CSAR effort is by its very nature a multi-dimensional and complex affair, and each scenario is different from another. The A-10 'Sandys' will try to accomplish their tasks as early as possible in the rescue effort, and CSAR forces in contact with a possible survivor must authenticate him before the rescue can continue. Authentication ensures that the person on the radio is actually the survivor and not enemy personnel trying to lure the CSAR force into a trap. The techniques used in authenticating the survivor centre around a document called the Isoprep card. This card contains statements and numbers memorised by that individual—information that only the actual survivor would know. Survivors are often injured, disoriented or in shock and may not be familiar with their survival equipment. 'Sandy 1' will therefore assess the survivor's physical and mental condition to determine how much help he can provide in the CSAR effort. 'Sandy 1' can also help the survivor maintain his composure by establishing a professional atmosphere and by making his instructions to the survivor as specific as possible. If possible, the 'Sandy' pilot should have an inventory of the survival gear carried by pilots on his mission. 'Sandy 1' will then advise the rescue helicopter of the survivor's condition, and this will allow the pararescue personnel to prepare medically and give them advance notice of the need to exit the helicopter and carry the survivor back.

Survivor information is high priority and is considered vital for any mission execution. Information that the 'Sandys' collect about the survivor include the aircraft call-sign and the number of survivors, their location, their survival equipment and their physical condition. It is also very important for the pararescue personnel to know if the survivor can walk or whether he needs medical attention. Information such as recovery area threats, elevation, terrain and enemy activity will help the rescue force know what to anticipate, and aid in the formulation of the rescue plan. This rescue plan will include such things as an Initial Point (IP) for the helicopters to use, a safe route in and out of the survivor's area for the helicopters and any ordnance or tactics the 'Sandys' will employ during the rescue. Once in the recovery area, the 'Sandys' will usually split into two elements of two aircraft, with Sandys '1' and '2' moving near the survivors and '3' and '4' orbiting in reserve. The efforts of the entire rescue force are then directed towards getting the helicopter to the survivor for the pick-up. Since the helicopter operates in a low-altitude, low-airspeed regime, visual look-out and the suppression of enemy defences are vital.

Helicopter escort missions will normally consist of rendezvous with the helicopter(s), ingress, helicopter escort/suppression, cover/suppression during the pick-up and egress escort/suppression to a safe area. 'Sandy 1' will initiate each phase of the pick-up and coordinate all actions with the CSAR force and the survivors on the ground. Once the survivor is on board the rescue helicopter the 'Sandys' will escort it quickly out of the area towards friendly territory. With all four 'Sandys' back together, they join forces to ensure the safety of the rescued survivor and that of the helicopter crews.

## The Gulf War: AFSOC's Challenge

With the invasion of Kuwait by the forces of Saddam Hussein in August 1990, it seemed only a matter of time until the crisis turned into a conflict. By now CSAR was firmly under the jurisdiction of AFSOC, operating its dedicated MH-53J 'Pave Lows' and MH-60G 'Pave Hawks' alongside its MC-130 'Combat Talons', HC-130 'Combat Shadow' tankers and AC-130 Spectre gunships. The US Navy were now equipped with their sea-going HH-60H Seahawks, the US Marines relied on their multi-aircraft TRAP teams and the Army carried with it the new MH-47D/MH-47E Chinooks and MH-60K/L Hawks, both from the 160th Special Operations Regiment (Airborne), which although dedicated to long-range, covert infil/exfil of Special Operations Forces still retained a creditable SAR capability. The lessons from 'Eagle Claw' were well learned, and the SOF helicopters and crews were now the recognised specialists, able to undertake missions at night or in adverse weather over any type of terrain and do so with an outstanding 90 per cent chance of success.

## PLS/TACBE

During the 1980s fast jet and special operations aircrew were issued with high-powered digital Personal Locator Systems, or PLS/TACBE. These 28oz, hand-held devices allow the user to talk to AWACS or other aircraft on a pre-programmed, encrypted frequency using 'burst' transmissions to reduce the risk of interception by an enemy. They are also capable of being programmed with their own individual codes, and the more advanced units can be automatically interrogated by CSAR/SOF/AWACS aircraft to verify their authenticity. Using the 'burst' transmission system, the PLS/TACBEs can also be automatically interrogated by CSAR aircraft in order to obtain a bearing and steering cue to the location. This allows the aircraft to remain masked against the terrain, using a fast 'pop-up' to interrogate the unit quickly in order to gain an update to the aircraft's navigation systems.

## Rescue in the 'Storm': The Recovery of Devon Jones

In the early hours of the morning of 21 January 1991 Lt Devon Jones, and his RIO, Lt Larry Slade, from VF-103 ('The Sluggers'), were tasked with flying their F-14A+Tomcat A212/161430, call-sign 'Slate 46', on an armed escort mission to protect a high-value EA-6B Prowler from VAQ-132 around the airfield at Al Asad, as part of a larger Navy strike package. The Prowler, carrying HARM anti-radar missiles, was briefed to fire a single missile from 45 miles out on to a set target, and take a second shot at any other target on an 'opportunity' basis. The Prowler took its HARM shot on cue, and the F-14 followed in a further fifteen miles with the EA-6, looking for more trade. However, since they were operating at around 28,000ft there was little chance of taking a second shot, so the duo turned for home.

Moments into the egress route, at 6.05 a.m. local time, the Tomcat crew, now 160 miles inside Iraq and some 30 miles from Baghdad, sighted a Soviet-built SA-2 SAM heading upwards in their direction through the clouds. Jones accelerated as briefed, and rolled in towards the SAM to give the missile tracking problems. However, as the aircraft rolled, the SAM continued on track and exploded behind the Tomcat, impacting blast fragments on it. The detonation was so fierce that it ripped the face mask off the pilot and sent the aircraft into a flat spin. It soon became apparent that the situation was irretrievable, and the pair 'punched out' at around 10,000ft, with the Prowler watching the event and 'calling in the hit'. Slade, the RIO, used his PRC-112 radio whilst parachuting down to call in a 'mayday' to the orbiting AWACS, before both aircrew lost sight of one another in the cloud and darkness and were separated.

Once on the ground, Jones could see the pall of smoke from his F-14, which he estimated to be some eight miles away, and the realisation of where he was and the consequences that might befall him began to wheel through his mind. Immediate action was required, however, to hide his tell-tale parachute and get a call-out on his older PRC-90 radio, hoping to spoof any Iraqi search party by calling his intended heading as 'east', when in actual fact he began to walk westwards. The SAR briefs had indicated that any downed aircrew should walk to the south-west, which would take them towards the Saudi border; however, disorientation following the ejection saw Jones walking in the wrong direction, and he realised this when the sun began to rise.

After a 2½- hour desert sojourn, Jones came upon a small patch of vegetation and began to dig in. After an hour of digging with his survival knife he had produced a hole measuring 4ft by 3ft, but he realised that the disturbed ground would be conspicuous from the air so he decided to lay top sand over it. He got into the hole, lay his radio near to his head and waited, wondering if any of his unanswered calls had been heard. At Arar airfield in Saudi Arabia a rescue package was being prepared and a 20th SOS crew, including Capt Tom Trask (pilot) and Maj Mike Homan (co-pilot) got airborne in an MH-53J 'Pave Low' helicopter. Battling through dense fog, they headed for the Iraqi border, which they crossed at 8.15 a.m. Flying at a mere 15ft above the deck to avoid Iraqi radar, the helicopter headed for the crash site. During this period an Iraqi MiG-23 fighter appeared, but it quickly retreated when it was locked by two USAF F-15Cs on RESCAP.

At around 10.30 a.m. Jones caught the sound of what he thought was a pair of Iraqi jets but in fact turned out to be the aforementioned brace of F-15Cs on RESCAP, looking for him. An Iraqi truck stopped at a nearby water tank but, much to his relief, departed. Jones turned his radio on again to listen in for any broadcasts, and in the hope that he might contact his RIO, whose fate was of great concern.

In fact, Slade had made a heavy landing, having already lost sight of Jones and watched the stricken Tomcat impact into the desert. Gathering up his parachute and hiding it as best he could, he also began to walk towards the south-west, using his radio every hour, until dawn began to break. Unfortunately for Slade, at around 10.30 a.m. he was picked up by two armed Iraqis in a truck who took him to Baghdad for 'interrogation'. Here he became part of the 'human shield', suffering six weeks in captivity before being released on 4 March. The MH-53 team were unable to locate the downed F-14 crew and returned to Arar to refuel, flying immediately back to the crash site to resume the search.

To Jones's surprise, the SAR frequency crackled into life with some-one calling up his call-sign 'Slate 47', though slightly out of range. The SAR aircraft used the directional abilities of Jones's radio to get closer into the area, authenticated both aircraft and downed aviator and fired off a flare from 18,000ft for Jones to see and position the aircraft. The first attempt, however, was to no avail. A second shot was sighted by Jones, and the aircraft, identified as a 'Sandy' A-10A, one of a pair flown by Capt Randy Goff and his wingman Capt Paul Johnson of the 354th TFW, dropped down to 100ft, overflew Jones and picked up his exact location by reference to the aircraft's INS. The 'Sandys' then exited the area to refuel, after speaking to the 'Jolly' rescue helicopter, which was vectored to Jones's position. The Iraqis were now alerted to the rescue attempt and again moved MiG-23s to intercept, but the presence of the RESCAP F-15s soon put paid to that endeavour. Jones once more heard the friendly voices of Goff and Johnson talking to the 'Jollys', which were now only 30 miles from his position. The 'Sandys' streaked in to sanitize the area while the helicopter waited on the ground. Jones was asked to shine his signal mirror and start looking for the MH-53.

At about 1.55 p.m., with Jones now in radio contact with the 'Jolly', one of the door gunners spotted an Iraqi truck heading in Jones's direction, obviously having been sent out with orders to capture the American. The two A-10s, now critically low on fuel, also spotted the vehicle and rolled into an attack posture at 100ft, squirting off short bursts from their Avenger cannon, the characteristic 'growl' whistling across the desert floor. Within seconds there was nothing left of the vehicle except smoke and flames. Looking east, Jones picked up the bulky sight of an MH-53J 'Pave Low' helicopter as Capt Trask landed the machine 150yds from the smouldering wreckage of the truck. With the helicopter in position, at 2.15 p.m. the exhausted Jones broke cover and boarded the aircraft with a little help from crewman Sgt Ben Pennington. The 'Pave Low' immediately got underway, whilst the two 'Sandys', now 'on vapour', continued to orbit the area to assure their safety.

The journey back to the MH-53's operating base was 140 miles and took 88 minutes. Jones had been on the ground for eight hours; the A-10s had been in the air for eight hours and the helicopters for three. A-10 pilot Capt Goff received the Distinguished Flying Cross and Capt Johnson the Air Force Cross for their part in the rescue. It is also worth noting at this point that the Slade pick-up during 'Desert Storm' was the first successful combat rescue since the Vietnam War.

## Casevac/Medevac

The Sikorsky H-60 Black Hawk saw widespread use in the Gulf War, the US Army deploying over 400 to Saudi Arabia. The 2nd Battalion 229th Aviation Regiment lost one of its UH-60s to Iraqi fire during an attempt to rescue Capt William Andrews, a downed F-16 pilot. As the helicopter approached the pilot's position it began to receive heavy anti-aircraft fire, which brought down the aircraft and an accompanying AH-64 Apache that was serving as its escort. Only three personnel survived the crash, Maj Rhonda Cornum (flight surgeon), S/Sgt Daniel Stamaris (crew chief) and pathfinder SPC Troy Dunlap, who along with the F-16 pilot were taken prisoner by the Iraqis.

## Desert Dustoffs

For most observers the UH-1 'Huey' is associated more with the Vietnam War than with any other conflict, and yet the invasion of Kuwait saw some of these valuable and venerable workhorses returning to the battlefield—even taking some Vietnam veteran pilots with them! One of the reserve Huey units sent to participate in 'Desert Shield'/'Desert Storm' was the 273rd Medical Detachment (AA), which was called into active duty on 17 November 1990, leaving its home base at Fort Sam Houston in Texas for Saudi Arabia. Operating from Al Qaysumak, the unit began receiving medevac missions from 30 December. Flying the UH-1V, the 273rd was the only medevac unit qualified for NVG work, and in the first four months of 1991 it flew over 700 sorties and carried out 190 patients. Normally the helicopters carried wounded and sick Iraqi prisoners, moving them from forward aid stations to POW camps or field hospitals, and, with the war concluded, the unit returned home in May 1991.

SSG Evacuation Platoon Sgt Mike Curtis of the 872nd Medical Company, 273rd Medical Detachment (AA)—the 'Cajun Medevacs'—recalls his 'Desert Storm' experience: 'Try to imagine a bar bell set vertically. The front lines are the set of weights at the one end, the hospitals are the set of weights on the opposite end, with the medevac's making the "bridge". At the front lines the wounded were cared for by a combat lifesaver, usually a first-aid level trained soldier (non-medic). However, if needed, a medic could be called for and the care of the patient determined. If this was out of the scope of the platoon medic/company medic they were sent to the Battalion Aid Station. Sometimes the wounds were so severe that only limited treatment could be effected, and if they were not able to provide full treatment on site then a medevac was called in. The patients were then flown to a TAC EVAC (Tactical Evacuation) station to the rear of the combat zone. The small mobile field hospitals had only limited assets and could easily be overloaded, and many times they were bypassed directly to the TAC EVAC stations. The C-130 Hercules TAC EVAC bird would also form the long bar of the bar bell. They would fly the patients to the rear for dispersal to the regional hospitals (all around Dhahran and outlying areas). At the TAC EVAC receiving station the patients that needed evac out to speciality hospitals (i.e. burns units, etc) would be placed on C-141 Starlifter STRAT EVACs (Strategic Evacuation) to be flown to Germany or back to the US.

'We flew over 118 missions with over 300 patients, mostly Iraqi POWs, and we did not lose a single patient or aircraft/aircrew. We also flew numerous missions on the "tapline road" for road accidents, explosions and crashes. One incident that sticks in the memory was the Saudi C-130 that returned from Mecca with Sengali soldiers on board completing their Haj. It crashed at Al-Mishab airport in low visibility due to the oil fires set by Iraq. Of 104 people on board, only four survived the crash, but two died later that day. We were the first medevac on the scene (out of eleven sent), and I was the flight medic. A sister ship made it 30 minutes later, with all other "high tech" medevacs turning around due to "poor visibility".

'I am certified in Critical Care Nursing (CCRN), Emergency Nursing (CEN) and Flight Nursing (CFRN) as well as being a Paramedic. The nurses I would get patients from would talk to us flight medics like idiots (assuming that we were lowly trained medics with the standard six-week course). It would blow their minds when they looked at my survival vest where I had my "credentials" sewn on . . . they read RN, CCRN, CEN, CFRN, EMT-P. Ask any one of the ER charge nurses how hard it is to obtain all of those, but we drew people like that into our unit. We were equipped with a Chemical (MOPP4) Flight Medic kit which included nomex flight suit, MOPP suit, M24 mask, gloves/booties, survival vest, weapon, a flak jacket for aircrew (heavier than what the infantry guys wear) and aidbag. We made our own training missions titled MCAT. We would fly fake, moulaged (blood-painted) patients out somewhere and have a crew set up for evac, with a flight medic/observer. Then we would call into flight ops, tell them what we knew and off they went. We would then would throw in alternate scenarios like sniper takes out the pilot in command, killed crew chief, wrong coordinates, etc. It was great, plus we learned a lot from our mistakes. Our pilots flew full time (90 per cent of them) with the oil companies in the Gulf, and had thousands of hours, while the active duty group had only hundreds. Our mechanics and crew chiefs also worked for the same companies—we had the best of the best.'

## HH-60 'Pave Hawk'

The HH-60G is configured for rescue and special operations work and incorporates an aerial refuelling probe; additional, internal, cabin-mounted, 117 US gal (443-litre) auxiliary fuel tanks; a fuel management system; Doppler navigation equipment; an electronic map display; secure HF (high-frequency) radio; FLIR; Bendix weather radar; GPS; an internal APU; chaff and flare launchers; and up to three .50in machine guns or 7.62mm miniguns. For an air rescue mission at medium altitude, the HH-60G can carry up to three rescue personnel, associated equipment and three machine guns and fly—with two 230 US gal (871-litre) external fuel tanks—to a radius of about 400 miles (644km); with the addition of two 450 US gal (1,703-litre) fuel tanks, radius becomes about 600 miles (966km), with a maximum endurance of 4hr 51min; and the aircraft can be refuelled in flight. The HH-60G also has a comprehensive suite of radios and SATCOMM (satellite communications), used in relaying information such as the survivor's coordinates to the Rescue Center. For utility duties or conventional operations—for which it would not normally be employed—the HH-60G can carry out various mission functions and can carry eleven combat troops or paratroopers, eight passengers or four hospital litters and an 8,000lb (3,628kg) load slung externally, operating to a maximum radius of about 650 miles (1,046km)

A small number of the USAF's 92 HH-60Gs are assigned to special operations forces, the remainder to combat rescue units of the active-duty, Reserve, and Air National Guard forces. The HH-60 is a in its basic form a conventional, medium-range helicopter with elastomeric (no lubrication) bearings carrying an advanced four-bladed titanium/glass fibre honeycomb rotor. The aircraft has a horizontal stabiliser, tail rotor and electronic FBW (fly-by-wire) flight control system. The HH-60 routinely has a crew of two pilots and one or more Pararescue technicians (PJs) for rescue and special operations

The USAF's operation of the H-60 actually began with a batch of UH-60A Black Hawks which were initially upgraded to 'Credible Hawk' standard. A total of nineteen helicopters were involved in this project, with all the surviving examples later being further updated to full 'Pave Hawk' status. Work on adapting these machines to the interim configuration began at the end of May 1986, with the final example of the initial batch of ten being completed in August 1987, whereupon a further nine were subjected to the same process. Prior to that, a single USAF UH-60A was earmarked to serve as a prototype for the proposed definitive Air Force model, namely the HH-60D. This was planned to be the full-system, all-weather version and was allocated the name 'Night Hawk', with the USAF expressing its intent to purchase no fewer than 243. Following the fitting of an in-flight refuelling probe, an additional fuel cell in the cabin and stub wings with external tanks, but still lacking mission avionics systems, the HH-60D prototype made its first flight from Sikorsky's Stratford plant in Connecticut on 4 February 1984.

As it transpired, a lack of funds forced the USAF to reconsider and it initially opted for a revised plan that involved the acquisition of 89 HH-60Ds plus 66 reduced-capability HH-60Es. Even that proposal proved too costly, with the result that both versions were shelved in favour of a model known as the HH-60A, which would be a hybrid using less complex and less expensive systems. Since the existing HH-60D prototype had yet to be fitted with avionics, it was chosen to serve as the HH-60A prototype and made its initial flight in this guise on 3 July 1985. At that time, the USAF anticipated taking delivery of 99 HH-60As, but, once again, a shortage of funds prompted a re-appraisal and the service eventually settled upon a programme involving the adaptation of nineteen UH-60As to 'Credible Hawk' configuration. As noted earlier, it was intended to update these to MH-60G standard and to obtain additional examples of both the MH-60G and HH-60G. This is basically what has happened, with the USAF utilising a mix of modified and new-build 'Pave Hawks' at the present moment.

The two pilots are separated by a console that rises between their seats, making it impossible for them to access the rear cabin. A flight engineer sits behind the right-side pilot, and a lead Pararescueman sits behind the left-side pilot. Both act as 'scanners' and both are capable of operating the guns if necessary. On a normal CSAR mission two PJs would be carried, and they have the expertise and know-how to operate the medical equipment carried on a rescue mission. Once in the rescue area the HH-60 may go directly to a survivor or may be told to 'hold' while the 'Sandys' clear the area. The retrieval mechanics depend on a number of factors, such as the casualty's condition, ground threats, air threats, terrain and weather. If threats are in the area, the PJs would be dropped and the helicopter would exit to a safe distance whilst they package up the survivor, calling in the 'Jolly' for a pick-up and fast exit. Alternatively, if the weather is deteriorating the aircraft may stay on the ground to avoid having to egress through a storm.

Specialised personnel are assigned to Air Force combat rescue units with responsibility for ground search, rescue and recovery. These PJs have skills in aircraft insertion/extraction methods, aerial gunnery, aerial scanning, scuba, surface team operations, land search/adverse terrain operations, emergency medical treatment, and survival, evasion, resistance and escape (SERE). Specialised pararescue teams possess the capability for advanced parachuting techniques, open-sea recovery operations, extended low-visibility or clandestine surface operations and high-altitude mountain recovery operations. During a rescue operation, the pararescue team leader will be the OSC for surface operations. PJs will carry various specially designed communications radios.

The HH-60G 'Pave Hawk' serves with a number of 'full time' and Air National Guard units. Two such examples are the 48th RQS and the 304th RQS. The 48th RQS are based at Holloman AFB and are part of the 49th FighterWing, and not only provide CSAR support to theWing's own assets but are prepared to move anywhere in the world at a moment's notice. The 304th RQS are based at Portland International Airport in Oregon and belong to the United States Air Force Reserve.

## MH-60G/K 'Pave Hawk'

The MH-60G's primary wartime missions are infiltration, exfiltration and resupply of special operations forces by day or night or in marginal weather. Other missions include combat search and rescue. The

MH-60G is equipped with an all-weather radar which enables the crew to avoid inclement weather. To extend their range, 'Pave Hawks' are equipped with a retractable in-flight refuelling probe and internal auxiliary fuel tanks. They are also equipped with a rescue hoist with a 200ft (60.7m) cable and 600lb (270kg) lift capacity. All MH-60Gs have an automatic flight control system to stabilise the aircraft in typical flight altitudes. They also have instrumentation and engine and rotor blade anti-ice systems for all-weather operation. The non-retractable undercarriage consists of two main landing gear units and a tail wheel. Aft sliding doors on each side of the troop and cargo compartment allow rapid loading and unloading. External loads can be carried on an 8,000lb (3,600kg) capacity cargo hook. 'Pave Hawks' are equipped with folding rotor blades and tail stabilator for shipboard operations and to ease air transportability. There are two crew-served 7.62mm miniguns mounted in the cabin windows, and two .50-calibre machine guns can be mounted in the cabin doors. The aircraft can be equipped with the external stores support system (ESSS) and can carry eight to ten troops. The MH-60K/Ls operated by the Army's 160th SOAR (A)—the 'Nightstalkers'—were one of the success stories of the desert war.

## MH-47 Chinook

The MH-47E will operate a 5.5hr covert mission scenario over a 300nm (556km) radius, at low level, by day or night, in adverse weather and over any type of terrain, and do so with a 90 per cent probability of success. The helicopters are operated by the 160th Special Operations Aviation Regiment (SOAR) (A) at Fort Campbell, Kentucky, and Hunter Army Airfield, Savannah, Georgia, and the 1/245th Aviation (SO) (A) Oklahoma Army National Guard (OKARNG) at Lexington, for long-range, covert infiltration/exfiltration of special operations forces.

The MH-47E's integrated avionics system (IAS) permits global communications and navigation, and the IAS is also the most advanced system of its kind ever installed in a US Army helicopter. The IAS includes forward-looking infra-red (FLIR) and multi-mode radar for nap-of-the-earth and low-level flight in conditions of extremely poor visibility and adverse weather. A contract was issued in December 1987 to provide for the development and flight-testing of a single MH-47E prototype and 25 production aircraft; a contract allowing for long-lead purchases and the induction of the first 25 production aircraft was awarded in June 1991.

The Army requires that the MH-47E and MH-60K avionics systems be common and interchangeable; thus, for example, the basic radios, mission computers and multifunction displays can be exchanged between an MH-47E and an MH-60K in a matter of minutes—a unique capability and one which means that missions conducted far from normal supply channels have a much higher probability of success. The MH-47E combines many proven Chinook systems and features, notably fuel tanks providing twice the capacity of the CH-47D and an in-flight refuelling system. MH-47Es have been remanufactured on the CH-47D production line, with most E-model systems installed during the final stages of completion.

### Vive la France

The US Air Force had the 'visible monopoly' on CSAR efforts during the Gulf War and no one seemed to pay much attention to a pair of French Aérospatiale SA 330 Puma helicopters from Escadron 1/67 'Pyrenees', based at Al Ahsa, a short distance from their Jaguar and Mirage colleagues. These rather unnoticed sand and brown camouflaged helicopters were part of COTAM, the French military transport command, and were tasked with search and rescue for the recovery of friendly pilots downed behind enemy lines. Whilst several US aircrew were rescued by AFSOC forces during the first weeks of 'Storm', French combat aircraft suffered no losses. However, in late February one of the French Pumas was given the task of recovering a US Navy pilot shot down in a heavily defended area of Kuwait. The rescue package of A-10 'Sandys' and F-15C RESCAP Eagles picked up the Puma off the Kuwaiti coast. The 'Hogs' then proceeded to escort the helicopter into the shoot-down area, where the pilot was quickly identified, picked up and flown back to Al Jubail air base. The SA 330 Puma is the standard transport helicopter for the French Army, and also serves in the medium-lift capacity with the RAF and other air arms.

### Firehawks: Sea SAR

HCS-5 is a Naval Air Reserve Squadron under the command of Commander Helicopter Wing Reserve, San Diego, California, and Naval Air Reserve Force, New Orleans, Louisiana. HCS-5, along with its sister squadron, HCS-4, remain the only Navy squadrons that perform both combat search and rescue (CSAR) and special warfare support (SPECWAR) for Special Warfare units such as the Navy SEAL (Sea/Air/Land) teams as their primary missions. Working from either forward-deployed bases or ships, 'Firehawks' HCS-5 helicopter detachments are ready at short notice to fly into hostile or enemy territory and seek out, locate and rescue downed aircrew. The unit flies the Sikorsky HH-60H Seahawk helicopter, which is especially suited for the CSAR mission. All HCS-5 pilots and aircrew are experienced at flying in complete darkness using NVGs and regularly train in all types of weather and over all types of terrain. The 'Firehawks' helicopters can act independently, flying in pairs or in concert with rescue escort (RESORT) aircraft such as Navy F/A-18 Hornets and F-14 Tomcats, Air Force A-10 Warthogs or Marine Corps AH-1 SeaCobras. Each HH-60 Seahawk is armed with two M-60 light machine guns, mounted on either side of the fuselage, and each aircrew member is armed with a CAR-15 automatic rifle.

Operating the Sikorsky HH-60H Seahawk, an aircraft first acquired by the Naval Air Reserve Force, HCS-5 can rapidly deploy four two-aircraft detachments to any location in the world, operating from ships as part of a naval task force or independently at remote shore-based sites. One of these detachments remains continuously on alert for deployment anywhere in the world within 72 hours. This capability was put to the test in December 1990 when HCS-5 deployed a two-aircraft detachment to Saudi Arabia in support of Operation 'Desert Storm'. While operating from tents at a remote desert airfield near the Iraqi border, HCS-5 provided 24-hour, seven-day-a-week CSAR coverage. During September 1994 HCS-5 was again tasked to forward-deploy, this time sending a detachment to Haiti in support of Operation 'Uphold Democracy'. Serving aboard the USS *Dwight D. Eisenhower* (CVN-69), *Vicksburg* (CG-69) and *Compte de Grasse* (CG-74), HCS-5's detachment provided total CSAR coverage. HCS-5 also continuously supports numerous carrier air wing and SEAL teams throughout the western United States, both on land and at sea, performing CSAR and SPECWAR missions.

HCS-5 was established on 2 October 1988 when the combat SAR mission of HC-9 and the SPECWAR support mission of HAL-5 were combined. Working under cover of darkness in hostile-threat environments, the 'Firehawks' perform those critical missions necessary fully to support deployed US forces. The HH-60H Sikorsky helicopter flown by HCS-5 is ideally suited to support CSAR and SPECWAR missions, especially during insertion and extraction. The 'Firehawks' can transport SPECWAR personnel to and from high-risk areas of operations under cover of darkness, and all the unit's pilots and aircrew are familiar with SPECWAR operational techniques and regularly train with Navy SEALS and Air Force Pararescue Jumpers (PJs) to hone inter-operable skills. These include regular exercises such as 'Desert Rescue', held annually at NAS Fallon, Nevada, and 'Cobra Gold', held annually in Thailand. Currently HCS-5 operates eight Sikorsky HH-60H Seahawk helicopters, and these aircraft were first acquired by the US Naval Reserve as a variant of the SH-60 family of Sikorsky helicopters. The HH-60H is optimised for night flight, with pilots wearing NVGs to 'see' in the dark. The running lights on the HH-60H are also modified for use with NVGs, allowing HCS-5 pilots to fly in tight formation in total darkness but remain invisible to the naked eye.

# 10

# CSAR for the 1990s: The Changing Battlefield

Operating over enemy territory has always been one of the most dangerous aspects of any pilot's service career, and over the modern battlefield this is made even more difficult by the plethora of sophisticated tracking, ECM, missile and location systems that are available throughout the world. Conducting any kind of mission in enemy territory now brings with it a constantly changing set of rules and threats, which immediately make CSAR one of the most demanding of all aerial functions.

The new long-range 'radar-invisible' aircraft such as the F-117 Nighthawk and the B-2 Spirit, designed to penetrate deep into hostile areas with little or no support, and with an unlimited range by virtue of in-flight refuelling, add to the problems of the rescue services. To balance the combat range of this type of aircraft, CSAR assets also need to match the 'stealth shooters" global reach, and to equate that with their own operating constrictions, which for rescue helicopters usually means working at low level and at relatively low speeds. If an airman has the misfortune to go down, he can be confidently assured that the enemy knows that his aircraft has been hit, the position of the strike and where to look for him. He will also know that unless the airman is seized quickly a CSAR mission will be mounted to recover him.

Captured military aircrew have never been such a valuable commodity, and have of late become something of a 'political football' to be bargained with. During the Gulf War few will forget the images in the media when downed airmen were paraded before the cameras in an attempt by the Iraqi government to influence public opinion at home and abroad. Even so, rather than having the desired effect, it only served to harden the resolve of the Coalition nations to bring the Iraqi leadership into line.

In order to counter some of these intrinsic disadvantages, considerable effort has been expended to ensure that modern aircrew receive intensive training in combat survival (CS) and escape and evasion (E&E) techniques. This instruction is designed to allow them to survive, get them away from the crash and allow time for a detailed CSAR mission to be planned and executed. The CSAR 'package' now involves large formations of fixed- and rotary-wing aircraft, which, depending on the area threat, will include escort/close air support fighters, tankers, command and control platforms, Special Operations helicopters and specialised Hercules, with crews specifically trained for long-range covert operations.

Detailed planning and the coordination between agencies are prerequisites for any modern CSAR operation, taking full advantage of all that technology has to offer, including detailed reconnaissance, either from satellites or 'high-tech' aircraft, and, time permitting, rehearsals in flight and mission simulators. The missions can also be 'viewed' in detail using systems such as SOFPARS or other interactive visual aids. Although CSAR missions can be tailored to meet the perceived threat environment, occasionally the risks to the rescuers can be too great, and in these instances downed aviators are required to use their E&E tactics. They will have been fully briefed on what to expect should they land in 'bad guy territory', as well as being forewarned of the terrain, climatic conditions and the likely location of enemy forces, and would be expected, if possible, to make their way to a pre-determined E&E lying-up/pick-up point (PUP), where either advance/special forces would have been inserted to receive them or they must await the arrival of a CSAR helicopter on a pre-selected day and time.

The pick-up will only then take place if the CSAR team can authenticate the identity of the aircrew, which usually involves a special code-word or signal. At night CSAR teams would use their NVGs and would be looking out for a signal from an IR 'Beta-Light' or Cyalume to flash out a code. Aerial refuelling, digital satellite communications, terrain-following radars, AWACS/C3 and dedicated SF teams who train together regularly for multi-agency recoveries all help reduce the risks and provide a realistic chance of recovering any downed aircrew.

### A Bitter European Conflict: Combat SAR over Bosnia

The Bosnian conflict brought home to the military the difficulties of recovering downed aircrew whilst they were operating over densely populated areas with no discernible 'front line' and the ever-present risk of landing right on top of an enemy position or amongst a hostile faction. Since the 1980s and the creation of the US Special Operations Forces, able to deal with combat rescue situations, many of duties concerning the recovery and rescue of downed NATO personnel has been passed into their hands, and so whenever a conflict looms AFSOC is placed on standby. However, not all rescues have been successful, and not all rescues have been AFSOC's immediate responsibility, as was demonstrated in the middle of 1995 near Banja Luka.

## The O'Grady Rescue: Freed by a TRAP

Capt Scott W. 'Zulu' O'Grady, an F-16C pilot from the 555th ('Triple Nickel') FS/31st FW based at Aviano in Italy, had the misfortune of being the first 'shoot-down' casualty of the United Nations' efforts to secure a lasting peace in troubled Bosnia. It was also the first time a NATO jet had been targeted by an SA-6 missile system. O'Grady spend six long days in the Bosnian countryside, not certain whether his radio beacon signal was being received and not knowing whether capture was imminent.

In the morning of 2 June 1995 O'Grady, together with his wingman Capt Bob Wright, was conducting one of the 75,000-plus Operation 'Deny Flight' sorties over Bosanski Petrovac in northern Bosnia, near the town of Banja Luka, reinforcing the UN exclusion zone set up to eliminate the use of hostile air power over the former Yugoslavia. Using the mission call-signs 'Basher 56' (O'Grady) and 'Basher 57' (Wright), the pair made several sweeps across their assigned area. During one of these patterns O'Grady's F-16C was targeted by a Bosnian Serb SA-6 SAM, which was then locked and launched from a stronghold to the south of Bihac.

Owing to a clandestine shift of many of the Bosnian Serb missile systems in the days preceding the event, the location of the missile battery had escaped the notice of NATO, and the Serbs carefully bided their time until a prime target came into their envelope and the opportunity was ripe for an ambush. Launched from directly below the aircraft, the SA-6 was able to hurtle up beneath the blind spot of the pilot and the underfuselage ECM pod, giving O'Grady barely a few seconds' warning of impact. The blast from the warhead cut the jet in half and created a huge fireball; however, through the inferno wingman Wright caught a glimpse of the cockpit section, still intact, before the plane plunged into cloud. Trying to suppress the horror of what he had witnessed, Wright 'called' the hit, marking O'Grady's position but being unable to tell if the pilot had managed to eject.

Miraculously, the front of the F-16 had held together long enough for O'Grady to grab the ejection lanyard between his legs ('the beautiful gold handle', as he was later to call it) and his seat exploded though the canopy into the 'clear blue' 26,000ft above the Bosnian forests. The blast seared O'Grady's face and neck, but the conscious pilot manually opened his parachute instead of waiting for the auto-release and sailed gently across the clear afternoon sky. He later commented that he seemed to be in the air a long while, and his trajectory took him over a main highway. He fell towards a crowd of watching Bosnian Serbs who were, he perceived, waiting to take him captive.

Landing in a grassy clearing, O'Grady shed his parachute swiftly, dashing into a clump of bushes, covering his face with mud and dirt and covering his ears with his green flying gloves so that no bare skin would be visible. His actions were well warranted, as within moments Serbs were swarming all over the area in a frenzied effort to locate him. Back at Aviano, and in the Pentagon, planners held little hope, thinking that the pilot had not survived the impact, or, if he had, that he would most certainly be captive.

Over the following days the Serbs continued their searches, sometimes coming within three feet of his position, beating the ground with their rifle butts, but throughout this O'Grady remained concealed on the frozen earth, moving at night to gather food and ranging out two miles from the spot where he landed. The terrain provided excellent cover, as the site was pockmarked with caves which had been used by the partisans in the Second World War to evade the Nazis. Freezing temperatures by night were complemented by heavy rain during the day, and the exhausted O'Grady quickly consumed his eight 4oz emergency water packs. He was, however, able to catch rain in Ziploc bags and even tried to squeeze water out of his sodden woolly socks, living off a diet of leaves, grass and ants!

Beneath his ejection seat O'Grady had a 29lb survival kit, which included a first aid bag, flares, radio batteries, a signal mirror, a compass, a whistle, water and a 9mm pistol. In his survival 'vest' was an 'evasion chart', a 3ft by 5ft waterproof linen map with cues concerning what food to find on the ground in Bosnia, and where to find it;

camouflage paint; another mirror; a second compass; a GPS receiver; and another first aid kit. Most important of all was his 28oz PRC-112 survival radio, a device not much larger than a personal stereo that could operate for up to seven hours on a single battery. The evasion chart could also be used to catch rain, to wrap clothing, as a splint or as a bandage to plug a wound. Early efforts by O'Grady to establish contact with friendly aircraft were thwarted by bad weather, which kept Allied planes grounded for days; but, undaunted, he searched for a site that would give him a high broadcast point, have sufficient camouflage and be large enough for a helicopter to land.

When the weather improved, NATO jets ranged out ceaselessly in the hope of getting a contact with him, with F-18 Hornets from VMA(AW)-533 clocking up the most search sorties. Although aircraft had reported intermittent transmission signals, it was not until five days after the shoot-down that the F-18s finally confirmed that they were receiving signals from O'Grady's beacon. Not knowing whether it was a Serb trick or the 'real thing', the Pentagon threw a massive intelligence net over the region, using CIA satellites to sweep the area continuously, hoping to photograph O'Grady on the ground, signals intelligence (sigint) aircraft to listen for messages and infra-red-equipped aircraft to detect body heat.

Early on the Thursday morning an F-16 flown by Capt Thomas 'T.O.' Hanford, also of the 555th, received direct contact from O'Grady during a sweep of the area. Hearing the familiar sound of the F-16, and listening intently to the SAR frequency, he transmitted: 'Basher 52 reads you.' It was O'Grady's first voice contact: 'I'm alive—help.' Hanford then asked him to identify the unit with which he served in Korea, authenticating the result and notifying the relieved and excited personnel at Aviano. He then peeled away to refuel over the Adriatic. He later recalled: 'It's hard to fly a plane with tears coming down your face.' Within minutes VMA(AW)-533 launched their alert aircraft to aid the recovery. The first Hornet to arrive on station was flown by Capt David Ehlert, who made a low, fast run over O'Grady's position—a sort of 'wake-up call' to let him know that things were happening. Moments later a second F-18 under the control of Capt Will 'Wheels' Thomas, an old friend of O'Grady's, overflew the site and made direct radio contact: 'Hey, Zulu, do ya hear me? This is Wheels.' He obtained accurate coordinates of O'Grady's position and left the area so as not to give away the location to any watching Serbs . . .

## US Marine Corps TRAP Rescue

TRAP is the United States Marine Corps acronym for their rescue system, translating to Tactical Recovery of Aircraft and Personnel. The main differences between the Air Force's 'Combat SAR' and TRAP is that the Air Force operates with as few personnel and aircraft as possible and is unable to recover any 'hardware', whereas for TRAP the function is to not only rescue the aircrew but also, where possible, to retrieve the machinery. A typical TRAP recovery team would comprise:

**Air assets:** two AH-1W Super Cobras; two CH-53E Sea Stallions; four AV-8B Harrier jets (CAP patrol); and an armada of joint assets such as AWACS, F-16s and A-10s which are 'nice to have along if available'.

**Ground Assets:** Security Element (approximately 15 Marines); and Search Element (approximately 15 Marines).

A TRAP team is designed to penetrate some 100nm into enemy territory in order to rescue a downed pilot, aircrew or any allied or UN personnel. The team are trained to defend against most modern surface-to-air weapon systems, and the ground element can defend against a small unit attack. Flying at tree-top level, the Cobras escort the CH-53s until they are about ten miles from the targeted position, when the smaller helicopters will push ahead to locate, identify and secure the area. They will then call in the CH-53s for the pick-up and escort them back to the ship via an extraction route. Waiting on the deck of the assault ship is another TRAP team of greater assets and strength, standing by to assist if needed.

Details of O'Grady's position were sent to Col Martin Berndt, commander of the 24th Marine Expeditionary Unit aboard the USS *Kearsarge*, a Marines helicopter carrier sailing in the Adriatic. Berndt was convinced that a rescue was viable and was given the immediate go-ahead from the Pentagon to execute a multi-agency recovery of the airman, with whatever means were at his disposal. Shortly after 3 a.m. Brendt called in 51 Marines, including ten helicopter crews, who were sleeping below. The Marines established their TRAP team, which consisted of two AH-1W SuperCobra gunships flown by flight leader Maj Scott 'Mick' Mykleby and co-pilot Capt Ian 'Blondie' Walsh and wingman Major Nick 'Festus' Hall with co-pilot Capt Jim 'Jinx' Jenkins; two AV-8B Harrier jump-jets; and two CH-53 Super Stallions which were to be used for the actual pick-up. These assets were to be joined by a pair of Navy E-A6B Prowler and USAF EF-111A jamming aircraft, a brace of Marine Corps F-18C/D Hornets to provide top cover and a pair of USAF A-10 Warthog 'CAS-busters'—just in case. This TRAP team was duplicated in case of emergency, and the aerial armada of some 40 aircraft came under the choreography of an orbiting AWACS platform.

After leaving the ship, the TRAP helicopters had to circle over the Adriatic for 45 minutes to allow the rest of the package to arrive on station, either from other carriers or from Aviano. When the 'push' authorization came from AWACS, the mission got under way in a calm, professional yet expectant manner. Within moments the aircraft were into Serb territory, with the package calling 'feet dry' as they crossed the coast. For the next 50 minutes the helicopters flitted over pine forests at 200ft until, around 6.35 a.m., they reached O'Grady's marked position.

As they made their approach, the pilots radioed O'Grady, authenticated his identity and then were talked on to his position by O'Grady himself. Once they had a rough position they requested that he 'pop' smoke in order to pinpoint his exact location on the hillside. As O'Grady's red smoke grenade quickly dissipated in the wind and bad weather, the Dash-2 Cobra hovered overhead briefly to drop a yellow smoke grenade in order to provide guidance for the '53s', which were now on their way in. The first CH-53, flown by Maj William Tarbutton, flared in his aircraft to touch-down, avoiding a crude pine fence strung with barbed wire just at the edge of the site. Immediately the rear ramp went down and twenty Marines poured out and set up a security perimeter, whilst the two SuperCobras trawled for any Serb opposition. Overhead the other aircraft of the team circled, waiting to be called in if needed. The second CH-53, flown by Capt Paul A. Fortunato and his co-pilot Capt James M. Wright, and carrying Berndt, 'removed' part of the barbed wire fence on its ingress, but the crews were delighted to see O'Grady running towards them, 9mm pistol in hand. The Stallion's side door was opened and O'Grady tumbled across the threshold, relinquishing his 9mm to the crew and pulling on a Gore-Tex parka and crash helmet. The Marines re-boarded their helicopter and strapped in and the aircraft took off. The event had taken just 8½ minutes.

Sgt-Maj Angelo Castro strapped O'Grady into his seat whilst the grateful airman repeatedly thanked his saviours. Shivering, dehydrated and soaking wet, he drank almost an entire canteen of water and ate four bites of a chicken stew MRE (Meal Ready to Eat) before uncontrollable shivering set in. He was quickly enveloped in thermal blankets and a pair of young Marines were detailed to protect him from the blast whipping in from the gun portals. At 12.49 a.m. EST, just as O'Grady was being whisked away, a call was made to President Bill Clinton, who had been monitoring the proceedings. A simple two word message said it all: 'Got him!'

However, the celebrations may have been somewhat premature. During the ingress to O'Grady's position the helicopters travelled at around 120mph, but on the way back to *Kearsarge* they let rip at 170mph, skimming the tree-tops in the hope of avoiding any Serb gunners and missile batteries below. For the first third the 87-mile home run was smooth, but when the helicopters entered a shallow valley three shoulder-launched SA-7 SAMs flew past, followed by volleys of small-arms and anti-aircraft fire, many of these rounds piercing the CH-53s.

Everyone on board leapt around as the shells tore into the rear cabins. Aboard Brendt's Sea Stallion some rounds smashed communications gear whilst others passed straight through. One bounced off the back of Angelo Castro's flak jacket, and the Marine behind him picked the slug up off the floor and handed it to the startled sergeant major, who handed the bullet back to the Marine with the comment, 'No big deal.' The pilots began violently rocking the helicopters from side to side, hugging the ground as close as they dared and occasionally executing stomach-wrenching 'pop-ups' to clear dangerous power lines. Inside the helicopters lifejackets, ammunition boxes and Marines were being pitched around. O'Grady clenched his teeth as the wild zig-zag ride continued. As one crew member later admitted, 'It was a terrifying ride . . . the roughest helicopter trip I've ever been on.' Suddenly they were clear. Berndt looked back from the cockpit to see how O'Grady was coping. A grin and a 'thumbs up' said it all.

Nine New River Marines received the Air Medal with a Combat 'V' for their heroic efforts in the rescue of Capt Scott O'Grady during the June TRAP mission in Bosnia. These included Maj William R. Tarbutton, the TRAP mission commander, and his co-pilot, Capt Paul D. Oldenburg; the pilots of the two CH-53E Super Stallions and two AH-1W SuperCobras, Capt Ian Walsh, Maj Scott C. Mykleby, Capt Jim Jenkins and Maj Nicholas J. Hall; and four AV-8B Harrier pilots.

'Almost any Marine unit that trains hard like this could perform this mission. In fact, it's a testimony to the whole squadron that the mission was carried out successfully. This is a perfect example of the types of things that the Marine Corps does and the types of things we'll continue to do in the future,' commented a proud Maj-Gen John E. Rhodes, Commanding General, 2nd Marine AircraftWing, MCAS Cherry Point.

Capt Ian 'Blondie' Walsh, the lead SuperCobra pilot for the O'Grady rescue, gave his personal account of the events: 'At 0300 a.m. in the morning of June 8th, my room-mates woke me, shouting, "Get moving 'Blondie'—you have a go!" When I asked what they meant they said I had missed the ship's loudspeaker announcement calling in the TRAP Determination Team to briefing. I then remembered hearing the call, which I thought was in my dreams, so I splashed some water on my face, jumped into my flight suit, grabbed my holster and dashed to the squadron ready room to meet with the other eleven pilots selected as the primary aircrew for this operation.

'The previous six days that we had spent on 6-hour alert status had been filled with conflicting news and intelligence reports regarding Captain Scott O'Grady and his situation. The more time that passed, the more skeptical I became of the pilot's survival. Nevertheless, no news was good news, and each day we conducted intelligence briefs, started and checked our fully armed aircraft and rehearsed our TRAP briefs. The only element missing was Captain O'Grady's actual location. As I ran into the ready room that morning I noticed the large red word 'LOCATION' written on the grease board followed by a six-digit grid. Before I could relax I was in my full flight gear, on the flight deck, strapped into my Cobra attack helicopter and waiting for my co-pilot to show up with any last-minute information. As I sat in the cockpit and watched the sun creep over the calm ocean's razor-line horizon, I kept thinking how this whole alert would be turned off any minute, for we had been told when we arrived in the Adriatic that there were other Special Operations forces in theater who were considered the primary option for any type of search and rescue mission.

'Before I could ask any more questions I was airborne, heading east and test-firing my weapons into the water. The ingress route had been carefully selected; we had to weave our way around two known SA-6 sites and other AAA gun positions. We were moving at 120 knots (135mph) between 200 and 300 feet above the ground as we crossed the outer islands and entered the first mountain range. I was amazed at how beautiful the countryside looked with its thick forests, rich green meadows and quaint, small villages. Yet, upon closer examination, I also noticed how all the windows and doors of the old stone buildings were blown out, and, even more puzzling, how the villages were absent of people. Granted, it was now about 0530 in the morning and everyone was probably sleeping or hiding—which was a definite advantage. Wires were everywhere, and even with the sun directly in our eyes I was somewhat relieved we were conducting this operation during daylight instead of at night, which is preferred due to the protective cover of darkness.

Within minutes we were flying even lower TERF (terrain following) profiles between 5,000-foot mountains. The route was approximately 90 miles through the southern portion of Croatia and then north-east into the heart of Bosnia. After the first set of mountains we encountered weather problems. There was a thick, low, overcast layer of ground fog in each valley which we had to cross. Our helicopter flight looked like four sharks as our fuselages and rotor blades sliced in and out of the surface of the fog. The upper layers of overcast clouds were between 5,000 and 6,000 feet right around the tops of the mountains. As we drove over one ridge line we would dash across the top of another foggy floor base. With hindsight, we believed this fog prevented us from receiving any ground fire by AAA gun pieces or small arms, as the enemy simply could not see us as we flashed past in the haze.

'We maneuvered to each checkpoint along our route until approximately 30 miles from O'Grady's believed location. "Magic", the Air Force AWACS, and its controllers circling high above picked us up on its radar and began giving us headings and a distance countdown to the last known position of the pilot. From this point we could see endless overcast layers of fog to the east with light rain showers beginning all around us. I began thinking about the plausibility of punching below the fog in order to find the pilot. At ten miles from the target site, our section of Cobra gunships, call sign "Bolt", increased power and pushed ahead of the pair of CH-53E Super Stallion transport helicopters to positively identify the pilot and make sure the zone and its surroundings were safe. We then switched to Captain O'Grady's survivor frequency on our radio and at five miles started calling for him by "Basher 52", his call-sign. I soon heard in response a weak and garbled tone: "Bolt, this is Basher 52." My co-pilot then asked O'Grady two quick questions from his personal information sheet. You could hear his voice become stronger and more anxious with each word as we closed in on his location. This was an incredible feeling, as I honestly thought after all this time that we may have been flying into an ambush, or perhaps would not find him! Once I heard his voice, however, I could tell it sounded like someone who had been evading and surviving for six days and nights.

'We called again as we approached three miles and climbed up the side of a small, round-topped mountain peak. "Basher" then said he could hear us, and told us to head south-east. I immediately banked hard right and told him to talk us into his position. He eagerly gave us another call to head south and we told him to "pop smoke". As we dived over the ridge line running down from the mountain top I was surprised at how high the fog layer had traveled up the mountainside. He said he could hear us circling and after a couple of seconds we saw red smoke filtering up through the fog. I called "I've gotcha Basher," and we told our wingman to stay "padlocked" (maintain sight on the smoke) and instructed the transport helicopters, which were holding ten miles away, to go "buster" (get here as fast as you can).

'My next thought was that the transports would have to hover and use ropes to extract him as the only hole I could see through the fog had dense, tall, pine trees below. I also started to worry about how awful it would be if we had to leave him here after finding him because the fog and terrain might prevent us from finding a suitable landing zone for the large rescue helicopters. However, I quickly dismissed this thought. The fog layer slowly covered the hole back up as "Basher" informed us he had heard small-arms fire and troop movement south of the area the night before. As I peeled around the hilltop again I searched south and spotted a dirt road winding up the mountain, over the top of the ridge line and back down into the fog towards his position. There were several old barns and shacks along the road but no approaching vehicles or people The transport helicopters sighted us and we directed them to "Basher"'s position. My Cobra wingman then hovered overhead the fog bank where the red smoke had dissipated and threw out a yellow smoke grenade to assist CH-53 transports into position for the final phase of the pick-up.

'The Stallions circled briefly as I saw them sight the yellow smoke, kick their noses up to level off and disappear as they descended into the fog. As I pushed overhead I saw that both transports had found a tight little field. They had pruned some bushes on the way down but were successfully in the zone. The longer the Marines and transports were on the ground the more uncomfortable I became. My co-pilot felt the same. We decided to pull our Harrier jet friends, call-sign "Boomer", in over our position just in case we needed the extra fire support. Captain O'Grady came on the radio again and yelled, "I have the 53s in sight!" We told him to move towards them. He responded, "I'm moving as fast as I can." "No kidding," I thought to myself; I would too!

'Suddenly I saw O'Grady jump from the tree line wearing his fluorescent orange hat from his survival gear which immediately blew away as he approached the rotor wash of the large transports. The lead transport radioed that his wingman had the pilot and all he was waiting for were the remaining Marines to withdraw from the zone. After serious urging from the Cobras, the transports finally lifted and were rolling back over the ridge line. From the time the transports had landed and taken off seemed like an eternity, yet it was only eight and a half minutes. As we pushed from the zone, "Magic" gave us a steer of 230 degrees back towards "feet wet", the safety of the Adriatic Sea.

'The next thought running through my mind—and each pilot's, I later found out—was not only the satisfaction of locating and extracting the pilot, but knowing the most dangerous part was still ahead. The morning ground fog had slowly risen and joined the bottom portion of the 5,000 to 6,000-foot overcast layer. As a result, not only were the enemy towns and villages exposed, which we had originally flown over while protected by the fog, but the new interlocking fog bank across the mountains had completely covered every pass. This time we had no choice but to push below the fog and clouds, increase to full power, and maneuver as low and as fast as we could. Even though we were now flying the way helicopter pilots like to fly, low and fast, our first problem occurred at the end of the first valley.

'We were rapidly approaching the next mountain range with no way out, for the clouds and fog trapped us in on all sides. As we reached the mountains the lead transport helicopter called he was "pulling up". Before anything else was said I saw both transports pull 30 degrees back-stick and shoot into the clouds. I pulled nose high on my Cobra as well, and started climbing as fast as she could go. At roughly 5,500 feet we broke out into daylight, at which point I nervously looked down to my left through a tiny hole in the clouds and saw the tops of pine trees below. We had just climbed up the side of a 5,000-foot mountain while in the clouds—the way helicopter pilots would rather not fly!

'We re-joined on top of the cloud deck and continued to press westward. As soon as we found an opening we punched back down through the clouds at maximum speed. Instinctively, we were down in the TERF mode again, maneuvering at 50 feet and below, and as fast as possible, 160 knots (175mph). We had to continually "bunt and roll"— climb up and over power lines, some as high as 300 feet. As we jumped the last major mountain ridge line and descended into a long, open valley the first enemy SAM launch happened; this was so unexpected that all I saw was the smoke trail pass from left to right behind my tail. I then remember looking up to the right at the transports and seeing what looked exactly like an artillery explosion hitting the dirt just below them. From the dust cloud came another spiralling missile's smoke trail across the whole flight. We had already called "SAM in the air! SAM in the air!" as we reactively triggered the fiercely burning decoy flares from each aircraft and began evasive maneuvers, hard-banking turns and hugging the ground as low as possible. I remember descending so low that I had to pull up to pop over houses.

'The transports then started calling out over the radio that they were taking "small arms fire" and "AAA" as they banked hard left, but my wingman and I could not attain a positive location on the guns as the enemy ground fire was completely sporadic. As we passed over a small outlying airfield my wingman called over the radio that they were also receiving AAA gun fire. My buddy Jim "Jinx" Jenkins, flying the other Cobra, said he could actually feel the *thud, thud, thud* of the double-barrel AAA gun before he looked right and saw the muzzle flashes and the bullets, which he later described as huge "orange baseballs" passing over him.

'The last shallow ridge line hid a narrow placid lake which we immediately descended over and flew across, just above the surface. As we skimmed the top, I remember looking out and behind and seeing the four rotor wash trails from our aircraft along the mirror surface of the water. The open ocean was just ahead—the safe zone. In minutes we were out over the Adriatic, racing towards our mother ship. Once on deck, de-armed and shut down, with Captain O'Grady safe in our medical facility, I noticed the crowd. I think the whole ship was top-side waiting for our return. What an amazing feeling. The Harriers landed behind the helicopters and after a bit of brow-wiping and handshaking we made our way down to the squadron ready room—job well done.'

### Profile: Captain Ian 'Blondie' Walsh

Capt Ian Walsh was born in Providence, Rhode Island, in 1966 and entered Naval Flight School in Pensacola, Florida, in 1990, graduating with Distinction from Advanced Flight Training. Subsequently he was designated a Naval Aviator in October of 1991 and despatched for training in the AH-1W SuperCobra attack helicopter, and was duly assigned to HMLA-269 ('The Gunrunners') at Marine Corps Air Station New River in Jacksonville, North Carolina, in 1992. In August 1993 he embarked aboard the amphibious assault ship USS *Guadalcanal* for his first Mediterranean cruise with the 'Golden Eagles' of HMM-162. Along with his squadron, he participated in Operations 'Deny Flight' and 'Provide Promise' in the Adriatic Sea and 'Restore Hope' and 'Unosom II' in Somalia. He was promoted to Captain, and his second deployment was with the 'Black Knights' of HMM-264 as part of a Special Purpose Marine Air Ground Task Force sent to Haiti. His third deployment brought him back to the Mediterranean and Bosnia-Herzegovina. During this period, as described, Ian flew as the lead Cobra pilot in the rescue mission for USAF pilot Scott O'Grady.

Not as fortunate as O'Grady were the crew of a French Mirage 2000, who also fell victim to a SAM near the town of Pale. Despite a vigorous campaign to locate the position of the two airmen, including constant sorties by MH-53s, nothing was heard from them until it was later announced that, despite the very best efforts of all the in-theatre rescue services, with all their sophisticated kit, they had been captured. Thankfully, they were alive and well. This serves to remind us all that 'who arrives first on the scene gets the spoils'.

### US Navy and Marine Corps CH-53E and MH-53E

Sikorsky H-53 series helicopters combine power and versatility like nothing else in the sky. They are at home in searing desert heat, arctic cold and everything in between. They fly a gamut of missions, including heavy-lift operations, military transport, search and rescue, vertical replenishment, vertical onboard delivery, airborne mine countermeasures, advanced early warning, minesweeping and the delivery of humanitarian aid and disaster relief. Powered by three 4,380shp General Electric T64-GE-416 engines, the CH-53E Super Stallion and MH-53E Sea Dragon can carry 16 tons of supplies, cargo, vehicles, artillery and troops for 50nm. They operate at cruising speeds of 170kts, and, with air-to-air refuelling, H-53E series helicopters have unlimited range. Sikorsky are currently developing an installation kit to put the 4,750shp T64-GE-419 turboshaft in the MH-53E, and cockpit upgrades are under way for both the Marine CH-53E heavy-lifter and Navy MH-53E minesweeper.

## Marine Corps Bell AH-1W SuperCobra

The AH-1W is the Marine Corps' 'ultimate gunship'. It began life as the AH-1T+, and subsequently 96 new-build aircraft were ordered, around 140 currently remaining in service. The AH-1W is able to carry BGM TOW and Hellfire missiles at the same time, as well as 2.75in rocket pods, Maverick missiles and Sidewinder AAMs in addition to its turret-mounted M197 cannon.

## Exercising Combat SAR

Training for CSAR is a continuing process, and the United States conducts many joint-service exercises to mould its rescue and recovery assets into a fluid unit. One such exercise was conducted in early 1998 from a Marine Corps base camp at Okinawa, Japan. HMLA-369 provided two of its AH-1W SuperCobra attack helicopters to assist the USAF's 33rd Rescue Squadron in a combat rescue mission, with A-10 'Hogs' also on hand to provide close air support as necessary. During the exercise a brace of HH-60 'Pave Hawk' helicopters were sent to locate and retrieve a 'downed' F-16 pilot in enemy territory, the Cobras providing integral fire support. On reaching the landing zone, the pilot was located by two PJs who 'fast-roped' to the ground and stabilised the casualty, placing him on a stretcher for recovery. Simulated enemy fire was suppressed by the Cobras as the 'Pave Hawk' took on board the injured airman, whilst the second HH-60 hovered nearby in case of an emergency and the A-10s flew a 'racetrack' pattern overhead.

## 'International Rescue'
Of necessity, military operators the world over have search and rescue units created within their ranks. However, because of budgetary constraints, and the need to employ a credible service to aid in civilian rescues, most of these recovery assets serve a dual purpose, with both aspects in their 'job description'. For the most part the United States is unique in having a complete force solely dedicated to recovering downed airmen using specialised aircraft and techniques. That is not to say that the other countries do not have the same capabilities, but their employment is narrower, and orientated to 'in-country' requirements. Most of the nations of the world use some helicopter or other aircraft for SAR, and listed here are just a few examples to show the vast array of 'talent' available to the civilian or military 'rescuee'.

In Great Britain, both the Royal Navy and the Royal Air Force have dedicated search and rescue units, both now operating the Westland Sea King helicopter and providing military and civilian recovery services around the coastline and inland. Since the 1982 South Atlantic conflict with Argentina, the RAF has a detachment in the Falkland Islands also.

**Royal Navy Rescue.** 771 Naval Air Squadron (motto: 'Non Nobis Solum'—'Not unto Us Alone') is based at Royal Naval Air Station Culdrose (HMS *Seahawk*), near Helston in Cornwall. Tasked primarily with military and civilian search and rescue, the Squadron's area of responsibility includes Cornwall, the Isles of Scilly, the western English Channel and the South-West Approaches. Operating the Westland Sea King Mk 5 SAR helicopter, 771 NAS has averaged more than 220 SAR missions every year for the past ten years. Its missions are as varied as they are far-reaching.

The Aeronautical Rescue Coordination Centre (ARCC) at Kinloss in Scotland issues both civil and military tasking. Local tasking comes from the Maritime Rescue Coordination Centre (MRCC) in Falmouth, while local military emergencies may be alerted by the Air Traffic Control at RNAS Culdrose. 771 maintains a fifteen-minute alert status from sunrise to 30 minutes after sunset and 45 minutes at night. In most cases, crews are airborne in less than five minutes from notification. Should an aircraft be scrambled away from the local area, a further aircraft and crew will be brought to immediate readiness to provide SAR cover for military aircraft operating from Culdrose. The Squadron consists of twelve pilots, three observers, seven winchmen, three SAR divers and a team of 60 engineering personnel. A typical SAR crew has two pilots, an observer, a winchman and an SAR diver.

In addition the Air Station Medical Centre provides expertise in the form of a doctor or medical orderly on 30 minutes' call to join SAR missions. The diver is unique to Royal Navy SAR. He is able to move swiftly into action by jumping from the helicopter and providing independent surface and sub-surface rescues in the open sea. Squadron aircraft are maintained to a high standard by dedicated maintenance personnel who run watch routines to ensure round-the-clock engineering cover. The Squadron has an additional function, which is the training of Royal Navy and Royal Marine aircrewmen in winching, vessel transfers, load-lifting and confined-area operations before they are posted to front-line units.

The hornets on the Squadron's crest originate from the unit's early days when, among other aircraft, it flew the De Havilland Sea Hornet. In addition, the Squadron long ago adopted the ace of clubs as a logo, and this is proudly displayed on the nose and sides of its aircraft. Since the Squadron's arrival in the South-West, the distinctive red and grey livery of its helicopters has become a familiar and welcome sight around the Cornish coast. In 1945 it received the Hoverfly helicopter, making 771 the first naval air squadron to operate helicopters. Disbanded in 1947, the Squadron re-formed in 1961 at RNAS Portland as a helicopter trials squadron for the Whirlwind and Wasp.

Early tasks included pioneering techniques now commonplace among many SAR squadrons—the free diver drop, the hi-line transfer and helicopter in-flight refuelling. 771 assumed a dedicated SAR role with the introduction of the Whirlwind HAR.3 and in 1974 moved to its present home at Culdrose. The Whirlwind was soon replaced by the Wessex Mk 1; later, in 1979, came the twin turbine-powered Wessex Mk 5. In 1988 the ageing Wessex was replaced by the Westland Sea King Mk 5. With this helicopter's greater lifting capacity, longer range and improved avionics, the Squadron then assumed a long-range, day/night, all-weather SAR capability. The Sea King also serves aboard Royal Navy aircraft carriers in the plane-guard role, being on hand to recover any errant Sea Harrier or helicopter crew that have the misfortune to jettison their aircraft or need to be recovered following combat damage or mechanical failure over the sea.

**Royal Air Force Rescue.** The backbone of the RAF's rescue capabilities for nearly two decades was the Wessex HAR.3, which replaced the Whirlwind as the service's primary recovery vehicle. The bright yellow Wessex was operated by two squadrons, Nos 22 and 202, which were dispersed into flights located around the United Kingdom. The Wessex itself has now been superseded by the Sea King HAR.3A, also instantly recognised by its high-visibility yellow colour scheme, in all rescue duties in Britain. As mentioned, the Sea King also serves in the Falkland Islands, where it has adopted a 'tactical' overall Dark Sea Grey colour scheme rather than that yellow of its British-based counterparts.

The RAF's Search and Rescue Training Unit, SARTU, is situated at RAF Valley, beside the Irish Sea on the island of Anglsey in North Wales, where it is co-located with 'C' Flight of No 22 Squadron. Until 1997 the venerable Wessex was used by both, normally five of the type belonging to SARTU, and two with No 22. These aircraft have now been replaced by the more capable Sea King HAR. 3, two in the active SAR role, whilst as part of the newly established Defence Helicopter Flying School (DHFS) based at RAF Shawbury, three Bell 412 Griffons now undertake the actual SARTU training tasks at Valley. As already noted, No 22 Squadron itself is spread into a number of flights around the country, and SARTU undertakes all the crew training for both No 22 and No 202 Squadrons.

The primary role of the RAF's search and rescue helicopters is to provide assistance to aircrew in trouble, but the majority of their call-outs are to save civilian lives. In an average year they will be called out on over 170 occasions. A SAR helicopter is ready to go 24 hours a day, 365 days a year. During daylight hours its response time is set at 15 minutes' readiness, stretching to an hour at night, though in fact

---

### Bell 412 Griffon

The 412 Griffon is a development of the famous UH-1 'Huey' helicopter. The cabin can accommodate up to twelve people, plus the two pilots, and the helicopter is powered by the Pratt & Whitney Canada PT6T-3B-1 Turbo Twin-Pac, which comprises two 900shp turboshaft engines. The SARTU aircraft are detached from the DHFS at Shawbury to train *ab initio* pilots and aircrewmen in SAR skills as part of their helicopter training course, and all potential rotary flyers attend this facet of their training.

*Specifications:* Length 56ft (17.07m); rotor diameter 46ft (14.02m); maximum speed 161mph (259kph); first based at Valley 1997.

## Westland Wessex HAR.3

In the Westland Wessex the engines slopes diagonally upwards from the air intake towards the pilot's cabin. Drive is sent to the main rotor assembly above the passenger area, where the gearbox is fixed to the aircraft by just four bolts. A long shaft runs directly from the gearbox to the tail rotor. The passenger cabin is capable of holding up to fifteen survivors with a low fuel state and the Wessex's crew comprises a pilot, a navigator/winch operator and a winchman. The pilots sit high up above the engines and set forward from the passenger cabin. Instrumentation has been upgraded to allow the use of NVGs, improving the aircraft's ability to work in arduous conditions.

Having navigated to the scene of the rescue, the winch operator assists the winchman as he is lowered down to the scene, relaying instructions to the pilot. The helicopter is often asked to hover in high winds over the sea, or in vicious downdraughts close to mountain sides. SAR training takes place most days in and around the base, and of course in the nearby mountains. The winch on the starboard side of the aircraft is able to swing out above the side door, and can be extended to 300ft, and one of the ground crew's tasks after it has been used is to pull the entire length out horizontally on the pan and rewind it, washing down the cable to remove salt water. As the cable is wound out, a reinforced glove is worn by a technician, wiping the cable with a rag. On the way back in again the cable is lubricated with PX-24 to help protect it.

The Wessex's tail unit is hinged to allow the aircraft to take up less hangar space. A failure in this component was discovered to be the cause of a tragic accident to befall one of Valley's helicopters. On 12 August 1993, while flying over Snowdonia, Wessex XR524 suffered a complete tail rotor failure. The pilot managed to avoid a nearby town before ditching the aircraft into a lake, Llyn Padarn. Sadly, of the seven on board, three lost their lives and the others were seriously injured.

The badge of No 22 Squadron comprises the Greek character *pi* over a Maltese Cross. This recalls the unit's time in Malta, where the badge was designed, and the *pi* recalls the time when No 22 Squadron regularly flew over the 7th Wing HQ, thus giving 22 over 7 = *pi*! At the time of writing a few Wessex helicopters remain in RAF service with No 84 Squadron based in Cyprus in the SAR and support roles.

*Specifications:* Length 48ft 4½in (14.74m); rotor diameter 56ft (17.07m); maximum speed 137mph (220kph); range 300nm (556km); maximum ceiling 13,500ft (4,115m).

the response time would usually be much swifter. No 22 Squadron's motto is '22 Rescue You'.

For short-range operations Sweden utilises the Eurocopter BO 105 (locally designated Hkp 9B) in the SAR role fitted with emergency flotation gear on its skids. For long-range operations the Swedish capability was increased with the delivery of twelve Aérospatiale AS 332s (Hkp 10), replacing the older Vertol 107s serving with F15 and F21. The service also uses its hard-working Bell Iroquois Hkp 3Bs for 'local' SAR.

Amongst the most colourful of the rescue helicopters are the Kawasaki KV-107s and the CH-113 Labradors operated by the Japanese Air Self-Defence Force and the Canadian Defence Forces/Forces

# Westland Sea King HAR.3

The Westland Sea King is product of GKN Westland, and a development of the Sikorsky S-61, which originated in the late 1950s. Westland initially developed the S-61 as an anti-submarine warfare helicopter (HAS) for the Royal Navy. However, the Sea King has also been developed as an operational search and rescue helicopter, the role prefix 'HAR' denoting Helicopter Search and Rescue. The Westland Sea King has been in service for more than 25 years; worldwide, more than 300 Sea Kings are in service and have saved thousands of lives in search and rescue, disaster relief and other humanitarian missions.

Westland were awarded a contract in 1995 to build three new Mk 3A search and rescue helicopters and to upgrade the existing Royal Air Force Mk 3 fleet to Mk 3A standards. The new systems included a lightweight ARI 5955/2 radar from Racal, a Racal RNAV-2 navigation system, Racal Doppler 91, an STR2000 Global Positioning System from Cossor, Bendix/King KDM 706A distance measuring equipment, a Bendix/King KDF 806 direction-finder, night vision goggles-compatible lighting and a main gear box emergency lubrication system, ELS. The AFCS Mk 31 aircraft flight control system installed in the Sea King Mk 3 was replaced by the AFCS SN500 developed by Smiths Industries Newmark. The SN500 consists of a duplex analogue ASE auto-stabiliser and a digital autopilot together with a set of yaw rate gyroscopes, accelerometers and a pilot's control unit. The automatic flight control system provides duplex stabilisation, attitude and heading hold, fly-through manoeuvring, automatic trimming, barometric altitude hold, airspeed hold, heading acquisition, area navigation (R-nav), radar altitude hold, transition down, hover with hover trim, transition up and overfly.

With the helicopter configured in the search and rescue role, the cabin can accommodate up to 22 survivors or nine stretchers for injured personnel and two medical officers, with the cockpit and cabin areas being equipped with ventilation and heating. On the top centre line of the fuselage spine is a rounded fairing which houses the radar, either the ARI5955 developed by Thomson Thorn or the RDR-1500B by Bendix King. The Sea King HAR.3 is powered by two Rolls-Royce H1400-1 Gnome turboshaft engines rated at 1,660shp and has a crew of four. The winch operator can fly the aircraft when hovering, enabling him or her to position the rescue harness with great accuracy. The Norwegian Air Force operates a dedicated SAR Sea King which is also equipped with an RDR-1300C nose radar developed by Bendix King.

*Specifications:* Length 55ft 9¾in (17.00m); rotor diameter 62ft (18.90m); maximum speed 143mph (230kph); range 280nm (519km).

Armées Canadiennes respectively. The KV-107s serve alongside a number of Bell UH-1Hs with the JSADF's rescue wing at Iruma and with the 11th Kokutai at Shimofusa, and are painted in a garish orange, yellow, black, white and red scheme. The JASDF also operate the Mitsubishi-Sikorsky S-61AH Sea King for its on-base Kyunan Hikotai (SAR Flight). The Canadian CH-113s are used in the local SAR role, again carrying a high-visibility yellow and red colour scheme, partnering the mountain rescue tasks of the DHC-5 Buffalo and, until recently, the Iroquois and Twin Otter. Two versions of the aircraft entered service in 1963, the Labrador, used by the Air Force for search and rescue, and the Voyageur, used by the Army for support of troops in the field. In the mid-1970s the Voyageurs were transferred to the Air Force and all were eventually modified to the current search and rescue configuration. This aircraft incorporates such features as a 6,400lb fuel capacity, for relatively long-range helicopter search and rescue operations; a 10,000lb cargo hook for external loads; a rear ramp for easy loading; a watertight hull for water landings; a rescue hoist; and special equipment for the rescue and care of survivors, including a rescue sling, 'Billy Pugh' net and Stokes Litter.

The US Marine Corps also utilises the CH-46D Sea Knight for local SAR work at MCAS Beaufort, Cherry Point, Iwakuni and Kaneohe Bay. Remaining with the United States, Aérospatiale developed the SA 366G1 for the US Coast Guard to answer an urgent requirement to replace the service's ageing HH-52s. To satisfy political objections to the purchase of a non-indigenous aircraft, the 'HH-65 Dolphin' is equipped with many US-manufactured components, including the FLIR and the rescue equipment. The first of 96 aircraft was delivered in February 1987. Also now in service with the USCG is the HH-60F Jayhawk, another variant of the highly successful Black Hawk family, carrying the familiar red and white Coast Guard plumage.

The Sud SA 316A/SA 319 Alouette II and III serve with many air arms in the rescue mission. Holland and Portugal are amongst the users of the Alouette III, which is able to carry two stretchers, two sitting wounded and medical attendants. The Alouette II, with its familiar 'bug-eye' cabin, can carry up to two stretchers and is used by, amongst others, l'Armée de l'Air, who also have use of the longer-range SA 321 Super Frelon helicopter. Portugal also operates a SAR version of the Aérospatiale Puma with a nose-mounted Omera ORB-31 Hercules radar and flotation gear. Austria flies refurbished Augusta-Bell AB-204 'Hueys' as air ambulances with HG III at Horsching, whilst the Italian Air Force has a number of Augusta-Sikorsky AS-61R Pelican helicopters, primarily for combat SAR missions. The AS-61R, a development of Sikorsky's HH-3, carries a dark green paint scheme and features revised RWR and chaff and flare launchers. So far these helicopters have been utilised in Somalia and have been operated in support of UN and NATO efforts in Bosnia. The Italian Air Force has also developed a SAR version of the AB-212 Grifone, whilst the Navy has on strength the Augusta-Bell AB-212 for sea-borne SAR work.

The USSR was renowned for its amphibian craft, and the CIS members still have long-range and coastal ASW and SAR amphibians on their inventories The latest of these is Beriev A-40 Albatross ('Mermaid'), developed as a successor to the piston-engined Be-12 'Mail'. The A-40 is a jet-powered flying boat which has a revolutionary single-step hull with unique double chines and a high-set tail. The largest amphibian ever built, the aircraft has a pair of Perm/Soloviev D-30KPV turbofan engines mounted on pylons just above the wing roots, with an RD-60K turbojet take-off booster fitted inside each pylon. Its principal tasks are ASW, minelaying and maritime patrol, with a secondary SAR role. A minimum-change, dedicated SAR version is planned, with medical attendants, LPS-6 liferafts, blood transfusion units, ECG equipment and other surgical items. Up to 54 survivors could be catered for.

The Kamov Ka-25 'Hormone' and Ka-27 'Helix' remain the Russian Navy's standard shipboard helicopters. Primarily used for ASW work, both have a useful SAR capability with flotation bags and rescue hoists. The Mil Mi-14 'Haze' is larger but similarly capable, and a number of former East German aircraft were converted to SAR operations following unification. Poland also operates the Mil-14BTs, in a dedicated SAR role. The Mi-8 'Hip' is used in SAR operations by various countries to which it has been exported, as well as by the Russian Air Force.

Israel, a country which has had a very turbulent aviation history, currently relies on its CH-53s for long-range combat SAR. Greece is the last of the air arms to operate the Grumman U-16 Albatross seaplane. Twelve of the type currently serve with 353 Mira at Elefsis in the SAR/transport role. China has a small number of Mil-4 helicopters, licence-built as the Harbin Z-6 and used for SAR, and also the huge Harbin SH-5 flying boat for long-range recovery.

# 11

# CSAR in the Millenium

*Preserving the life and well-being of our service members and civilians, who are placed in harm's way while defending our nation's interests, is, and must remain, one of our highest priorities, both now and throughout the coming century.*—Former Secretary of Defense William J. Perry, 1996

## The United States JRCA

The United States alone continues to operate an indigenous combat SAR force, dedicated not only to its own affairs but also to those of its allies. In the changing face of global politics the work of the Special Operations Forces, and within them the specialised recovery services, are taking on a higher-profile and more demanding role. In recognising this, and to coordinate the various agencies involved in rescue and recovery, the US Government created the Joint Combat Resources Agency (JRCA) in order to manage future efforts.

The JCRA was activated as a Field Operating Agency (FOA) on 29 November 1996 at Langley AFB, Virginia, to carry out the tasks assigned by the US Secretary of Defense (SecDef). The JCRA's responsibilities are as follows: to provide CSAR functional expertise to Department of Defense (DoD) components and assist them in implementing SecDef CSAR policy and directives; to conduct coordination within the DoD and within the Department of Transportation insofar as it relates to the Coast Guard for the implementation of policies and instructions concerning CSAR; to provide advice to the Unified Combatant Commanders and Military Services concerning CSAR training, planning and operations; to make CSAR policy and operational recommendations to the SecDef and Chairman of the Joint Chiefs of Staff; to recommend CSAR doctrine, procedures and capabilities to the Chairman, Joint Chiefs of Staff, and ensure that they are integrated into the DoD Personnel Recovery programme; within the Joint Requirements Oversight Council process, to address CSAR procedures, training and equipment standards to ensure interoperability of service CSAR assets; to identify budgetary requirements

167

to support the CSAR executive agent functions; to review periodically CSAR employment concepts and capabilities and recommend improvements to the SecDef and Chairman, Joint Chiefs of Staff; and to develop and maintain a fully integrated national Personnel Recovery (PR) architecture that ensures the nation's capability worldwide to recover, through diplomatic, military or other means, Americans who are isolated in dangerous situations. The JCRA mission's is to enhance the nation's ability to recover isolated personnel in wartime or contingency operations; to advise military services and combatant commanders on organisation, training, planning and operations; and to make CSAR operational and policy recommendations to service secretaries, the Chairman, Joint Chiefs of Staff, and the Office of the Secretary of Defense.

## The UH-60Q: Dustoff in the Twenty-First Century

Following the Gulf War the US Army quickly realised that one of the major lessons to be learned was the need to update its medical evacuation capability, so that wounded soldiers could be treated for their injuries more quickly. To meet this need, the Army began to develop the UH-60Q Black Hawk as its latest type of medevac helicopter, for decades having been using the venerable 'Huey' helicopter to airlift soldiers in medical emergencies. This new Black Hawk 'hovering hospital' is crammed with $1.5 million worth of medical gear and at just two minutes' notice it can be switched to any of three modes, medical evacuation, troop transport or cargo carrier. In the medical mode, the converted Black Hawk holds six patients on motorised stretchers that move up and down, a configuration that allows for better patient care, as Sgt Stacy Swallows, a medic with the Tennessee National Guard, explains: 'In the event of an emergency medevac, patients are loaded feet first, so you always have the face of the person available to you. You also have the capability of moving around inside the cabin—so accessibility is the keyword in the new "Dustoff".'

The equipment available to medics inside the Black Hawk also includes an on-board oxygen generating system (OBOGS) and suction devices for cleaning out wounds. 'This is the same kind of OBOGS system that can be found on the F-15 and F-18 fighter jets,' continues Stacy Swallows. 'We no longer carry bottles of liquid oxygen; we generate oxygen whilst we are airborne, using the bypass air from the helicopter's engines.' Ergonomic design has maximised the UH-60Q's cabin space, placing sophisticated, life-saving instruments and equipment at the fingertips of the medical attendants.

The UH-60Q medevac Black Hawk is specifically designed to meet the demands of the twenty-first century battlefield, and can be operated thus: battlefield evacuation, deep operations, aircrew rescue operations, force entry operations, joint operations, hospital ship lifeline, patient regulating, hospital medical re-supply, forward surgical team transport, physiological patient evacuation and rescue of distressed personnel. The UH-60Q is a derivative of the basic UH-60A and incorporates all the UH-60A's major characteristics. Building on the Black Hawk's heritage of saving lives in Grenada, Panama, Kuwait and Somalia, the UH-60Q delivers exceptional patient care, increased survivability, longer range, greater speed and added mission capability.

The UH-60Q's leading-edge technology incorporates an improved environmental control system, cardiac monitoring systems, distribution and suction systems, an airway management capability, provision for stowing IV solutions, an external electrical rescue hoist, NVG-compatible lighting throughout and advanced communication and navigation gear, including an infra-red camera that can find the wounded at night.

### 'Hammer Hog' FACs: A-10s in Control

For many years prior to the Gulf conflict the US military had been looking at ways of utilising other assets to fulfil the FAC role, following the retirement of the trusty OA-10 Broncos after the Gulf War. Developmental work had already begun on a dedicated attack version of the Fighting Falcon, the F/A-16C, which would have all the necessary kit to carry out 'in-touch' close air support work and act as an area controller. Also on the 'list' was the ageing A-10 Warthog, which, it seemed, was destined for retirement in the mid-1990s. However, the Gulf War changed all that when the A-10 proved just what a versatile and deadly platform it could be, and one ideally suited to the modern FAC role. Alan 'Boots' Vinson a 'Hog driver' and FAC specialist from Barksdale AFB, takes up the story:

'Forward Air Control personnel conduct the required coordination and control of close air support, providing detailed integration of air-delivered firepower with friendly ground force fire, and coordinate the ground commander's scheme of maneuver. The OA-10 is also an excellent "Sandy" machine, and we train specifically for the rescue role as part of our inventory. FAC personnel include A-10 airborne forward air controllers (AFAC), Ground Forward Controllers (GFAC), Air Liaison Officers (ALO), Enlisted Tactical Air Controllers (ETAC) and personnel from other services/countries who have been properly trained to perform terminal attack control duties. FAC personnel contribute to CAS efficiency by ensuring air attack forces are used on the most critical targets at the right time. The degree of control required during the attack may vary from directing individual attack aircraft against individual targets to coordinating a flow of attack aircraft into an area of enemy concentration. Regardless of the control requirements, past combat experience has demonstrated that successful integration of air and ground operations requires FAC personnel with detailed knowledge of the fire and maneuver plans of supported friendly forces. The typical OA-10 AFAC is a fully qualified and experienced A-10 fighter pilot who carries an additional qualification as an AFAC.

'The dynamics of a modern-day battlefield, combined with the necessity to sort the friendly forces from the enemy, makes communication imperative for close air support missions. Real-time communications are essential to integrate air support with the fire and movement of ground forces. The Army commander, through the Tactical Air Control System (TACS) network, tells the fighters exactly where CAS is needed. During the attack, a FAC provides positive control to ensure the mission is carried out to the ground commander's specifications and may provide threat warnings while the fighters are on the attack. In essence, CAS and communication are inseparable. Many threat environments will include a communications jamming threat. The A-10 carries three communications radios with special anti-jamming, frequency-hopping capabilities. This equipment and good radio discipline reduces the effectiveness of enemy communications jamming. The FAC will typically be acting under "positive control" of attacking fighters. This means the FAC can see the attacking fighters and confirm that their attack is directed against the correct target. The fighters are not, in this case, allowed to deliver ordnance without the final clearance from the FAC on the radio.

'Much as in an A-10 ground attack scenario, the A-10 FAC collects all sorts of mission data several hours prior to take-off. Intelligence briefings on the current situation, location of friendly and enemy troops, and surface-to-air missile and threat systems are very detailed. The A-10 FAC pilot further collects coded radio frequencies for controlling agencies and ground maneuver forces. All this information is recorded on a "flight data card" carried on the Hog pilot's knee-board. Several scale maps, usually covered in a clear flexible plastic, are used to plot targets, friendly forces and known enemy threat systems. The Hog FAC begins formulating a battle plan of action including safe locations to hold inbound fighters and altitudes for holding and attacking. The Hog FAC will step to the aircraft carrying maps, information cards, coded frequency listings, authenticator tables and binoculars for spotting small targets from high altitudes.'

Forward Air Controller missions, unlike any other flown by the 'Hog', are for the most part 'single ship'—that is, instead of flying in multiples of two the aircraft are launched alone, which is an extremely demanding mission for the 'Hog' pilot. He must protect himself and perform the myriad tasks required of him without the support and that extra pair of eyes normally available to the A-10 flight lead in the form of a wingman. En route to the target area, A-10 FACs will generally follow a typical flow of communications. Once airborne, the aircraft will normally contact a radar controlling agency such as Control and Reporting Center (CRC) or Airborne Warning and Control (AWACS) aircraft for threat warning. Then they will normally check in with the Air Support Operations Center (ASOC) or Airborne Battlefield Command and Control Center (ABCCC) to confirm or update their tasking. They may then be handed off to a tactical air coordinator airborne (TAC-A), who will direct them into the target area.

The Airborne Forward Air Controller's mission is one of the most demanding in the 'Hog''s 'bag of tricks'. The FAC is charged with the responsibility of coordinating between the ground manoeuvre units and a wide variety of fighters sent to support those ground forces. He spends time prior to fighters arriving on station accumulating data and plotting targets, friendly forces, artillery battery fire and enemy threats on very accurate and detailed 1:50,000 scale maps of the target area. The FAC will then relay this detailed information to arriving fighters in a structured format called the 'J-fire' (or more commonly the '9 line') briefing. This briefing format allows the FAC to communicate specific necessary target area information to the fighters in an order that they expect and understand. The items in the 'J-fire' briefing are:

**1. Initial point (IP).** The IP should be a readily identifiable ground feature from which to initiate the attack.

**2. Heading to target and offset.** This is stated in magnetic heading from the IP to the target. Offset direction, when specified, tells the flight that deviating on the specified side of the line to the target is approved while deviations to the opposite side have been restricted. Offset direction is simpler to execute than more detailed attack restrictions. When possible, the FAC will modify detailed attack restrictions so that they can be stated as an offset direction. When deviation to the offset side must be restricted, the restriction will be stated in simple terms, for example, 'Offset right, no further than three miles out'.

**3. Distance.** The distance from the IP to the target is given in nautical miles and tenths.

**4. Target elevation.** Stated in feet MSL.

**5. Target description.** A brief description helps the attacking flight to picture what the target will look like. This may encourage early acquisition.

**6. Target location.** Coded map coordinates are given, in Universal Transverse Mercator (UTM) format, latitude/longitude format or visually in reference to some easily identifiable feature of the terrain.

**7. Type of mark.** If laser-designation is used, the laser-to-target line will be stated in degrees and the four-digit laser code will be specific. Otherwise the target mark will be by light or white phosphorus marking rocket fired by the FAC or artillery.

**8. Friendly location.** The friendly location is normally stated in reference to the target. Friendly position marks may be described. Once the flight is in the target area and understands the situation, the FAC may mark the target and/or ask the friendlies to mark their location.

**9. Egress direction.** Stated in cardinal direction or magnetic heading.

## Example of FAC 9 Line Briefing Order

*1. 'Alpha one zero nine':* The IP designated A-109 on the map.

*2. 'One five zero degrees':* The magnetic heading to the target from the IP.

*3. 'Four point seven nautical miles':* The distance to the target from the IP.

*4. 'Three hundred and fifty feet':* The target's mean sea level elevation.

5. *'Tanks and armoured personnel carriers in the open':* The target description.

6. *'Whiskey Foxtrot five one seven seven, three two four seven':* UTM coordinates WF51773247.

7. *'Two white smokes':* The target will be marked by two puffs of white smoke.

8. *'Three kilometres north in the tree line':* Friendly forces are 3km north of the target.

9. *'Egress back to the IP':* Where to go after the attack.

The A-10 FAC's job is never really done—even when he is back on the ground. After the air strike the FAC will account for the location, type and number of targets destroyed by the air strike and report this Battle Damage Assessment (BDA) to the fighters in a coded format. The fighters, in turn, report this information to controlling agencies on their return to base. The A-10 FAC must fight his way out of the target area just as he fought his way in—alone. He may return to base or, depending on the tasking and his ordnance remaining, proceed to a air refuelling point to continue controlling additional air strikes. In some cases these FAC missions may last in excess of eight hours. Upon egress from the target area, the communications process is generally reversed. BDA is passed in the form of an in-flight report to the ASOC or ABCCC, and en-route threat updates are obtained from the CRC or AWACS. There is no room for error. Accuracy and timely communication is absolutely critical, and one small error may be disastrous for friendly forces on the ground.

The latest 'Sandy' role for the A-10 is increasing the chances of survival for shot-down crews. 'Hog' pilot Capt Ron Stuewe has been breaking new ground with the latest OA-10 role in combat search and rescue. 'This is one of the best missions in the Air Force and I'm glad to be a part of it,' comments Stuewe. 'I've been flying the A-10s for more than two years now, but the OA-10A combat search and rescue mission is something I've only done for six months. When something goes wrong, the OA-10s are ready.'

Fighting off any enemy attacks so that helicopter rescue crews can get to downed pilots quickly is the latest role of the OA-10s based at Al Jaber in Saudi Arabia. The Warthogs remain on alert on the flight line 24 hours a day, reflecting the importance of preventing such a crisis. 'It doesn't take much to shoot the gun and it doesn't take much

# Fairchild Republic OA-10A

The A-10 and OA-10 Thunderbolt II are the first Air Force aircraft specially designed for the close air support of ground forces. They are simple, effective and survivable twin-engine jet aircraft that can be used against all ground targets, including tanks and other armoured vehicles. The A-10/OA-10 have excellent manoeuvrability at low air speeds and altitude, and are highly accurate weapons delivery platforms. They can loiter near battle areas for extended periods of time and operate under 1,000ft (303.3m) ceilings with 1.5-mile (2.4km) visibility. Their wide combat radius and short take-off and landing capability permit operations in and out of locations near front lines. Using night vision goggles, A-10/ OA-10 pilots can conduct their missions during darkness. Thunderbolt IIs have Night Vision Imaging Systems (NVIS), compatible single-seat cockpits forward of their wings and a large bubble canopy which provides pilots with all-round vision. The pilots are encircled by titanium armour that also protects parts of the flight control system. The redundant primary structural sections allow the aircraft to enjoy better survivability during close air support than did previous aircraft. The aircraft can survive direct hits from armour-piercing and high-explosive projectiles up to 23mm. Their self-sealing fuel cells are protected by internal and external foam. Their redundant hydraulic flight control systems are backed up by manual systems, permitting pilots to fly and land when hydraulic power is lost.

The Thunderbolt II can be serviced and operated from bases with limited facilities near battle areas. Many of the aircraft's parts are interchangeable left and right, including the engines, main landing gear and vertical stabilisers. Avionics equipment includes communications, inertial navigation systems, fire control and weapons delivery systems, target penetration aids and NVGs. The weapons delivery systems include head-up displays that indicate airspeed, altitude and dive angle on the windscreen, a low-altitude safety and targeting enhancement (LASTE) system which provides constantly computing impact point freefall ordnance delivery and Pave Penny laser-tracking pods under the fuselage. The aircraft also have armament control panels and infra-red and electronic countermeasures to handle surface-to-air-missile threats. The Thunderbolt II's 30mm GAU-8/A Gatling gun can fire 3,900 rounds a minute and can defeat an array of ground targets, including tanks. Other equipment includes an inertial navigation system, electronic countermeasures, target penetration aids, self-protection systems and AGM-65 Maverick and AIM-9 Sidewinder missiles.

The first production A-10A was delivered to Davis-Monthan Air Force Base, Arizona, in October 1975. It was designed specially for the close air support mission and had the ability to combine large military loads, long loiter time and wide combat radius, which proved to be vital assets to America and her allies during Operation 'Desert Storm'. In the Gulf War A-10s, with a mission-capable rate of 95.7 per cent, flew 8,100 sorties and launched 90 per cent of the AGM-65 Maverick missiles.

*Specifications:* Powerplant two General Electric TF34-GE-100 turbofans each of 9,065lb thrust; length 53ft 4in (16.16m); height 14ft 8in (4.42m); span 57ft 6in (17.42m); maximum take-off weight 51,000lb (22,950kg); speed 420mph (Mach 0.56); ceiling 45,000ft (13,636m); range 800 miles; armament one 30mm GAU-8/A seven-barrel Gatling gun plus up to 16,000lb (7,200kg) mixed ordnance on eight underwing and three underfuselage stations, including 500lb (225kg) retarded bombs, 2,000lb (900kg) of general-purpose bombs, incendiary and Rockeye II cluster bombs, combined effects munitions, Maverick missiles and laser-guided/electro-optically guided bombs, infra-red countermeasure flares, electronic countermeasures, chaff jammer pods, 2.75in (6.99cm) rockets, illumination flares and AIM-9 Sidewinder missiles; crew one.

*Active force:* 72 × A-10, 72 × OA-10; Reserve 24 × A-10, 12 × OA-10; ANG 64 × A-10, 30 × OA-10.

to drop bombs,' Stuewe continues. 'Rescuing someone from an unfortunate incident where the priority of getting that guy back so he can look forward to another day is a sense of accomplishment. From a tactical aspect you have to be aware of what others around you can do and what their limitations are: it's not just going up there and working with a helicopter to get someone who's down. There may be assets from other places. If an F-15 shows up with air-to-air missiles and an F-16 shows up with air-to-ground missiles you gotta know what's going on. The primary function of the Warthog is to provide close air and rescue support. It is the first Air Force aircraft specially designed for that purpose.'

## Bell Boeing V-22 Osprey

For the new millenium, a new doctrine in airborne concepts was required. What was needed for the missions of the new era was an aircraft that could hover like a helicopter, have the payload of a small transport and possess a performance better than any of the current array of rotary aircraft. Enter the Bell-Boeing tilt-rotor design, the V-22 Osprey. The V-22 is a highly survivable, low-maintenance, tactical transport and combat assault aircraft that combines the vertical take-off, hover and vertical landing qualities of a helicopter with the long range, fuel efficiency and speed of a turboprop aircraft. The V-22 will provide military services with an entirely new combat and rescue capability never before attainable.

The Bell-Boeing CV-22 Osprey is scheduled eventually to replace AFSOC's entire fleet of MH-53J 'Pave Low III' and MH-60G 'Pave Hawk' helicopters, and, additionally, some HC-130P/N 'Combat Shadows' and MC-130E 'Combat Talons' will be phased out. In all, the 50 Ospreys will replace up to 89 current AFSOC aircraft. The CV-22 will be capable of a 230kt cruising speed, with a combat radius of 500nm. It will be able to fly over 2,100nm with only one in-flight refuelling. The Osprey will have a crew of four, with two pilots and two flight engineers, and it is designed to carry eighteen combat-equipped troops. The aircraft will have terrain-following and terrain-avoidance radar, extended-range fuel tanks and an integrated navigation system. The unique special operations equipment will allow the CV-22 to penetrate adverse weather, flying at altitudes as low as 100ft, and the Osprey will have a forward-looking infra-red sensor, a digital map display and a mission computer capable of storing hundreds of navigation waypoints. An integrated electronic warfare suite, a reduced acoustics noise level and a strong ballistic damage tolerance will also aid the aircraft's survivability. The US Marine Corps will get 425 MV-22 aircraft for combat assault and combat support missions whilst the Navy will get 48 examples of yet another version, the HV-22, for fleet logistic support, special warfare and combat search and rescue. The CV-22 is designed for night-time infiltration and exfiltration of special operations forces and has been approved as the Air Force Special Operations Command's next operational aircraft. The schedule calls for AFSOC to receive its first Osprey in 2003 and establish an operational capability for twelve Ospreys in 2005. Hurlburt Field is scheduled to have 22 CV-22s assigned to it by 2010.

The CV-22, which will be a special operations variant of the Marine Corps' MV-22, will fulfil a long-standing need for a long-range, high-speed, vertical take-off and landing aircraft that can deliver, extract and resupply special operations forces in enemy territory in complete darkness. It will enable the command to do what it cannot do now, that is, conduct long-range, high-speed, vertical-lift missions in an aircraft capable of getting troops into and out of an area. Lt-Col James Teeple comments, 'We've had a requirement for an aircraft such as the CV-22 since the failure of the Iran embassy rescue sixteen years ago. The 1980 mission left eight servicemen dead and was eventually aborted after two of the eight helicopters on the mission broke getting into Desert One and a third crashed into an EC-130 at the desert location. The mission was designed to free 53 Americans who were being held hostage in the embassy in Tehran. Due to the limitations of the C-130s and helicopters, the rescue plan would have taken three nights to complete, and, by today's special operations forces standards, would have violated the maxim for covert operations—get in fast, get out fast and not be detected. If the CV-22 had been available, rescuers could have completed the mission in one night. The CV-22 is acoustically quieter and less likely to be heard coming in, and it has a cleaner design which means it will have less drag and be more efficient to fly.'

Teeple continues: 'The CV-22 also will be more reliable than any of AFSOC's current aircraft, which means special operations forces can do their job with fewer aircraft. For example, if we have to deploy six aircraft today, we have to send eight to ensure six will be operational for a mission. With the CV-22 we'd only deploy seven, and since the CV-22 is self-deployable worldwide, special operations forces won't have to rely on a large strategic lift requirement.' The CV-22 can deploy rapidly and be ready for a mission within minutes at forward locations. The CV-22 has an additional 900-gallon fuel capacity over its Marine counterpart, giving a combat unrefuelled radius of 500nm. Considering that the CV-22 has in-flight refuelling capabilities, its ultimate range is limited only by crew endurance. With an internal air filtering system for both the cabin and cockpit, the CV-22 will protect special operations forces from nuclear, biological and chemical agents.

## Eurocopter's Cougar AS 532: Sophistcated SAR

Within the European nations, the Eurocopter company has developed the AS 532 Cougar family of twin-engine helicopters, of which more than 350 have been ordered, based on the already proved Super Puma design. The Cougar is already in service with 28 air forces, eight armies and five navies. The specialised AS 532 A2 combat SAR version is a dedicated search and rescue helicopter and is used for the recovery of downed aircrew from hostile territory; this particular machine has been selected by the armed forces of France and Saudi Arabia for its future needs.

In order to locate survivors, the user country's air crew are provided with a Personnel Locator System (PLS), which is based on an encrypted communications homing system. This communicates with the AS 352's Nadir Mk 2 navigation computer, which selects the navigation mode according to the phase of the search and rescue mission and controls the integrated flight display which is presented on four flat screens. The integrated flight display system, IFDS, includes a four-axis autopilot which covers the search and rescue functions. The Nadir Mk 2 navigation computer supplied by Sextant Avionique interfaces with the positional and navigation equipment on the helicopter, the global positioning system, the inertial navigation, the Doppler radar, the VHF omnidirectional radio range equipment (VOR), the Tacan tactical air navigation, and distance measuring equipment (DME). When search and rescue missions are carried out at night, the crew use the very latest third-generation night vision goggles, and the Cougar aircraft cockpit and cabin area is NVG-compatible. For the critical detection phase of the mission the Cougar is equipped with observation domes to the cabin doors, a searchlight, a FLIR sensor and panoramic view detection radar with homing and PLS functions.

These features enable the helicopter to locate and reach the pick-up zone very quickly, even under adverse weather conditions. In search and rescue missions involving pick-up from the sea, higher operating modes of the helicopter's autopilot are used and manoeuvres in transition and hovering flight are performed automatically. The digital autopilot, PA 165 from SFIM, incorporates redundant architecture for high efficiency and safety. For very long range missions the helicopter can carry auxiliary fuel tanks in the cargo hook well, sponson tanks and cabin floor tanks. Ground refuelling during a mission can be carried out using flexible tanks air-dropped on the route by aircraft or helicopter and fitted with locator beacons. Refuelling can also be carried out while hovering above a ship system. The Cougar also has radar and infra-red jammers and a chaff and flare decoy system and comes equipped with two outboard 20mm cannon, pod-mounted rockets and two 12.7mm machine guns.

The helicopter is fitted with a 272kg capacity rescue hoist and an external sling. The enlarged sponsons provide additional stowage for carrying extra fuel, liferafts, floats or other equipment, and are also equipped with emergency flotation gear for over-water missions. The AS 532 Cougar has an exceptionally large cabin volume for a 10-tonne class helicopter, which enables it to airlift stretchers, medical equipment and rescue personnel such as winch operators, doctors and paramedics and allows for up to twelve stretcher patients or 29 seats. Powered by two Turboméca Makila 1A2 engines, the Cougar is also well able to perform fast operations and nap-of-the-earth flight.

## Westland's Super Lynx

The Royal Navy is equipped with Lynx HMA Mk 8 helicopters, which are operational on escort ships. The naval Super Lynx is a rugged multi-role helicopter for anti-surface warfare, anti-submarine warfare, search and rescue and utility operations. It is equipped with a 360-degree Seaspray Mk 3000 scan radar and a Sea Owl thermal imager, the latter fitted on a gimballed mount in the nose of the helicopter, above the radar. The Sea Owl has an elevation range +20 to −30 degrees and azimuth +120 to −120 degrees, with ×5 and ×30 magnification optics. The Super Lynx also has the GEC Marconi Sandpiper FLIR fitted.

The helicopter can be fitted with a range of surveillance equipment, including the Vipa 1 reconnaissance pod from Vinten or the Agiflite reconnaissance camera. In the search and rescue role it is equipped to carry out its missions in all weather, by day and by night. For SAR the Lynx is usually manned by three crew members, and the two-man, 270kg capacity rescue hoist on the starboard side is hydraulically operated. The cabin can accommodate up to eight survivors. Power for the Lynx is provided by two Rolls-Royce Gem 42-1 turboshaft engines.

## The EH-101 Merlin

The Royal Navy's new medium-lift helicopter will be the Merlin from EH Industries. The primary roles of the helicopter are anti-surface ship and anti-submarine warfare, tracking and surveillance, amphibious operations and search and rescue missions. The Merlin is a variant of the EH-101 series of helicopters developed by European Helicopter Industries, a cooperative company formed between Agusta of Italy and GKN Westland at Yeovil, England. The helicopter will operate from the Royal Navy's Type 22, Type 23 and 'Horizon' class frigates, the *Invincible* class aircraft carriers and various amphibious warfare ships and land bases.

The dimensions of the helicopter have been selected to be compatible with the size of the frigates' hangars. The main rotor and the tail pylon fold to minimise the dimensions for stowage, and the Merlin is able to fly out at more than 150kts from the fleet to an extended range and can spend three hours on station, with the autonomous capability of searching, locating, identifying, tracking and attacking targets such as the new-generation fast, quiet submarines. The Merlin is regarded as a powerful and highly manoeuvrable helicopter which can be launched and recovered from a Type 23 frigate in conditions up to sea state 6 with 50kt winds from any direction. The rotor blades are able to generate negative thrust to provide stability on landing and a rapid-attachment harpoon system secures the helicopter on to the deck grid. The helicopter is powered by three Rolls-Royce/Turboméca RTM 322 02/8 engines which provide continued high performance if one engine becomes inoperative, and the Merlin's range and endurance can be extended by the hover-in-flight refuelling procedure.

## Canadian Cormorants

The Cormorant search and rescue variant of the EH-101 has been selected by the Canadian Defence Forces to replace their fleet of CH-113 Labradors. After an extensive and demanding sequence of evaluations, the Cormorant was chosen over the rival Boeing CH-47 Chinook, Eurocopter Super Puma and Sikorsky S-70 Black Hawk. GKN Westland has announced that fifteen Cormorants, worth some $C550 million, have been ordered, with deliveries due to commence in 2000.

Canada has one of the most hostile search and rescue environments in the world and the decision to acquire the EH-101—effectively endorsing the type's credibility—gives the whole programme a much-needed boost. The 101's performance in export markets is likely to be the yardstick by which the success of the entire development and production programme is judged. The helicopter's ability to operate at long range (750nm) in extreme IMC makes the aircraft a serious contender for operators looking for a replacement medium-lift helicopter, whether it be in the SAR, civil and military utility or naval roles. The 101 is in a strong position to capitalise when the benefits conferred by life-of-type extension (LOTE) programmes on current helicopters begin to expire in the next century. The political wrangling that is stalling development of the NH90 will also give Merlin an additional advantage. Obvious other potential buyers of the naval Merlin are the Australian and Canadian navies, whose Sea Kings are approaching the end of their service lives.

## SAR from the Sea

During late 1979, and giving due recognition to the need to have standardised search and rescue training and equipment throughout the United States Navy and Marine Corps, the Chief of Naval Operations established the Search and Rescue Model Manager at Helicopter Combat Support Squadron 16. HC-16 then initiated numerous advances for SAR operations. They established a rescue swimmer curriculum, developed the SAR Tactical Aid, introduced 'A' and 'B' level medical kits and introduced the SAR-1 vest for rescue swimmers. In 1990 the SAR Model Manager responsibility was transferred to Helicopter Anti-Submarine Squadron 1 (HS-1) in Jacksonville, Florida. Under HS-1, SAR continued to develop and adapt, and their tenure saw the introduction of an improved rapel harness, a rewriting of the Navy Search and Rescue Manual (NWP 3-50.1) and the intro-duction of the SAR Medevac Litter. In March 1997 HC-3 assumed the duties of SAR Model Manager, continuing the fine tradition of Navy SAR and promoting the continued standardisation of training, equipment and procedures.

# Appendix

## Super Jolly Green Giant Inventory

### HH-53B

*66-14428:* Currently in service with 551st SOS at Kirtland AFB, New Mexico.

*66-14429:* Currently in service with 551st SOS at Kirtland AFB.

*66-14430:* Combat loss January 1969, 40 ARRS, Udorn RTAB; all killed. Loss circumstances unknown.

*66-14431:* Yarrawonga rescue off coast of Ireland (35 saves) January 1989. 'Desert Storm': Corvette 01 rescue attempt in Northern Iraq (21st SOS). Currently in service with 20th SOS at Hurlburt Field, Florida (on loan to 551st SOS).

*66-14432:* Currently in service with 551st SOS at Kirtland AFB.

*66-14433\*:* Prototype HH-53H, roll-out 18 September 1975. Currently in service with 51st SOS at Kirtland AFB.

*66-14434:* Combat loss January 1970, 40 ARRS, Udorn RTAB; 5 killed. Shot down by IR missile from a MiG-21 while attempting rescue of F-105 pilot (only H-53 lost to a fighter).

*66-14435:* Ops loss, September 1981, 1551 CCTW, Kirtland AFB; all killed. Main rotor blade struck tree and aircraft impacted ground during evasive manoeuvre training.

### HH-53C

*67-14993:* Currently in service with 20th SOS at Hurlburt Field.

*67-14994:* First MH-53J, roll-out 17 January 1987. Currently in service with 20th SOS at Hurlburt Field.

*67-14995:* Currently in service with 20th SOS at Hurlburt Field.

*67-14996:* Logistics loss October 1969, 55 ARRS, Eglin AFB, Florida; all killed. Aircraft went out of control during aerial refuelling over Gulf of Mexico and crashed into water.

*68-8283:* Combat loss June 1970, 40 ARRS, Udorn RTAB; circumstances and details unknown.

*68-8284:* Currently in service with 20th SOS at Hurlburt Field.

*68-8285:* Ops loss 21 July 1971, 40 ARRS, Udorn RTAB; no fatalities. Son Tay raid ('Apple 4') November 1970; settled with power and crashed during a picture-taking mission.

*68-8286:* Nine lives! Son Tay raid ('Apple 3') November 1970. Took 37mm round in cargo hook in SEA. Crashed in Virginia during brown-out landing in 1988. Currently in service with 20th SOS at Hurlburt Field.

*68-10354:* Ops loss October 1986, unit unknown, Hill AFB, Utah; no fatalities. Aircraft settled with power and crashed short of LZ during ridgeline approach; destroyed in post-crash fire.

*68-10355:* Logistics January 1985, 3494 TG, Hickam AFB; all killed. MRB separated from head while hovering over ship during rescue attempt.

*68-10356:* 'Desert Storm': first mission of war, first Coalition aircraft at Kuwait City International, first Coalition aircraft at US Embassy in Kuwait City. Currently in service with 20th SOS at Hurlburt Field.

*68-10357:* Lead H-53 for Son Tay raid ('Apple 1') November 1970. Currently in service with 20th SOS at Hurlburt Field.

*68-10358:* Currently in service with 20th SOS at Hurlburt Field.

*68-10359:* Combat 27 March 1972, 40 ARRS, Nakhon Phanom RTAB; all killed. Son Tay raid ('Apple 5') November 1970. Shot down on escort mission in southern Laos and burnt

*68-10360:* Currently in service with 20th SOS at Hurlburt Field.

*68-10361:* Combat 18 August 1972, 37 ARRS, Da Nang RSVN; no fatalities. Son Tay raid ('Apple 2') November 1970. Destroyed on ground during VC rocket attack.

*68-10362:* Logistics June 1973, 40 ARRS, Nakhon Phanom RTAB; 3 of 5 killed. Aircraft went out of control in roll axis and crashed inverted into Lake Tonle-Sap, Cambodia (suspected primary servo hardover).

*68-10363:* Currently in service with 20th SOS at Hurlburt Field.

*68-10364:* Assault on Koh Tang Island ('Jolly Green 11') May 1975. Currently in service with 20th SOS at Hurlburt Field.

*68-10365:* Combat April 1972, 37 ARRS, Da Nang RSVN; all killed. Shot down by large-calibre AAA during 'Bat 21' rescue attempt.

*68-10366:* Combat November 1971, 37 ARRS, Da Nang, RSVN; 4 of 5 killed. Returning to Da Nang low-level down river, pilot shot in belly, slumped over on to controls.

*68-10367:* First 'Pave Low' in combat: Operation 'Just Cause' December 1989. Led first mission of 'Desert Storm' Jan 1991. Currently in service with 31st SOS at Osan AB, South Korea.

*68-10368:* Ops June 1977, 67 ARRS, RAF Woodbridge, UK; no fatalities. Settled with power and crashed during a hurried approach at airfield. Now cockpit trainer at Kirtland AFB.

*68-10369:* Flew first mission of 'Desert Storm' January 1991. Currently in service with 31st SOS at Osan AB.

*69-5784:* Currently in service with 21st SOS at RAF Mildenhall, UK.

*69-5785:* Assault on Koh Tang Island ('Jolly Green 42') May 1975. Currently in service with 20th SOS at Hurlburt Field.

*69-5786:* Logistics July 1980, 1551 CCTW, Kirtland AFB; 1 killed. Assault on Koh Tang Island ('Jolly Green 44') May 1975. Lost cyclic roll authority and crashed due to auxiliary tank fuel imbalance during 'Honey Badger' exercises at Dugway Proving Grounds, Utah.

*69-5787:* Ops February 1979, 33 ARRS, Kadena AB, Japan; 4/5 killed. First helicopter trans-Pacific flight (lead) 1970. MRB struck drogue during aerial refuelling, tail rotor pylon separated due to severe vibration, aircraft crashed into sea.

*69-5788:* Combat 27 December 1972, 40 ARRS, Nakhon Phanom RTAB; no fatalities. First helicopter trans-Pacific flight (wingman) 1970. Aircraft took round through probe and could not refuel, abandoned and destroyed by A-7 'Sandy' with napalm; multiple hits in main and auxiliary fuel tanks and engines; co-pilot wounded.

*69-5789:* Currently in service with 20th SOS at Hurlburt Field.

*69-5790\*:* Currently in service with 20th SOS at Hurlburt Field.

*69-5791\*:* First production HH-53H 'Pave Low', roll-out 13 March 1979. Currently in service with 20th SOS at Hurlburt Field.

*69-5792:* Ops 27 July 1982, 1551 CCTW, Kirtland AFB; all killed. Assault on Koh Tang Island ('Jolly Green 43') May 1975. Impacted ground during descent from air refuelling at night.

*69-5793:* Assault on Koh Tang Island ('Jolly Green 12') May 1975. Currently in service with 20th SOS at Hurlburt Field.

*69-5794:* Assault on Koh Tang Island ('Jolly Green 13') May 1975. Currently in service with 20th SOS at Hurlburt Field (on loan to 21st SOS).

*69-5795:* Assault on Koh Tang Island ('Jolly Green 14') May 1975. Currently in service with 20th SOS at Hurlburt Field.

*69-5796:* Currently in service with 20th SOS at Hurlburt Field.

*69-5797:* Currently in service with 20th SOS at Hurlburt Field.

*73-1647\*:* Ops October 1984, 20 SOS, Hurlburt Field; all killed. Impacted ridgeline during night TF mission in heavy rain squall during Exercise 'Cope Thunder' near Clark AB, Philippines.

*73-1648\*:* First fully SLEP'ed MH-53J. Crashed during CAPEX in September 1987, killing 1 Ranger. Currently in service with 21st SOS at RAF Mildenhall.

*73-1649\*:* Currently in service with 31st SOS at Osan AB.

*73-1650\*:* Logistics Nov 1984, 20 SOS, Hurlburt Field; no fatalities. Tail rotor and tail rotor gearbox separated from aircraft in flight, auto-rotated to field near Pope AFB, North Carolina.

*73-1651\*:* Ops May 1986, 20 SOS, Hurlburt Field; 1 killed. Impacted ridgeline at night during formation approach on Exercise 'Elated Cyclone' near Nellis AFB, Nevada.

*73-1652\*:* Currently in service with 20th SOS at Hurlburt Field.

## CH-53C

*68-10922:* Ops November 1971, 1551 CCTW, Kirtland AFB; unknown no of fatalities. Impacted ground during night unaided approach to remote LZ.

*68-10923\*:* One of two CH-53Cs modified to HH/MH-53H configuration to replace early losses (73-1647 and 73-1650). Currently in service with 31st SOS at Osan AB.

*68-10924:* Currently in service with 20th SOS at Hurlburt Field (on loan to 21st SOS).

*68-10925:* Combat May 1975, 21 SOS, Udorn RTAB; 1 killed (2/Lt Richard Vandegeer—last name inscribed on Vietnam Memorial). Destroyed by ground fire on beach of Koh Tang Island ('Knife 31') during *Mayaguez* rescue.

*68-10926:* Combat May 1975, 21 SOS, Udorn RTAB; 1 killed. Crippled by ground fire on beach of Koh Tang Island ('Knife 21') during *Mayaguez* rescue, took off, limped offshore, crashed.

*68-10927:* Logistics 17 Mar 1976, 601 TASS, Sembach AB, Germany; all killed. Assault on Koh Tang Island ('Knife 51') May 1975. Rolled over and crashed inverted from a hover due to primary servo bolt breakage.

*68-10928:* Assault on Koh Tang Island ('Knife 22') May 1975. Currently in service with 31st SOS at Osan AB.

*68-10929:* Combat February 1971, 21 SOS, Udorn RTAB; no fatalities. Lost tail rotor due to ground fire during infil, crashed in LZ.

*68-10930:* 'Slate 46' pick-up during 'Desert Storm', first successful combat rescue since Vietnam. Currently in service with 21st SOS at RAF Mildenhall.

*68-10931:* Combat March 1971, 21 SOS, Udorn RTAB; 2/4 killed. Took severe ground fire on exfil, crashed and burned in LZ.

*68-10932:* Logistics June 1995, 31 SOS, Osan AB; no fatalities. Assault on Koh Tang Island ('Knife 32') May 1975. Catastrophic engine failure on short final, ruptured fuel and oil lines caught fire, aircraft burned in LZ.

*68-10933:* Logistics May 1975, 21 SOS, Udorn RTAB; all killed. MRB separated from head in flight.

*70-1625:* Currently in service with 21st SOS at RAF Mildenhall.

*70-1626:* Assault on Koh Tang Island ('Knife 52') May 1975. Currently in service with 21st SOS at RAF Mildenhall.

*70-1627:* Combat May 1975, 21 SOS, Udorn RTAB; no fatalities. Disabled by ground fire on beach of Koh Tang Island during *Mayaguez* incident.

*70-1628:* Logistics January 1975. Currently in service with the 21st SOS at RASF Mildenhall.

*Note:* Original design: HH-53B—8; HH-53C—44; CH-53C—20; total 72. All original USAF HH-53Bs, HH-53Cs and CH-53Cs are now designated MH-53J. The list above does not include CH/NCH/TH-53As obtained from the US Marine Corps. The symbol * indicates aircraft modified to HH/MH-53Hs prior to becoming MH-53Js.

# Index